Creativity

Conversations with 28 Who Excel

Creativity

Conversations with 28 Who Excel

Susan Charlotte

with

Tom Ferguson and Bruce Felton

Momentum Books Ltd.

© 1993 by Momentum Books, Ltd.

All rights reserved. No part of this book may be used or reproduced in any manner without prior written permission of the publisher, except in the case of brief quotations embodied in critical reviews and articles.

Manufactured in the United States of America

1996 1995 1994 1993   5 4 3 2 1

Momentum Books, Ltd.
6964 Crooks Road, Suite 1
Troy, Michigan 48098
USA

ISBN 1-879094-11-8

Library of Congress Cataloging-in-Publication Data

Charlotte, Susan.
    Creativity : conversations with 28 who excel / Susan Charlotte with Tom Ferguson and Bruce Felton.
      p.   cm.
    ISBN 1-879094-11-8 : $24.95
    1. Artists--United States--Interviews. 2. Creation (Literary, artistic, etc.) 3. Arts, American. 4. Arts, Modern--20th century--United States. I. Ferguson, Tom, 1942- . II. Felton, Bruce. III. Title.
NX504.C47 1993
700'.92'273--dc20
[B]   93-17201
                                                                          CIP

*To the Memory
of Joe Raposo*

Whose contributions to
the Facets of Creativity Series
planted the seeds from which this book grew,
and whose music will sing out long.

Contents

Preface ix
Foreword xi

JoAnne Akalaitis 1
Tony Bennett 17
David Brown 29
Eric Fischl & April Gornik 43
Morgan Freeman 61
Martin Garbus 71
Philip Glass 89
Carlin Glynn & Pete Masterson 107
Sheldon Harnick 125
Ernie Harwell 145
Al Hirschfeld 159
Anne Jackson & Eli Wallach 177
Judith Jamison 199
Balthazar Korab 213
Robert Krulwich 229
Elmore Leonard 245
Dr. Paul MacCready 259
E.G. Marshall 279
Frank Pierson 295
Jimmy Schmidt 315
Ntozake Shange 333
Kenneth Snelson 349
Gloria Steinem 365
Grant Tinker 381
Jimmy Webb 397

Preface

We have the misfortune of living in an age of analysis. When we are not analyzing ourselves, we are probing the secrets of the universe. For every action there must be a reaction. For every effect there must be a cause. We have parsed ourselves into trivia. We have split the atom into quarks. We have recorded the cosmic echo of creation. But, thankfully, we have not yet explained the mystery of Creativity. Some things, apparently, are still sacred.

Nowhere is this passion for analysis more resolute than in the field of advertising. And no quest more intense than the quest for Creativity. No philosophical mystery is being sought. Just the magic ingredient that turns lead into gold.

Yet for all this analysis, nobody inside or outside advertising knows what Creativity is or how to get it. At DMB&B we knew we wouldn't be able to split this dense atom either. But we thought we might be able to define its characteristics by following the tracks it leaves in a cloud chamber.

We invited some of the most creative minds of our time to talk to us about Creativity. The stimulating conversations recorded here are far more than tracks in a cloud chamber. They are intimate glimpses into the private heaven or hell of creation by people who must endure it to make a living.

Is there a common thread? Perhaps. Or does the definition of Creativity preclude commonality? There are some fascinating clues here. While we may not find an answer we can all agree upon, a feeling slowly emerges as to what Creativity is and is not. I suspect a feeling is as close as we'll ever get to the resolution of this sublime riddle.

RON MONCHAK
Chairman, Bloomfield Hills Office
DMB&B Advertising, Inc.

Foreword

On June 25, 1987, Elmore Leonard walked into an advertising agency auditorium and talked for two hours about finding his voice as a writer. Thus was born a unique lecture series and, not indirectly, this book.

Many of the subjects who appear in the following pages were interviewed when they appeared as guest lecturers in the ongoing Facets of Creativity series. Some will appear in the future. Others were interviewed exclusively for this book as we sought to mine the broadest possible vein of creative ore.

In all, we talked with some 50 creative achievers whose disciplines range from novelist to chef to sculptor to baseball announcer. Half of them do not appear in this volume, merely because of space limitations. Further *CREATIVITY* volumes might remedy our sins of omission.

One paperback volume already has been spun off from this hardbound edition. *CREATIVITY IN FILM: Conversations with 14 Who Excel* includes eight subjects from this book, plus another half-dozen cinematic artists—from screenwriter to costume designer.

Several potential subjects declined to be interviewed, but even their demurrals could be revealing and educational. Norman Mailer, for example, wrote a note to Susan Charlotte:

"I'm afraid I'm going to say no to your invitation to an interview on creativity for I think the subject is dangerous. I don't think I want to know too much about it, at least not for myself, and don't relish the idea of poking into the gears of it and possibly the wiring—it's one machine (if it is a machine) that I don't wish to get near. All I can do is wish you good luck on your book even if I'm not contributing to it."

Some of our subjects, as you will see, do not even believe themselves to be "creative." We disagree, and include them.

These are *conversations*. We wanted to keep that flavor and texture, as much as possible in print. So there are no footnotes, and only slight parenthetical intrusion. If a few references are unknown to the reader, we apologize; on the whole this seemed to be the best way—to let the reader hear what we heard, while correcting factual slips and clarifying ambiguities wherever possible.

The first interview occurred six years ago; most were conducted in 1991 and 1992. Hence, a prolific interview subject might seem frozen in the year, or even the month, of a particular conversation. On the other hand, a movie producer—working in a discipline with a similarly slow turnaround time—might find one of his projects picking up an Academy Award or two just as we go to press.

Susan Charlotte, New York playwright, screenwriter and journalist, conducted all but three of these interviews, as well as writing the precedes for her subjects. New York free-lance writer Bruce Felton interviewed Elmore Leonard and Kenneth Snelson. Tom Ferguson, managing editor of Momentum Books, interviewed Ernie Harwell. Ferguson and Felton copy edited the manuscript. Ferguson designed the pages.

We very much enjoyed producing this book. We hope you will enjoy reading it.

SUSAN CHARLOTTE
TOM FERGUSON
BRUCE FELTON

JoAnne Akalaitis: "It's naive to think theater can change things in a major way. Like politically and socially. But I do think that theater is a profound encounter between groups of people . . ."

❝ It's very important for me not to listen to everybody because everybody wants to say something, and there are moments when a director is very vulnerable and somewhat paranoid... ❞

JOANNE AKALAITIS
Theatrical Director

Once a pre-med major at the University of Chicago, JoAnne Akalaitis made a radical career shift to theater. She went on to co-found a theater company, Mabou Mines—named after a town in Nova Scotia where she likes to go every year. That was in the early '70s. In 1992, at age 54 and after considerable work as a director, she succeeded the legendary Joe Papp as head of the Public Theatre in New York.

Akalaitis the director gained a reputation as an innovator for such productions as Genet's *The Balcony*, in which she brought to life a revolt that the play merely implied. She has also taken to the works of controversial West German playwright Franz Xaver Kroetz—including *Through the Leaves*, which won her an Obie in 1984; *Help Wanted*, and *Request Concert*, a brilliant wordless play that traces the premeditated suicide of a woman. *Dressed Like an Egg*, based on the works of Colette, opened by showing two pairs of feet in high-heels dancing backwards. She had another hit in 1980 with *Dead End Kids*, which dealt with nuclear destruction and showed a "sleazy lizard making overtures to a dead chicken."

Born to a working-class Lithuanian family in Chicago, Akalaitis has balanced her theatrical career with raising two children by her former husband, composer Philip Glass (see interview, Page 89). She is a woman of many sides, who teasingly refers to herself as a "wimp" but also enjoys power and her new position at the Public Theatre; who does not at first seem to be nurturing and yet whose face lights up at the mere mention of cooking; who does not like to talk about her own creative process and yet can be extremely articulate on the subject; who hates institutions, but is director of one of the largest not-for-profit theaters in the country. She was interviewed prior to Papp's death in 1992.

You once said you had a fear of institutions.

I think artists are traditionally wary of structure in life or in art, and that's basically what institutions represent. The concerns of an institution are often antithetical to the concerns of an artist. The strange thing about doing theater is that theater is a collaborative art, and one of the entities you need to collaborate with is the institution. But for me, institutions represent routine.

So why are you accepting this new position?

I've been given a lot by theater and maybe I should give something back. And working at the Public Theatre provides an interesting challenge. It gives me the opportunity to do good work. So my taking this new position is based on curiosity and a certain idealism.

The kind of work you do is experimental. Do you plan to do a lot more of that at the Public?

I think it will be mixed. I don't even think what I do is experimental at all.

Really?

No, I think what I do is classical. But I don't usually think in terms of what's experimental and what's not.

What do you think about when you're approaching your work?

I think about the particulars. I never think about the overall aesthetic, or an overall point of view. I take each project as it comes along. I know there are similarities in my work. I know there are things that I seem to be interested in.

Like what?

Well, politics, perhaps. Certain ideas about movement, acting style. I'm aware of that. I'm not acting unconsciously. I certainly have ideas about what I like and don't like. But if I don't like something it doesn't necessarily mean it's bad or good. At the Public it will be interesting for me to present work that is not like my work.

Will that affect your own work?
No. I don't see my work ever being affected by an institution. But things that really are outside creativity can affect my work, like money or time or facilities. You have an idea about what you want to do, and a bunch of people say there's no money for it or you can't have this set. Well, the set is part of your creativity. So then you have to come up with some sort of compromise.

If something happens in your life that's traumatic or extreme, does that impact your work?
Of course. In one sense, everything does. Everything is part of your work.

What about raising a family—has that had an impact on your career?
Yes. It's very time-consuming to be a mother; and if you work in the theater it practically and emotionally leads to a lot of juggling and a lot of negotiation. I believe children want to be with their mothers a lot. But I happened to have been a very selfish, driven person who needed to have this career, and I also wanted children.

Did your children pay a certain price?
If there was a sick kid I'd go home. But certainly the children must have suffered, because I'd be at rehearsal late at night.

Did your children influence your work?
Yes. They have ideas about my work and their ideas are useful to me.

Someone wrote that you had a dream about your daughter, actually a recurring nightmare, and it influenced your play, *Dead End Kids*.
I don't remember that particular dream, but I do dream all the

time. It gets to be exhausting. In the midst of a show I always have bad dreams. Horrible dreams. Always.

Any specific examples?
They're anxiety dreams.

Have any helped your work?
I've gotten certain ideas from my dreams. My play *Like an Egg* came to me in a dream. There was a dress which had eggs on it. And I often have good ideas right before I fall asleep. Sometimes I even get up and write them down.

You once said you used Genet's advice where you tell the actors to play each section as if it were a complete play, and then start the next one.
I'm very influenced by a particular book, a series of letters written by Genet. He talks about how important it is for actors to understand how to stop and how to start. Sometimes it's very hard for them to do.

Why is that?
I guess, like everyone else, they have to make transitions. I often prefer to work without emotional transitions.

How do you help them make those transitions?
One exercise I give them, where they move to music, deals with understanding what it is to stop and then to be able to start from nowhere. This exercise can be very frightening, because it leads to a kind of rhythm which is quirky and aggressive, as opposed to a rhythm in which one thing flows naturally or logically from one event to the next.

How do you personally get started? Do you begin with an idea or an image?
I get a clear picture in my mind and I see how I can do something, and then I proceed. And sometimes there's a particular project that's already been written and I want to work on it.

You directed a play about a woman who planned her suicide step by step. It was fascinating because there were no words—it was all action.

That was *Request Concert*.

Right. Is it true that you rehearsed it in slow motion?
Maybe we did. We probably did.

Can you talk more about the rehearsal process?
It was hard because I was working with just one person and the material itself was depressing. Also, it was during the winter, so it was really, really gloomy. The rehearsal process was not exactly fun.

Since that was a one-person show, were there special things you did with the actress to help her relax?
Joan MacIntosh is great. I didn't have to do anything special with her.

And you worked through all the details about her daily life?
It was a lot about details. We worked very realistically—like what kind of toothpaste does she use?

Can you talk about Mabou Mines, the group you co-founded?
We really wanted to have a theater so we could control our own work. So we could be independent: to decide on all levels, practically and economically, how we should be paid—how money is distributed—how work is done.

How has your work changed since then?
It was the late '60s, early '70s. My work now is much more accessible to theater audiences. I'm interested in working with bigger and bigger situations. It's less elitist, less art-oriented.

Do you miss working with that group?
No, I'm doing a project with them now.

What do you like about working at the Public Theatre?
Well, it's close to my house. And I know that sounds like a joke, but I believe in community in a very literal way. This is my neighborhood and it means something to me that I can walk out the door and walk to the theater, which is downtown. I went to see *Casanova* last night. It's very nice for me to walk to the the-

ater, see the play, then go have a drink with the costume designer who also lives in this neighborhood. There's something exciting about going to theater in New York, but there's something difficult about it. And there's nothing like it.

Do you think theater can change things?
It's naive to think theater can change things in a major way. Like politically and socially. But I do think that theater is a profound encounter between groups of people, performers, say, and members of the audience. It opens certain doors and those doors can be inspiring, disturbing, enlightening, horrifying. And I think that theater does change people in those ways. I frequently change because of theater.

In small ways?
In major ways. But not in ways that are programmed, or clear.

Are there specific times you've been changed?
Sure. When I saw *The Blacks* I was changed. When I saw Beckett's play, *Endgame*.

In what way?
I don't want to articulate it. I saw the Living Theater's production of *Frankenstein*, and it forever changed the way I think about theater. In different ways you see the potential, you see what art is, you see something about social reality.

Are there times when one of your projects has changed you?
They all do. But no one stands out. I feel very attached to whatever I have recently done. And then it takes me a while to have a distance to see whether I think a thing is good. But I love Shakespeare and he did really change my life. He made me think I should continue to direct.

Can you talk about your experience directing *Endgame*?
I think it is *the* contemporary, 20th-Century masterpiece. I had a great time doing it. It was very rewarding.

How did you feel about the legal controversy? [Involving Beckett's objection to Akalaitis's staging. See interview with lawyer Martin Garbus on Page 73.]

It was just a mess. It's too bad it happened. Because it basically was a smoke screen—it was a red herring. It was not really what that experience was about. It made it something else. It brought in something from the outside. The experience was a theater experience, not a legal experience.

You had directed Beckett before and won an Obie for it. Had you met Beckett before?
Yeah.

And there had been no problems before?
No. I think a series of things that were almost accidents caused this controversy. I think Beckett was misadvised. He didn't see the play—he never saw his work. He was upset by something someone told him. He may not have liked it. But that wasn't an issue for me—whether Beckett liked it or not. Because I liked it.

What finally happened?
It became a legal battle and they tried to bring an injunction to stop it. And it was settled out of court. There were certain agreements—like Beckett's name couldn't be on the poster. It was a distraction from the performance.

Do those things affect you—people's reviews or opinions?
Bad reviews always have an impact. But I can say honestly that they don't have a terribly long-lasting impact on me. I read all reviews. I enjoy reading reviews. I enjoy reading really bad ones, too, because I think they're funny. I think I'm saying I feel very confident about myself and my work after the show opens, not before previews.

Was there a specific time when a review affected you?
Yes, when I did Shakespeare's *Cymbeline*, which got unbelievably bad reviews, it had an after-effect. Like a month later. I didn't question my own talent at all. But I was depressed by the situation, so I had to think about that.

How did you get out of it?
I don't know; it wasn't a major life event. I think it's foolish to be crushed by reviews. But who am I to say? We are who we are.

And some people really are devastated.

Whose opinions matter to you? Do your children see your work?
Yes, and they're pretty honest about what they like. Some things they haven't particularly liked.

Do you show your work in progress to friends?
Yes, a lot. I invite the whole theater staff to come to rehearsal if they want to.

And then you listen to...
No. They can come because they work with the theater, but I'm not that interested in what everyone has to say.

But you have certain friends...
Yes. It's very important for me not to listen to everybody because everybody wants to say something, and there are moments when a director is very vulnerable and somewhat paranoid—and if you're not strong at that time, people in a bigger institution will be very pushy about certain things. Like money. And they have a right to be. But that's when you have to figure out how you're going to protect yourself and who you're going to listen to. It's not being snobbish not to listen to certain people; but the creative process is so fragile that at certain moments it could all just fall apart.

What do you do when you think it's falling apart?
Ride it out. Sometimes there are people who are connected with the same organization that you are, like producers, and they're not patient enough to see how a play is going to shake down. They want changes at moments when there shouldn't be any changes.

When is that moment that you're truly fragile?
Well, I think there are several moments. One is doing the first run-through. I invite several people to come, including the designers. And I feel I need the designers to like it, and I'm worried if they don't. Because I respect them a lot. And a couple of other friends. And there are moments in the first preview when I think it can be very hard.

Isn't there a difference between defending your work and being defensive?

Yes, but in recent years I decided not to say anything when people started to tell me how they felt about my work. Because once you talk you become part of the discussion and you start to become defensive. But when you just listen you may find that someone has something valid to say. Now I wait to see if I really want to defend my work. To defend it is to say, "Look, this is why I'm making this choice." Of course there are times I listen to people who are wrong.

Is there anybody in particular whose input you feel you really need?

Yes, the set and costume designers I work with. It's very creative for me to talk with them.

And you have a closer relationship with them than with the actors?

It's very different. The designers talk about the whole concept, whereas the actors don't see the whole thing—nor should they. I often find it disastrous when they want to. Actors have a lot of input with me. But the input is about their work, not my work.

What do you do with the actors to bring out their creativity?

I help them really understand space. And to understand their body—and their body in relationship to other bodies.

What about yourself? What helps bring out your own creativity?

It helps when I'm paid well or when I'm in good health. Or when my work supports me not only financially but also morally.

Do you think there are different levels of creativity? If you're a creative businessman, does that make you an artist?

No. I think people are creative or not creative—it's either there or it's not there. I tend not to think of creativity as belonging to business or, say, medicine. But it may be my prejudice. I also don't worry or think about it much. Maybe being creative means something else, maybe it means inventing solutions to old problems—which can apply to anything. But I don't think businessmen or doctors are artists.

What do you think an artist is?
I think to be an artist you have to live in another state of being, a higher spiritual state of being. And your art affects your state of consciousness.

Can you talk about how you started working in theater?
I did it in high school and college, but I didn't study it. It just seemed like something I was destined for.

Were there influences from your family?
No. I come from a working-class family in Chicago. But I think growing up as a Catholic had some sort of influence on me. I'm very ritual-oriented.

Were there turning points in your life that affected your art?
No, not really. There were times when I saw movies, like *Citizen Kane*, and I said, "This is something else. This is art." I also love Fassbinder's work—his ability to tell a story, to direct, his consciousness of movement and design, and his political awareness. I think he's brilliant.

What part does the unconscious play in your art?
It's hard to talk about it. But I know I'm in touch with it—with images and movements on stage that I don't understand and I can't explain but I know come from somewhere very deep.

How do you deal with it?
By letting myself be open and by not censoring it or rationalizing it or explaining it. I am able to trust that side of myself. But the other side of it is that because I'm so intuitive I often don't understand the plotting or logic. So I depend on other people to watch for the plot. I have a friend and dramaturge who may come to my work and say, "It's clear that he's in love with her." And I say, "Oh really," because I don't think that way.

Do you ever worry that you are missing something in your work by being more intuitive than logical?
Not usually. Not often. I'm not plagued by self-doubt, which

is an experience a lot of people have had, or that I often hear about.

So you feel fairly confident?
I guess I do. And I guess I don't want much. Maybe others want something that I don't want.

Which is?
Money and fame. I think once you get involved with ambition and competition, then self-doubt and rejection play a much heavier role.

So you don't feel you're ambitious?
I'm very ambitious, but because I'm a woman I'm exempt from certain kinds of playing to win that are part of a man's life. And a man's life in art.

Has being a woman in this field been difficult?
I think in one way theater is pretty non-sexist. But its organization is totally sexist because it's run by men. I know there are certain situations in which I would be treated totally different if I were a man. But I think it's sad that some women in theater don't know that. A woman at the Public said, "I've never been treated like a second-class citizen around here." But I'm not talking about that. Everyone treats you nice but that's not the point. I say look around. How many heads of departments are there?

But you've had a big breakthrough with your new position at the Public.
I hope so. But there should be more. And in a way I'm not grateful for it. I don't consider it a break. I deserve it. And I feel sort of irritated when people say there are more women directors. So what? There should be.

What attracted you to directing?
It's very creative. You get to have these ideas and put them on the stage. It's a lot of physical stress, but it's very exhilarating.

More so than acting?
Yes, because you have total responsibility. You have a chance to work with great poetry—like Shakespeare and Beckett. And

great artists. And there's a sense of power, since you're the person who puts it together. Directing is not for people with small egos. It's an enormous task and it's very exciting.

What do you look for in an actor?
I'm interested in actors who really understand their bodies, who are not conceited and who don't want to be alone on stage. I'm interested in actors who can use their voice, their instrument, who can go deep, who are willing to give over their heart.

How do you know when you've found that kind of actor—from the audition?
It depends what the audition is. Basically I don't like auditions. And sometimes I make mistakes. So I try and rely on what the casting director knows about a particular actor. But auditions can be very deceptive. Once an actor gave a terrible audition, but I wanted to work with him so I called him back. And I wound up working with him for years. I cast another actor because I needed a certain type. I didn't see how deep she was in the audition, but I did in the rehearsal. So that was luck.

What kind of material do you ask people to bring for the audition?
They only work from the script I'm doing. I never let actors do monologues or prepared work. That could be very unfair. But I can't stand monologues and I get bored by work that's been prepared.

What do you look for in designers?
I look for people who are artists, not just craftspeople who do what the director wants. I want them to be truly creative, which means going deep into the play. And I want them to constantly change, to be in the heady atmosphere of throwing ideas around.

Which means sharing your vision?
It could mean that—and it could mean being very stubborn, and being willing to argue with the director. That's when they're really collaborating on an equal level.

You work quite a bit with your ex-husband, Philip Glass. What appeals to you about his work?

Well, it's rich. There's a real fabric to it. I know it well because I know him well and I know how to work with him. I also feel he understands my work.

Has he or anyone else influenced you?
I think I've been influenced by Fassbinder. And certain writers, like Melville and Genet. But it's not like an influence, it's just there. I'm sure you find as you get older your art is not as influenced; you sort of create your own world.

What about Genet interests you?
Oh, he's a delinquent poet. He's a wild genius.

What do you want to do now?
I'm interested in very small and very big pieces, in working with lots of people.

Why big pieces?
It's a lot of fun. It's a real challenge to have a community with 50 performers. To make something with that many people is tremendously exciting.

But you do a lot of research when you're getting ready for a show.
Yes. I think it gives you a chance to really enlarge yourself. I didn't know anything about English history, for instance, and then I started to learn about it. Now I'm going to read *The Iliad*. In a way I'm ignorant—I don't know anything even though I'm an educated person. I believe the more you know the more it feeds you. I'm appalled at people who start projects when they're ignorant about a certain subject that is relevant. The interesting artists I know are people who read a lot.

What are the most important qualities for a director to have?
I think a truly creative director has a sense of wandering, curiosity and awe. That's why I like to travel—to go anywhere, to go to Kansas City. I'm interested in what all of it is. I feel I should know more about Africa or the Third World. I'm going to Palestine in a couple of weeks. It will feed into the Genet project. I didn't intend that. But I know it will be important.

How do you prepare for a show?
By refurbishing myself. And sometimes I have to go away. I go to Nova Scotia for a month every summer. But it's not a vacation. I work very hard in a way that I'm not able to in New York. I read and read and read and think. And I make plans—like what actors will play what roles. And I'll write out the scheme of the play. If I don't have that I'm in trouble, because then I'm sort of doing it in the rough. I need that time to provide a base, so that when I walk into rehearsal I'm prepared.

Do you know just what you're going to do when you start rehearsal?
No. All I know is we're rehearsing Act Two, Scene One. But I'm very open, and then I start to get ideas. And the time away provides a base for me. I don't understand directors who go from one project to another, who knock these things out.

Any regrets?
No, I think I'm so lucky to be doing what I'm doing. I can't believe it. I could have been a doctor; I was in pre-med for four years. I'm so lucky. I can't be doing anything better.

Is there anything we didn't cover?
Yes. The other creative thing in my life is I love to cook. I'm almost as obsessed about food as theater. I think it's completely creative. That's the only other thing I would do.

Why?
It's so much fun. It's being in touch with your body. Instead of just putting stuff in your body you are inventing something that is beautiful and nourishing at the same time.

Are there similarities between directing and cooking?
Both have managerial aspects. You plan certain things. You boss certain people around. You have to get it there on time and you're doing it for other people. It all has to come together so it can be presented.

Does it feed your art?
I use it to relax. When I was in Chicago, I'd make pinto beans in various ways and give them to the actors. I often bring food to

rehearsals. Some artists are meeting at my house tomorrow, and I'm going to cook for them.

What will you make?
Wild rice, salad, squid salad, I don't know. But I do know I'm already thinking about it.

Tony Bennett: "It's like what they say in sports: You have to hit a zone, where everything becomes right. All of a sudden there's a flow."

❝ I believe the one rule that is definite and applies to everyone is that you need sweat and pain and a lot of hard work, and then it has to appear effortless. ❞

TONY BENNETT
Singer and Painter

"I'm listening to music from Rio, Maria." The words were sung spontaneously in the middle of an interview as the subject chanced across them in his notebook of ideas and observations. In more formal settings he has recorded 91 albums, performed hundreds of concerts worldwide and given five command performances. He is Tony Bennett, talking in detail about his two loves: singing and painting. Sitting in his Manhattan apartment, singing lyrics he had written long ago, he communicated something special, more than just the beauty of his voice. It was the way he suddenly began to sing and the passion he felt. He had talked about a "wind" that pushes him to perform his art, and here was living proof. The song just seemed to sing itself.

Anthony Dominic Benedetto was hired by Pearl Bailey to sing in her show in Greenwich Village, where he was discovered by Bob Hope. Bennett had changed his name to Joe Bari because his father was from Bari, Italy. Hope said that was too affected. When Bennett told him his real name, Hope said, "That's too long for the marquee. Let's Americanize you and call you Tony Bennett." Hope then took him on the road and, as Bennett says, "showed me how to walk on stage and greet the public."

Four decades later, having just returned from a concert in Anchorage, Alaska, Bennett said his plans for the future are "just to learn more and more about the mechanics of singing." Surrounded by his paintings, photographs of many of the greats, including Sinatra, and of his daughter Antonia (the youngest of four children), he talked about how difficult it has been to juggle a family and career. His very busy schedule upsets friends and relatives, but in his mid-60s he clearly does not intend to slow down. His two sons (who manage him), and Antonia (who performed with him at his most recent concert in New York) and his other daughter, Joanna (an actress in New York), seem to understand.

How did you get started, both as a singer and as a painter?
I don't remember. It's not like I had an ambition; I just always had to sing and paint. And I've been doing it my whole life. The only way I can describe it is that I feel like I've always had an insistent wind behind me, just pushing me to do my art. I was on the right track from the beginning but I didn't know it at the time. It's not like I didn't have other jobs. I grew up in the Depression and I was forced to take a lot of jobs I didn't like. But they didn't last very long. All I know is that when I sang I loved it and when I went to art school I loved painting. And so I migrated to both. Somehow I insisted that if I have to work, I'm going to do something I love.

Did you start to sing before you started to paint? Or did the two happen simultaneously?
I always did both.

Jonathan Winters always wanted to be a painter. What's the relationship in your mind between performing and painting?
Well, they have the same rules.

Which are what?
They both deal with the economy of line, balance, proper attention, nuance, finesse, the whole creative process. You go by all the same rules whenever you're working in the arts.

So you don't feel that working as a painter takes away from your work as a singer?
Not at all. But I think American society says you have to be one thing or another. We live in a very specialized society, so if you're a singer you can't be anything else. But that's not true. I

think if you're creative you can do anything creatively. You just have to open up your brain and get rid of the laziness. They say that we only use three percent of our brain. I really don't know if that's a theory or if it's been scientifically proven, but it's true.

What appeals to you specifically about painting and singing?

I like the search of getting into the subconscious, getting into the creative process. The fact that I do two things keeps the creative process rolling all the time. It's a matter of keeping my finger on the pulse. I notice that throughout my life, if I took two or three weeks off I would get very rusty and have to get back on the track, and I don't like that. I don't like stepping away. Other people love vacations, I dread them.

You'd rather just keep working?

Yes. I'm on perpetual vacation when I'm creative. To me it's just like a beautiful trip that takes me somewhere I didn't expect to go.

How do you prepare? Do you vocalize every day?

I do now. As I got older I learned certain facts. We kind of live in an anti-disciplined society. And really the search for freedom comes out of discipline. When you have great discipline you get freedom. And it took me half a lifetime to learn that. About 35 years ago I made a commitment to my art. It happened after a friend of mine, a dancer by the name of John Brascia said, "You paint every day; stretch out and make it an occupation." So I took him up on it and just became disciplined. I paint every day now and sing every day.

Do you think that discipline helps you tap into the subconscious?

Yes, without using drugs. You keep working at your craft and every once in a while you hit something that's right. It's strange how you keep going by the rules, concentrating on what you're doing and then all of sudden it works and you say, "How did I do that?"

So it comes down to working at your craft every day?

Yes. Just going for it and making yourself stretch. Especially with improvisation. I really improvise every night. I'm not a jazz singer—I mean, I'm not Billie Holiday or Louis Armstrong. But I think that one of my commandments is that on the stage you always have to appear vital. And the only way you can do that is by thinking in an improvised way.

How do you do that?
I surround myself with jazz musicians all the time, like Ralph Sharon, who's a great jazz piano player.

You once made an album with Bill Evans, just piano and voice.
I worked with many jazz artists like Bill Evans and Stan Getz, and Count Basie and Duke Ellington and Woody Herman and everybody who's in jazz. But Ralph's been with me for 25 years and we have a jazz trio, which includes Joe LaBarbera on drums and Paul Langosch on bass. And we all think in an improvised way. Every time we walk out on stage we psych ourselves to believe it's the first time we're doing it. And that's what keeps the music alive and vital, so it always seems new.

Do you have a favorite kind of music?
I like good music, I like good performances, good performers. That's the only way I can describe it. I don't categorize people. I love an Art Tatum, a Vladimir Horowitz, or Caruso, or Pavarotti. And I like the ones that you put up on a shelf somewhere like an Oscar Peterson, or a Fred Astaire or Bing Crosby, Sinatra, Ella Fitzgerald. I like the ones that really hit the gold ring somehow. They know how to do it on a consistent basis.

What kind of influence did your family have on you? Did anyone sing or paint?
My father died when I was nine, but I heard he was a magnificent singer.

You never heard him sing?
I never heard him sing. But my brother sang beautifully when he was small. He sang at the Metropolitan Opera when he was 12. They called him a little Caruso. So I was very steeped into opera, listening to opera, and I had a great appreciation of good music.

Have you had any mentors?
Many. Louis Armstrong, and Bing. You hear them do something good and you say, that's it, that's right. And Duke Ellington, who I call the great, classical American composer. He always reminded everybody that they could be creative. He was ready to paint, or make a film or write a sacred concert or write a Broadway play. He just took it all on. He had no rules or inhibitions and he was very successful. He wrote more music than any composer in the history of the world. I think down the line it will be evaluated and everybody will realize he was a great classical composer, and a wonderful one to listen to. But we live in a very bigoted society. People have been afraid that he might move into their neighborhood. It's very sad.

What did you learn from him?
He taught me to eliminate all negativeness and be positive. He said that worrying is man's biggest disease, bigger than cancer. In fact, worrying creates cancer. So he said try not to worry, and study the philosophy of not worrying and just go for it.

Have you been able to do that?
I study it every day. I haven't been able to do it on a consistent basis, but I think about it all the time.

But what happens when you're warming up or vocalizing and thoughts about your life enter your mind?
I don't think of my life when I'm vocalizing. I think of the notes and the intonation, and what I have to do. It's a matter of just finding your center, to see where you're at each day. It's almost like a Zen thing. You just think, where am I at today, and you hear where you're at, and then you have a certain kind of control.

What happens if you're rusty, so to speak?
You just have to wait. It's like a car warming up—you wait till it warms up and then you're ready to go.

Is discipline the most important element in terms of creating?
Yes. There are so many different rules that you can't say this is the one way to do it. Some rules work for some people and they

don't work for others. But I believe the one rule that is definite and applies to everyone is that you need sweat and pain and a lot of hard work, and then it has to appear effortless. I remember reading something Ginger Rogers said once in the *New York Times* when they were doing a salute to Fred Astaire. She said that at many rehearsals their feet would bleed. Remember how easy it looked? That's high artistry.

What effect do you think an artist's life has on his work?
Again, there's no one rule. You can't generalize. There were Nazis who were great performers. Wagner was an out-and-out fascist. These were great musicians who were not great men. That's a mystery to me. I mean that these kind of people, who you couldn't trust, knew how to create. But on the other hand there was Duke, who was a beautiful person and who loved beautiful music.

But it's interesting how someone who's a Nazi, who acts out his darkest side, is able to separate from his life and create beauty. It's a contradiction.
It is. Look at the great Winston Churchill, who was a magnificent painter. He was better than most people think, and yet he was involved in sending hundreds of thousands into war. And then there's Charlie Chaplin, whose personal life did affect his work sometimes. I was reading this wonderful book called *Chaplin* by David Robinson. I think it's the best book ever written on Chaplin. And in it they talk about how he ran into marital problems and everything and he couldn't get going with his art.

What category do you belong in?
I don't know. I've been recording for many years. I've done 91 albums. And sometimes I remember having a terrible cold and the performances were wonderful. Other times I felt on top of the world and the records weren't that good. So it's hard to analyze.

Have specific events in your life affected your art, the way Chaplin's marital problems affected his ability to work?
Well, I had to go through the misery of divorce. It's a very strange culture that we're into now, just stepping away from

family life, which I think is very important for everybody's welfare.

Did the divorce affect your work?
Oh, definitely. But it's funny, when I'm dejected and put to a point where I'm absolutely by myself—when I look back at my own life, that's when I got most of my work done. I had to justify everything I was doing. I had to fight my way out of a box. And all of a sudden I would show up with something that would work, and lift me up to feeling all right about things.

You mean because of the divorce?
Whenever I'd go through a low period, I'd find myself really feeling creative. Maybe I just had the freedom of being alone and having more time to concentrate on what I was doing.

Did that go on for a while, that dark period?
It goes in and out, in and out.

What about now?
I'm past it now. But you know you go through tragedies—personal friends die—and then you go into a pit. It's never one quick road, you're not in heaven. There are just moments that are beautiful, certain moments that are unexpected and thrilling, and others that are mundane and you go along with it.

And your art helps you deal with that?
Absolutely. It's the only thing that makes you happy. Your work makes you happy. It's not my personal opinion. I mean, I wish everybody knew that. Because I think that if everybody was forced to do only what they like to do, it'd be a better world—rather than "I have to do this for a living so I hate it." I just feel so sorry for people who are forced to work at something they don't like. I admire them for sticking it out, if they're breadwinners for other people. But I think when you're doing something you love to do, it just comes out a little better. And when someone's fortunate enough to do what they like, really do what they like, I think they have a better life. They have something to live for.

What do you think brings out the creativity in you?

Consistency. It's like what they say in sports: You have to hit a zone, where everything becomes right. All of a sudden there's a flow. This is an interesting conversation, 'cause I think about this a lot.

What specifically?
About inspiration and where it comes from. I'll be going along and I never know when it's going to happen, but all of a sudden, on some incongruous day, I get this surge of creative excitement within me. And then I pick up a pad and write down notes and there's a flow of activity.

What kind of notes do you make?
I write down titles that I've thought of, songs that I have to learn, ideas that I have.

Do you write these notes in a certain kind of book?
Yes. They're special books and they're all the same.

Do you ever write down your feelings before or after a performance?
Not really.

Do you usually accomplish the things that you want to do?
Ninety-nine percent of the time. I look back six months later at my notes—about how to do a certain song or performance—and usually I've accomplished the things that I've thought about. In fact, in the early '80s Bob Wagner, the movie actor, who was my next-door neighbor in Hollywood for a while, asked me about my plans. So I told him everything I was going to do on this three-block walk. And when he met me a couple of months later he said, "My God, I read your review in *Variety* and you did exactly what you said you were going to do."

Which was?
I did a salute to Nat Cole in this one little section of my show, because he was a dear friend of mine and a great pop singer, and I sang "Unforgettable," which is a number one song now with Natalie Cole doing it with her father. And I did "Nature Boy," just with piano, and at a certain spot I blacked out the whole room and then had his voice over the loudspeaker sing the end

of it. The great thing about keeping these notes and then seeing things happen is that it reaffirms that you just follow your secret heart and not compromise.

Do you feel that you had to compromise at the beginning?
Yes. When you start out your knees are knocking and you're ordered by producers to do things their way. But lately I'm really committed to just not compromising at all. About anything. I don't mind suggestions—but not orders.

Do you have any kind of censor?
What do you mean by censor?

A lot of people have an instinct but they judge it or put a veil over it. Do you do that?
Not really. I know that sooner or later I'll be able to do what I want to do. I don't know when it's gonna happen, what moment it'll happen, but I know I can do it. We all start out really struggling for acceptance, one audition after another, and getting turned down when you're not known.

And did you ever feel that you wanted to give it all up?
No, I don't remember a day where I said I want to throw the towel in. I never felt that for a second. I just figured it was a bad day and I'd go at it tomorrow. It didn't matter how tired I was or anything like that, I never felt, I don't want to do this anymore. Even now, I'm 65, but down the line I've never felt, "Well, someday I really want to stop doing this." This is what I do. I don't do anything else.

It's great that you have that clarity, because most people don't. They're always searching for something.
Even when I've had some doubt—like when I was 50 years old I said, "What am I doing? What is this? Who made this one up?"—there is some soft wind that's pushing me, saying "Go, do it, it's all right, it'll be all right."

Were there any major turning points in your life?
Oh, so many of them.

Can you think of one or two?

I had a lot of hits doing sentimental stuff with strings and ballads. And Ralph Sharon, my piano player and conductor, who had an astute awareness of what was happening, told me to break the format and do jazz. Otherwise, he said, I'd be too predictable. So he did an album for me with drums and flutes and trombones, very avant-garde. To this day it still sounds way ahead of things, with great drummers like Art Blakey and Candido and Sabu. And all of a sudden I acquired a whole jazz audience and everybody said, "We didn't know you sang jazz."

And that changed things for you.
It changed my whole career and opened up a whole new field. It taught me to be unpredictable. And by just being different all the time, you can survive. The interesting premise now is just longevity. It's 40 years later and I'm still rolling as a result of doing unexpected performances and great songs. I asked Sinatra once, "Why do you think we lasted so long?" and he said, "Because we've always done great songs."

Do you remember your first real public appearance as a singer?
Yes. It was with Bob Hope at the Paramount Theater. I remember he told me to walk out positive and come out smiling and enjoy yourself when you hit the stage. When he met me I was a complete amateur and he really boxed my ears back. He did a couple of musical numbers with me and a little comedy number and it was unforgettable. Les Brown's band was there and it was a great, great moment in my life.

Were you frightened when you started out?
Yes. For the first five or six years. I'll never forget when Pearl Bailey said, "I could start you out son, but it's gonna take you 10 years before you become a performer." And she was very accurate. It takes time. No one gets it right away. It takes time to learn what to leave out, what not to do.

What don't you do?
Sometimes you do something a little too much, or you stay on the stage too long. It's a timing thing. You have to know just when to do a certain number and why, and how it builds and how to communicate with the audience. You need a certain sen-

sitivity toward the audience and toward yourself. You have to learn who you are, and how to be natural rather than affected on the stage.

How do you think people perceive you on stage?
I think people trust me. I do 200 dates a year, and they know that I'm going to show up and they know I'm going to sing honestly for them and that they're gonna end up feeling good at the end of the night. So I think after so many years of traveling, in front of so many audiences all over the world, they know they're going to see a good show. I did it the old-fashioned way. I didn't take any shortcuts; I'm still in vaudeville. I mean I go from town to town and I play concert halls, bistros.

Do you have any regrets?
I could be humorous at this point.

Sure, why not?
All I know is when I heard Pavarotti sing I was at the Ford Theater and we were rehearsing with a whole group of people, like Lena Horne and other wonderful performers in Washington, D.C., and when Pavarotti sang I was so shocked by what I heard. The walls were shaking so much in the theater, that I wanted to run up on the stage and look in his throat to see how he did that. Not really. I'm really happy doing what I'm doing.

What has helped you get through the tough times?
My peers. Whenever I had feelings of self-doubt or something like that, my peers were always there for me. Whether it was painting or singing, you know, I've had Sinatra and Crosby and Judy Garland endorse me as their favorite. And in painting, Everett Raymond Kinstler, who's the greatest portrait painter in America today, and David Hockney both endorsed me. And that's very encouraging. You get the best artists in America and they say don't worry, just go straight ahead, you're doing it right. Just recently, my old art teacher, James MacWhinney, said in a magazine called *Jazz Link*, "In the 40 years that I've been teaching art, Tony Bennett was my best student." Comments like that make you try and live up to those accolades and inspire you to try and top yourself.

❝ Change has never been hard for me. What I find difficult is no change. I think that's typical of most creative people. ❞

DAVID BROWN
Producer/Writer

David Brown is best known for producing Hollywood hits such as *Jaws*, *The Sting* and *Cocoon*. But he began his career as a journalist, and an eye for a story remained a long suit when he moved to the world of film and theater.

After growing up in New York and graduating from Stanford University and the Pulitzer Graduate School of Journalism at Columbia, Brown took a reporting job in San Francisco. In 1937 he returned to New York, wrote for the *New York Times* and *Women's Wear Daily* and moved on to magazines, becoming the managing editor of

David Brown: "I'm not one who can live on the coast of Maine and write a book."

Cosmopolitan in 1951. A massive career switch occurred when the head of 20th Century Fox, Darryl F. Zanuck, summoned him to Hollywood.

Brown, now a distinguished-looking man in his mid-70s, later worked with Zanuck's son, Richard, on such notable films as *The Sound of Music, Patton* and *The French Connection*. In 1972 they moved to Warner Brothers and set up their own company. They had an unexpected hit with *Jaws*. "We never knew whether people would laugh at the shark, because it was well-known that the shark was a mechanical one," says Brown. "That was a very big gamble."

Brown ended his partnership with Zanuck after 19 years and started his own production company, the Manhattan Project. Another of his long-term relationships seems like it will go on forever—his marriage to Helen Gurley Brown, editor of *Cosmopolitan*. They met more than 30 years ago when he was executive story editor at Fox and she was a copywriter at the Foote, Cone & Belding advertising agency.

Brown has tasted failure along with his share of success. Richard Zanuck, his future partner, fired Brown after he almost drove the studio into bankruptcy under the exorbitant costs of *Cleopatra*. And he was fired a second time by Darryl Zanuck, who thought Brown and Zanuck's own son were trying to take over the company. The son was fired, too.

Brown writes, and produces films and stageplays with no hint of stopping. At the time of this interview in his Manhattan office, Brown was preparing for a three-week trip to Europe. Part of his journey would be spent lecturing in Berlin and Madrid on the art of writing cover lines and titles—an art form he knows well after spending a quarter of a century in what he calls "his other life," journalism.

What is the most creative part of what you do?

Well, I have a multifaceted occupation. I'm a writer. I've published four books. And I'm a producer of films and plays. And occasionally I'm a journalist.

Didn't you start out as a journalist?

Indeed. You see, everything I do is creative. The perception of producers is that they bring in the money. That's true; but basically I bring in the script, the story, the idea and then begin to assemble the numerous people required to make a movie or produce a play. So I'm involved in all aspects of the project. I guess you could say that creativity for me is a free-floating, unconscious life force.

How does your role differ in each of the various facets of your career?
As a producer in the world of entertainment, of course, you're dependent on other people—and your creativity is your ability to evaluate other people's visions, be it a script or an idea. In the theater it's the ability to respond to a completed play. But when you're writing a book you start with a blank sheet of paper. And when you read it, you cannot imagine how you got it all down; you think it was written by someone else. And then there's the creativity that comes into play when you are trying to translate a book into a film.

Which you did with *Jaws*.
And with *Cleopatra*, which to my sorrow was my suggestion.

Why to your sorrow?
Cleopatra was one of the great calamities of motion pictures. In my own memoir, called *Let Me Entertain You*, I refer to the memo at Century City—where 20th Century Fox Studios used to be. If not for *Cleopatra*, Fox would still own the land, and there's quite a chapter on that.

Aside from *Cleopatra*, are you generally good at coming up with film ideas?
Yes. I'm good at ideas and visions rather than the nitty-gritty. I'm not much on budgeting, though I am good at the bottom-line cost of a movie. And I also like to get involved with casting, although the director is the final judge of that.

What is a typical day like? Or is there no such thing in your business?
You come in the morning and no one tells you what to do. You have to start everything yourself. Once things get rolling, you

have a lot of things to do. But it all starts with a blank sheet of paper.

Is it hard for you to get started?

I think starting anything that's creative is hard. It's hard to write a book. It's incredibly tedious to make a movie. Sometimes it takes years. Most of the time you're trying to convince other people of the rightness of your vision. And you may not even be able to convince yourself. It's a very difficult and stressful job. People think it's glamorous, but it isn't. And by the time it all works out you've moved on to other things. I hardly every see a movie I produce except the 90 times you look at it in the various stages of completion.

But not when it's in the theater?

No, I hardly ever look at it then. I come in after the film has been run and then I greet everyone.

How do ideas come to you?

It's hard to describe. It's more like a dream than reality. No one knows. You cannot sit down and say, "Today I'm going to think up an idea."

Do you have specific memories of an idea coming to you?

Well, the only thing I can recall of that nature—which I wrote about in my book—is when my wife and I were living in California. She was complaining about her job at an ad agency and how her ideas were not being paid attention to. I remember her describing an article she wanted to write called "The Apartment." And I thought it would be good for *Esquire*—it described her years as a single woman. And I said "Why don't you write it as a book?" That was the beginning of *Sex and the Single Girl*. That I can remember. I even recall where we had that discussion.

Where was that?

It was in the Will Rogers State Park in Palisades. And from that came not only *Sex and the Single Girl* but about five other books and *Cosmopolitan* magazine. That I can remember. As for other ideas, all I can remember is getting the idea to form my own company.

Can you talk about why you broke up with Zanuck?
Richard Zanuck and I were together, oh my, close to 30 years in one form or another. We were together with our company from 1972—about 17 years. I was 18 years older than he, and at that point in my life I wanted to do something more than I was doing within the company itself. I had no complaints about the films we made, but I wanted to make different kinds of films. And I was ready for a change.

What kind of a change?
I wanted to go into the theater and I wanted to write books. I wanted the freedom that comes with having your own company, and therefore I formed the Manhattan Project. And then a couple of years later I became president of a major company called Island World, in conjunction with making movies and TV series. And I wanted to continue writing books.

Are you the kind of person who needs change in his life?
Yes. My theory of life is that one changes things every 10 or 11 years. In this case I went almost 17 years without a basic change. When Dick and I started the Zanuck/Brown company it was liberating, because we started with nothing. And the same thing happened with the Manhattan Project. Now we have four pictures completed, including *A Few Good Men*—directed by Rob Reiner and starring Tom Cruise and Jack Nicholson—and Robert Altman's *The Player*.

What do you need to be creative? Some people need chaos, others need quiet.
I need not to be in a tranquil place. I don't think I could write in the south of France or an island in the South Pacific. I find that doesn't work for me. My most creative times are in large cities like New York or London or Tokyo.

So you need to have people around you.
Yes, that's it. I'm not one who can live on the coast of Maine and write a book. Although I can write under a tree.

What about your particular work habits? Do you use a computer or do you work with pen and paper?
I write in longhand. I don't use a word processor. I have all

the high technological stuff rusting in my apartment.

Why do you write in longhand? Do you feel closer to your work?
Exactly. I like crossing things out, and for some reason the technology gets between the creative process and myself. I've even given up the typewriter, which I used for many years. It's fatiguing. I find it easier to have a pad in my hands and start writing. Then I get someone else to type it up. Then I make a lot of changes. Then it goes to a word processor so it can be readily spewed out.

What is the difference between working with a partner and having your own company?
Dick and I were so close that we finished each other's sentences.

Like a marriage.
Exactly. I still work with partners. But I have partners for a specific project. So I have a partner in the theater, Lewis Allen, and I have several partners in the movies. I like working with a partner. It gives one an opportunity—you know, a two-against-the-world kind of thing. And you need that because as a creative person you are always living with rejection. You live mostly in an environment where most people tell you you're wrong. "The book isn't right." "The movie will never work." "Why would anyone think this play would be successful?" And most of the time the naysayers are right. But for that 20 or 30 percent of rightness you stay in the business.

How do you deal with the rejection?
You go into mourning. It's very tough. A rational person always feels like the naysayers are correct. John O'Hara told me that when one of his novels received rave reviews but a son-of-a-bitch in Indiana wrote a bad review, he always wondered if the latter was right.

So there's a period where you have to...
Get over the failed book, the failed movie or play. And that's tough.

Is it tougher if you have doubts within yourself about the particular project?

You always have doubts. I don't know any professional who doesn't. I was talking to Robert Altman, who's directing *The Player*, which took four years to make. It's a wonderful movie. Everyone is happy. It looks great. But Altman is a worrier and so am I. We always worry. It's very tough with a stage play; opening night at Sardi's is a killer. Maybe one out of 10 times you get a good review from Frank Rich. Then it's fun, but not usually.

Can you remember times when you had a particular vision for a film?

Yes: When we saw Peter Benchley's book *Jaws*. It seemed like it would make a good movie. But the most important part of the project was getting Steven Spielberg to direct it. Once that happened, he entered into the nuclear club of filmmakers.

What about *The Sting*?

The Sting was an almost perfect script when we saw it. But you see, in this country movies are not of an auteur nature. So as a producer you decide you want to make a movie based on a particular idea or script, like *The Sting*, and you assemble the people who will help you get it on. And then you harness your vision to the vision of the people you're working with. Whereas in the theater, the prevailing vision is that of the playwright's. You simply pray a lot! You may have an idea for casting, which you discuss. But basically it's the playwright who dominates the venture.

Do you lean more toward theater or film?

They're all my children. The theater is wonderful—it's manageable, everyone is on stage, every performance is slightly different and you have a direct relationship with the audience night after night. When you make a movie you're playing to your crew. So you haven't any idea whether the film will work.

How did you get into this work?

I guess you could say it was an accident. My real dream was to be a scientist. I was admitted to Rensselaer, and I was quite influenced by books like *Arrowsmith*, the study of the nobility of being a doctor. But all my dreams dissolved in the physics lab at

Stanford University, where I finally wound up. I couldn't get the hang of physics or higher math. It was just too tough. I was looking for something softer. And I realized that the social sciences and journalism might be an easier way to go.

So then you switched into journalism?
Yes. Journalism seemed most closely related to my need for action. I also was a news junkie and I read a lot, and as a young man I had always wanted to write. So I started writing for the school paper, *The Stanford Daily*. Everything I've done since that time relates to the written word, even though it's now on film or in the theater and it's spoken and visualized. I got into this work through my preoccupation and interest in writing.

Are there any writers in your family?
No. My father was one of the early public relations men. The only book he wrote he paid to have published.

Can you talk about when you were editing *Cosmopolitan* **and Darryl F. Zanuck invited you to Fox?**
I was going through a painful divorce—is there any other kind? And I received a telephone call from my agent in New York, Carl Brandt. He said, "Zanuck is looking for the best editor in New York and I've suggested you." I later learned that I was one of three—the editor of the *Saturday Evening Post* was also being considered. Zanuck wanted an editor to come to Hollywood to be his chief creative aide and to run the studio in much the same manner as a national magazine. At the time there were 28 producers under contract, plus directors and stars.

When was that?
1951. Without telling anyone at work, I snuck out to Hollywood pleading a family emergency in San Francisco. I visited Darryl Zanuck, whom I had met as a journalist, and had lunch in his dining room with all his producers. I never went into his office. After lunch he simply said, "Tell Joe Moskowitz (who was Zanuck's vice-president in New York) to make a deal with you." And that's how I came to Hollywood.

So you didn't have a background in films.
Not at all. I had to take a crash course, in a sense. Times were

different. People didn't kill to get into movies. They went to Hollywood to make money so they could get back and write the great American novel or play.

How did the people in New York respond?
Dick Berlin, who was my boss, said he'd offer me as much money to stay. But as I said, I was going through a divorce and I thought it would be a good change of life. So off we went to L.A. and that was the beginning of my movie career.

How did you respond when you first got to Hollywood?
It was wonderful. It was the Golden Age. Nunnally Johnson said, "They're very forgiving out here. They don't expect anything for two or three years, so don't be discouraged if only part of your ideas are accepted."

Can you talk about your relationship with Zanuck?
He was my mentor. And it was wonderful to be around him because he was immensely creative, a person of wild enthusiasms. He took on the aura of the second coming. I like the fact that he was always on the positive side. When he criticized a script, usually he would start by telling what was good about it, and then he would go into details about what he would do to improve it. I also liked the fact that he was action-oriented—let's do it now.

When he commented on a script would you meet with him in his office or would he call you on the phone?
He commented entirely by memorandum, almost never by telephone. He had an office boy who stood by properly attired, in a jacket and tie, if you can imagine that in Hollywood. The boy would get on his bicycle and deliver Zanuck's notes immediately. He never kept files. He had his secretary type comments like, "Fine, go ahead." Or, "Make the best deal you can but don't lose it." Then he would go into a long memorandum in which he would analyze our mistakes—but he would say they were his mistakes, not yours. I liked that about him. I also liked the fact that he was genuinely a cosmopolitan person. He didn't just live in Hollywood. His world was much broader. He spent three months a year in Europe and had friends everywhere.

Can you talk about working with his son?
Dick and I were partners, but Darryl was my boss. Dick has a lot of the traits of his father but he's much more practical. He's more of a realist. He worried about his father's enthusiasms and rightly so.

Why is that?
Because some of Darryl's choices were not good and we had some terrible bombs. So Dick became much more practical.

Do you feel you need both—enthusiasm and a sense of realism?
Yes. But times were different when Darryl was producing. I don't think he could have survived in today's world.

In what sense?
The film business is now a world of super agents and actors who dictate how a script should be written. In Darryl's world the story was the primary element in the film. If he were working today he would have to make a profound change. On the other hand, Dick grew up in a Hollywood that was in rapid transition, where the actors were not under contract. It was no longer possible to cast a movie by a chart on your desk which showed that you could put Betty Grable here and Don Ameche there.

And you lived through both.
Yes. I lived in the old Hollywood and I'm right now red-hot deeply involved in the new Hollywood. Dick is old enough to remember the old Hollywood but he wasn't working in that world. When I started working for his father, Dick was still a student at Stanford University.

Has it been hard for you to make the transition from the old to the new Hollywood?
Change has never been hard for me. What I find difficult is no change. I think that's typical of most creative people. I couldn't function where everything is stagnant.

What's the greatest challenge for you?

Staying alive! Number two is finding a wonderful script. Most of them are garbage.

How have you changed?

One gets more secure in one's responses; one becomes less secure in one's knowledge. You know that almost every problem has been faced before. And you realize that all you're making is a movie. It's not life and death, which is what it feels like in all young careers. There's such anxiety about making it in today's world. In the words of Alan J. Lerner, "I'm glad I'm no longer young." It's a tough world, and I feel for these kids who are trying to break in. Especially when I think of how accidentally I got in, with very little background in the film business itself.

Theater is also much different now. How has that affected you?

It costs so much to get a play going. You hardly ever think of Broadway.

Though you have had several Broadway hits.

Yes, I produced *Tru* with Lewis Allen and *A Few Good Men*, which Rob Reiner and I have made into a movie. And I did a play called *The Cemetery Club*, which wasn't a success in the theater but which I'm now turning into a movie. The point is, it costs so much to get a play on stage that you just can't produce that many.

You once said in an article, "I'm an incomplete person working against time." Do you still feel that way?

I don't remember saying that, but I'll take credit for it. Actually, I'd say everyone is incomplete. But I'm more complete now than I've ever been.

Do you still feel you're working against time?

No. I don't feel what I'm doing has to be finished or the world will be a less perfect place. My friend John O'Hara did feel that way, because he had a medical condition. If I were Mozart or a major novelist with a big work in progress, then I'd be working under a time constraint—but everything I do is fairly short-term.

Whose opinion matters most to you?

My wife's, but not on movie matters.

Should I ask on what matters?
On plain matters of surviving and just on life and how you feel about things and people. I'd say she's an important influence.

What about movie matters?
I'll appropriate the words of Darryl Zanuck, immodest as they are: "I listen to myself. Always." I'm subject to other people's opinions because I have to go out and get approvals in order to get money. But I listen to myself. When I haven't listened to myself, I've been wrong. And sometimes when I have listened I've also been wrong. But I prefer it that way because I wouldn't know how else to play it. It's the only reliable barometer I have.

What do you feel your limitations are?
I suppose not being thorough enough in my analysis of a script on a first reading. Sometimes I'm impulsive, and after reading something for the second time I say, "My God, is that what I liked?" Or after seeing a film I might think, "Is this what we've been working on?"

When you think back on your most successful projects, what do you think was most helpful to you? Would you say it was your experience?
Actually it was the opposite; it was my naivete.

How so?
I remember being interviewed by David Susskind right after Dick and I produced *Jaws*. We both agreed that a certain naivete and innocence is necessary to successfully participate in this business. Because if you knew what you were up against, you wouldn't venture into so many dangerous places. You could say I share Ruth Gordon's philosophy, "Never, ever face the facts."

When did you venture into dangerous places?
When Dick and I produced *Jaws*. Had we read the story carefully we never would have acquired the book rights, because we would have thought it was an impossible film to make. How do you make a movie in which a shark jumps onto the stern of a

boat and swallows a man? How do you do that? There's a certain need not to be practical and not to be so bloody certain. You have to be able to take a risk based on emotion or creativity or whatever you want to call it. And so I think a liability can become an asset.

But you're not naive now.
Yes I am. I'm still naive. I mean, some harebrained scheme is just as likely to get me going now. Perhaps what is most important to being a creative producer is protecting your innocence. When I read a script it's as though I were a moviegoer, not a producer.

So, in a way, you have to put all that you know and all your experience aside.
Yes. I believe that experience does not necessarily count except in very pragmatic and specific things. I know, for example, when someone writes in a script, "The Indians burned the fort down," that two weeks of shooting might be in that one sentence. But experience would not lead one to some of the greatest hits of our time, because you might say this would never work. But times change and it does work.

Do you have any regrets?
I don't think in those terms. I think you'll find most creative people don't think about their failures. They think the public is wrong.

And is that what you think?
Probably not as much as most people. Actually, I usually think the public is right, that the public knows. I guess you could say my one regret is that I didn't make more out of my career in journalism. I like that very much. I came into entertainment accidentally. I enjoyed it, but I still kept my hand in the world of news.

If you were to come back in another lifetime would you return to journalism?
Yes. My ambition in another life would be to become the editor of *The New Yorker*, *Esquire* or *Time*. Frequently in life it's a choice between wants; and one can't have everything.

> I have a great fear that eventually they're going to find out that my work wasn't that good—it was a weird aberration and they're going to come and want their money back.

ERIC FISCHL
Painter

> I'm so obsessive that the only way I really like to work is to bulldog a painting till I get it done . . . I'm afraid I'll lose the germ of what made the painting interesting.

APRIL GORNIK
Painter

When April Gornik—who has given new meaning to landscape painting—first met Eric Fischl, who has given new meaning to anxiety in painting—her reaction was, "Who is this jerk?"

Gornik and Fischl were interviewed amid construction chaos not long after a fire had gutted their apartment near Ninth Street and Fifth Avenue in Manhattan. At one point, an architect stopped by to confer with Eric. The apartment served as a metaphor for their 15-year relationship—tumultuous and explosive, yet always there and always being rebuilt.

With Fischl out of the room, Gornik described their first meeting. Eric, who was raised in Port Washington, a suburb on Long Island, taught at the Nova Scotia College of Art and Design. April, who was raised in suburban Cleveland, was a student there in the mid-'70s. "We met because Eric started criticizing my work and making nasty remarks," April recalled. When Eric returned and was asked to confirm that account, a mischievous, boyish smile formed on his face. "Well, it worked," he said.

Fischl is known for provoking people in his work, so why not in his personal life? He created *Sleepwalker* in 1979 because "I wanted to shock people." And paintings such as *Bad Boy*, which shows a naked woman lying near a boy who has his hand in her purse, have earned him the title of "the painter laureate of American anxiety."

Fischl says the suburban backdrop in his paintings helps show "that tragedy operates even in supposedly ordinary, middle-class life." Fischl's mother was an alcoholic "who tried being an artist. It was tragic," Fischl said, "because she could never realize what she wanted. She knew more than she could realize." Fischl's paintings often reflect the disparity between the external calm of suburban life and an individual's turmoil.

Unlike Fischl, Gornik "never tries to startle us with oddly juxtaposed motifs," said art critic Carter Ratcliff. Though she likes to challenge, she also wants to create a sense of peace and calm. And while Fischl focuses on people and the environment, Gornik focuses on the environment alone. "Gornik's uninhabited landscapes are themselves personages—I mean, emblems of the world understood as an analog to oneself," Ratcliff said. "Landscape allegorizes emotional states, so when Gornik imagines and reimagines the pictorial structure of a space, she is shaping her own emotions."

While Fischl often returns to his suburban roots in his paintings, Gornik likes to reinvent places she has visited, such as Lake Powell, Arizona, which appears in *Two Rocks* and *North*. *The River Allee* was influenced by a trip to France.

There is another significant difference between the two painters—their degree of success. Not surprisingly, Fischl's acclaim as a major artist—he has been compared to Edward Hopper and two of his paintings recently sold for a million dollars— has affected Gornik's feelings about her own success. She has been on the cover of *Art News* and has had one-person shows, but Gornik said she often demeans her own success by comparing it with Eric's.

The interview began with Gornik alone, while Fischl attended to construction matters.

Can you talk about what it's like to live with another artist?

Gornik: When we first got together I felt very competitive with everyone, not just Eric. But living with another painter is a particularly tricky, risky business. There's so much ego involved. And one compares oneself to other people unless you're from, you know, Jupiter! Most artists want attention. I'm no exception. Neither is he.

If you hadn't received recognition, would you still be painting?

Gornik: I'm not sure. It's almost a moot point now. We've been through some very strange times where it's been like a seesaw.

Such as?

Gornik: When we first came to New York I was getting more attention, and then Eric moved quickly past me. And he has continued to be more successful most of the time we've been together.

How do you deal with that?

Gornik: Ideally you'd have a certain self-esteem that would carry you through the times when you're being ignored. But I don't know many people who are actually like that. Intellectually I'd say things to myself like, "I know my work is good." But emotionally I'd feel angry and jealous.

Eric Fischl:
Cattle Auction
1990
Oil on linen
98" x 114"

And how does that affect the relationship?
Gornik: There's much less tension now. It's so much easier to talk about it now that we've had moderate success—or in Eric's case a great deal of success.

What was the most difficult time you've been through?
Gornik: When we moved to New York. We were poor and we'd argue about money. We were just like everyone else. I suppose it would be more exalting to say that our problems stemmed from a kind of creative tension, but they were really about paying the bills.

What's the most rewarding thing about being with an artist?
Gornik: There's always so much to talk about. We mostly agree aesthetically.

Do you show each other your work?
Gornik: Often. I trust Eric. You know the fundamental thing about us both being artists is that we have tremendous respect for each other. I don't mean just respect for the principle of making art. We both really like each other's art.

What if you didn't?
Gornik: That would make the relationship impossible. Because there would be a level of hypocrisy in the support you're trying to give. Or there wouldn't be any support that you could give because you wouldn't be able to give in to the hypocrisy. It seems unlikely that someone would be attracted to someone whose work they didn't like. But maybe that's not true.

So you share the same kind of vision?
Gornik: Yes. I don't think Eric's just a good artist. I think he's a truly great artist, a lasting artist. I mean that sincerely. And I've felt that for a long time. I have a really solid appreciation of his work based on my own firm sense of aesthetics. I've never felt unsure about my perceptions, even when I've gone through a bad period creatively.

Can you talk about some of those bad times?
Gornik: I think a lot of it has to do with fatigue. Sometimes you've worked through something and you're tired. Or psychi-

cally you've worked very hard. I paint large canvases and I have to make whole areas come together in a solid way that gives them weight or gives them weightlessness. So just physically it's demanding to keep observing something in a concentrated enough manner.

Has an event in your life ever affected your art?
Gornik: Oddly enough, I don't think my art has much to do with what's happening in my life. Certainly it's affected by it. But I don't think I've made better art when I'm feeling stress than when I'm happy.

(Fischl enters the room)

I was just asking if a trauma in your life has ever affected your art?
Fischl: I don't think it relates when you paint. You're working off something deeper. Something closer, hopefully to the core being which is...
Gornik: It would almost be nice if suffering created great art. We could all do something unpleasant to ourselves to make greater work come out—but it's absolutely not...
Fischl: One of my favorite stories illustrates that. It's about Matisse. During the war his wife, daughter...
Gornik: Daughter.
Fischl: ... was arrested by the Gestapo and held for questioning. And he was informed of that while he was working on a painting—and he continued to work on it. What's important is that you can't tell what painting he was working on. A trauma might screw you up in terms of working but not in terms of altering the work. I think, in fact, art is a way of controlling trauma, tragedy, things like that.

In what way?
Fischl: I think art reorders it. So it reconfigures traumas. Sort of like as kids, boys get into fights and don't perform well. So they sit there and obsess for years—"I should have done that." Or they relive the fight in a way that they win eventually. So maybe art is sort of analogous to that. You sort of rework a situation. You limit the language, like games or sports. The simple language stands for the kinds of things that you keep reworking

until you get it right.

Gornik: I think my work, too, has been about a kind of expression of my own private emotional strength in the face of trauma. It's really on an abstract basis. But there's kind of a sense of privacy in my work, and I think that's something I emphasize unconsciously. I want you, the viewer, and myself to be able to be alone in a painting. It's sort of a protective space where feelings can happen.

Which seems like the opposite of your work, Eric.
Gornik: I don't know if it's the opposite. In some of my work there's a mood of ominousness or threat. So it's not exactly the opposite. There's something about nature that's so outside myself. Something unknown, sort of fascinating, frightening. But some of the paintings are kind of joyous and light. So it depends...
Fischl: Some of your paintings are joyous and light?

You don't agree? I wish I had a video of this so I could capture the look on your face right now!
Fischl: "Joyous" and "light" are two words I wouldn't use.
Gornik: But you know the one with the pink and blues—that to me is about light and peace—inner peace.
Fischl: But it's a heavy peace.
Gornik: But some of the work for me is about not being agitated, not feeling an ominousness. What I was going to say, more importantly, is that people still read those feelings into my paintings—especially the ones that I think you can move into and not have any kind of emotional threat. It's amazing how various the interpretations are.

Do you want that sense of ambiguity?
Gornik: Yes. I want to build it into the work so that there are a lot of possible interpretations. For instance, there is a painting I've done of two rocks, and they read to me as two hands that say, "Don't go any farther." They read like a portal you can pass through—so they can be inviting. They read as twins—like the bizarreness of seeing two identical things right in front of you. I look at paintings in a very abstract, formalist way. They're about this kind of configuration, mysterious and inviting a kind of contemplation of them. Rather than giving the viewer the sense that

something is scary and that's that.

Eric, what do you want your viewers to see? You once said that you wanted them to feel like they shouldn't be there.
Fischl: What I was talking about was embarrassment, an emotion in which you feel you shouldn't be there. Even though you are. So it's a double bind.

What comes to mind is your painting of the young boy masturbating in a wading pool in his backyard.
Fischl: That's *Sleepwalker*.

Right. One art critic said that in this painting the boy's masturbation is defiant of his parents, who are represented by the empty lawn chairs. So if I'm there, looking at this painting and I feel I shouldn't be there, how do I get out of what you call a double bind?
Fischl: By confronting your self and confronting the scene. I want people to know that they are there, this is happening, they do see it, they do have a response to it and that their response is perfectly fine. Whatever their response is.
Gornik: It's like a therapist.
Fischl: No, it's like reality therapy, a reality test. It's just verifying that this happens, you recognize it, you feel this way and you make a choice as to how you deal with it.

Do you ever feel your work is misunderstood?
Fischl: Yes, when I'm accused of painting pictures that are alienating. I don't really accept that because I think that if you confront a scene that's charged with meaning, and you recognize yourself responding to that, then you come in contact with people. You come in contact with the emptiness or need, and that pulls us together rather than alienates us. It's much more alienating to deny experiences and their meanings.

But you do make people confront things they don't want to confront, which is why April compared your work to therapy?
Gornik: It's not that they don't want to confront them. They're confronting things they're afraid to confront. I mean, in an ideal universe, you look fearlessly ahead to your future...
Fischl: But I never look into the future. I look strictly into the

past to understand the present.

But isn't the reason people are hesitant to confront because you're dealing with a lot of taboos—such as incest.
Fischl: Which is what's nice about art. Art is not something one necessarily wants to deal with every day. So you have places where art exists and you go there to have an experience that you don't have on a daily basis. But to say that art should be off-limits to that kind of exposure is wrong. Art is a very secure place. And if you avoid having an experience there, then you're going to have it in real life. You're going to have it where you can't even talk about it, and it's going to be a nightmare.
Gornik: In a funny kind of way we're both dealing with emotions. Except Eric's is much more specific to reality, to the reality of experience.
Fischl: I don't think the emotions are specific. What I try to do is put the work in a place which precedes what we think about it. So that when you see it you then have to wonder, "What is going on here?" and "Why do I feel this way?" It's not like you come there knowing what you're going to feel.

That's why it's provocative.
Fischl: It's become much more ambiguous. It provokes a vague feeling of ominousness or danger or sometimes discomfort, physical discomfort. But the reasons are not specific. Even the scenes that people say are incestuous—I don't see how they can know that for sure.
Gornik: It's interesting that people jump to that. Like the picture *Daddy's Girl*. He didn't even have the intention of . . .
Fischl: And I knew people would interpret it negatively.
Gornik: And I knew the scene because I was there when the photograph, from which he painted the picture, was taken. There was a daddy hugging his little girl. It was a sunny day at the beach and she was so happy. And then Eric paints this painting and people were like—incest!
Fischl: The potential for incest is there, and it has to do with the fact that they're alone. Which means you don't trust that they have their own limits. You assume that it will go the whole distance.

Why?

Fischl: I think we have a huge distrust of privacy. Privacy's antisocial. It means people are doing things they can't do openly—usually sexual things because we put sex in the darkest corners. It's interesting that architecturally western houses are open to the public with huge, uncovered windows. People from the outside can see in. Yet inside there are locked doors. We're not open to ourselves inside our own houses.

So then you don't think your paintings are about incest?

Fischl: In order for paintings like *Birthday Boy* and *Bad Boy* to be incestuous you have to assume that the women in those paintings are the child's mother, not just adult women.

Gornik: But considering how young the boy is, chances are whatever woman he's with is going to be more like a mom or aunt—I mean there definitely is a suggestion of incest in those paintings.

Fischl: I think it comes not just from the characters but also the environment. In *Daddy's Girl*, for example, there's a feeling of isolation to the house and a feeling of class privilege. So in a way it talks of a situation that has no limits, no limits that are self-imposed. So that you think this could go all the way. But that's totally subliminal. It's not really spelled out.

Gornik: What's good about your work is that people think it's an invitation to deal with things they're afraid to deal with. Potentially it permits a kind of catharsis.

How do you two affect each other in your art?

Gornik: I think Eric influenced me to even think about painting. Just by being around him and watching him paint.

Fischl: And April's the first person I show my work to. Usually I bring her in to look at a painting before it's finished. She knows it very well, and she knows what it would take to go the distance. So she encourages me. I think it's a support thing, very much. It's OK to feel this way and push that feeling.

Gornik: That's what I mean about we both trust each other aesthetically. Maybe it's a little less definite, that I'd bring him in to look at a painting at a certain point. Nevertheless, his OK means much more than anyone else's, because he's a great painter, not just because I know him so well. I trust his eye.

April Gornik: *Flood Light*, 1991, oil on linen

Have there been times when you disagreed on each other's work?

Fischl: It's seldom that you look at anything without a kind of prejudice. There are certain things you want to see and you don't want to see. April has a very different sense of finish. She doesn't let things hang. If she's painting a tree, there are different points where you can stop. You can do a simple flat silhouette, you can put leaves in and you can punch holes in so you can see the sky behind it. She takes it farther than I do.

Gornik: A tree to me has a lot of weight. For Eric it's usually a little thing in the background. So "finish" is relative. The way he paints is more drippy. For me it's important to build this more. It has more openness. And it doesn't let the viewer see me.

Fischl: It has to do with the kind of detail that's required to convey something that's concrete. If you paint people in a room, how much stuff do you have to put in the room to get across that kind of rhythm that is consistent with the expression of the event? So it's like talking. Sometimes you can convey the intent without finishing the sentence. So things hang. The same can be true with brush strokes. You can intimate a gesture or a light or a light source without having to be specific about it.

You once said that you know you're finished when you become like the viewer.

Fischl: My process is one of painting into a thing and then painting out of it. As you begin to define and clarify it you remove yourself from it. Then there's a point where you stand back and look at the painting and you can't really think of anything else to add or subtract. It's done and you find yourself wondering just like any other viewer, "Why are they doing this? What is this? Where is this coming from? Why am I feeling this way?" And you don't have the need to further answer it.

Gornik: I always get a physical sensation when the work's done. I mean it's like receding from me—visually. The way I begin working is that I get an idea and I want to see it and I have to make it no matter how long it takes. I get this obsessive kind of feeling about why I'm making something, what I want from it.

But when it's finished you said you have a sensation.

Gornik: There's a point where it's all done and it's almost like it removes itself from you. It almost feels physically like it's gone back a couple of feet. I can see it as a whole for the first time. I don't focus on certain parts. Like the whole thing goes click.

Is it difficult when it's over—do you feel sad?

Gornik: Not me. I feel happy that it's over.

Fischl: There are moments. It's a letdown after painting for a year. There also has to be a point in the painting when the worst is over.

What is the worst?

Fischl: The worst is not knowing where you are. Whether you actually have a painting there.

Gornik: The worst for me is not knowing whether I'll be able to approach the thing that I'm trying to do. And once I feel I'm starting to approach it...

Fischl: Then it becomes much more satisfying. When you

know what you're painting toward. It happens at different points. The first crucial point is to be able to slow down and paint just a small section and get it right. And then I know everything else has to come up to that. Then you get to put that together. But until I find that out...

Do you have a lot of this kind of self-doubt—that a particular painting won't be good? Or that you'll never be able to paint again? Or that you won't still be successful in a few years?
Gornik: All of the above!

How do you deal with those doubts?
Gornik: Usually I tell myself, even though I don't always believe it, if I would just put myself in the studio and work I'd feel better. I'd feel like myself, if not my ideal self. So usually...
Fischl: You fool yourself.
Gornik: Yes, I fool myself constantly. I start a new painting. I hate starting a new painting.

Is that when your self-doubt is really at play?
Gornik: Not necessarily. It's just something I detest. Sometimes I luck out and I have a painting that only takes a month to do and it just comes together all by itself. It's like it was waiting in the wings, just kind of saying, "Give me the chance. I can do it." And it's so easy. But nine times out of 10 it's not like that. There's a middle point where I'm pulling teeth trying to get the thing to happen. Sometimes it's so discouraging. I just don't want the challenge. And I don't want to look at it and think, "This isn't great." I'm not trusting it and I don't know where to go next.

Eric, do you fool yourself?
Fischl: Yes, in moments of doubt, when I feel I have to do something really good and I'm afraid I can't, I'll convince myself it doesn't matter even though I know it matters. Or I'll start a painting by not painting, by throwing paint on the canvas.

And that helps?
Fischl: Well, you know you're happiest when you're painting. So if you could just start painting, the thing you're feeling would lift and the process of painting will begin to flow. You tell your-

self that kind of stuff even though you're scared to death it's not going to help, and you're not going to be able to do it.

Do you have more self-doubt or less now that you're successful?
Gornik: I think one of the worst things that ever happened to me after I started to sell the work was the first time I walked back into the studio. I thought, "Now I'm going to paint an April Gornik painting."

And that felt like a lot of pressure?
Gornik: What was pressuring was that I didn't want to paint one of my kinds of paintings. I didn't want to feel like I was manufacturing them. I thought, "Where's the spontaneity going to be?" Where's the sense of fresh wonder and curiosity? In a way that still exists.

How do you get away from that sense of repetition so you can paint something new?
Gornik: Sometimes you rely on devices, things that you know will make a painting more interesting.

Can you give me an example?
Gornik: Recently I was working on a painting that really needed something. And I thought, "What if there was a lightning bolt?"

And you thought that would give the painting more life?
Gornik: Exactly. But that kind of thing doesn't usually work. You have to look inside yourself and find out if you're using a device, like a lightning bolt, because it belongs in the painting or because it's something you know, something to fall back on.
Fischl: There are things you cannot control on the conscious level. I think what April's talking about is there comes a point when you become highly conscious of the devices you've always used to create the work and you usually come to that point when they are no longer satisfying an unconscious need. So you have to find something else. And there are different ways to approach that. You can't rush it. Some people like myself can't stand waiting, so they'll keep doing a lot of things that don't work. Some people can just sit back and wait, knowing that all

of a sudden it will occur to them.

Gornik: I'll pick at an area on the canvas. But I can't stand the idea of not working. I think that's a similarity. I never start a new painting until I finish the one I'm working on. Almost never.

Fischl: Right—because then you just bring the same problem into the next situation.

It doesn't free you at all to move on to a new painting?
Gornik: Actually it does free me.
Fischl: I paint different paintings. They just all happen on one canvas. When I'm lost, the painting will become another painting.

But you won't stop working on one and go on to another?
Fischl: No, because it's the same problem—I don't know what I'm doing. I don't know what I want. I don't know what I need.
Gornik: I'm so obsessive that the only way I really like to work is to bulldog a painting till I get it done. But sometimes I think it would be smart if I were to change my tactics. Maybe I will; it would be therapeutically smart. But I'm afraid I'll lose the germ of what made the painting interesting if I start a new one. It will seem removed for me, but not in a good way; I'll be out of touch with it. I'm afraid of that psychologically.

What about you, Eric? How has success affected you?
Fischl: I think it's helped quite a bit. I am more who I am.
Gornik: He's happier.
Fischl: I function very well in terms of that kind of attention. I mean I am probably so filled with self-doubt that I need that outside reinforcement.

What do you think your strengths are? And your weaknesses?
Gornik: I think my strengths and weaknesses are sort of the same thing. I'm obstinate and that helps the paintings, but it also means it takes me a long time to make a necessary change. I think most of my character traits work both ways.
Fischl: I think my weakness is feet. I haven't figured out what my relationship to feet is.
Gornik: The way I work I don't even put in things I don't feel I have a relationship to. Like I don't put in...

Fischl: Leaves.

Gornik: It's true. I don't have a relationship to them, they don't mean anything to me. Even if I can't explain to you why something means something to me, I know when it does—like two rocks mean something to me. Three rocks mean nothing to me.

So you won't put in anything you're not connected with...

Gornik: Occasionally I have to do things that are hard to do. But there are things like—trees, actually. I had this experience of seeing these trees standing in water. It was this amazing thing. Like architecture, but weightless. It was too good to be true. So now I've figured out a device to make those parts of the tree more interesting for me to deal with.

Fischl: There's a certain kind of shortcut, too—a way of codifying detail, so that you're not necessarily obsessed with it. And the viewer doesn't become aware of it. They just accept it.

Gornik: So people will read a smudge as leaves.

You were talking about feet and I thought of Hitchcock, whose work reminds of me of yours...

Gornik: What a nice compliment.

I know you've been compared to Edward Hopper, but hasn't anyone compared you with Hitchcock?

Fischl: No, but that's very nice.

What reminded me of him was that he was obsessed with feet and hands and his obsession is evident in his movies again and again.

Fischl: Well, the thing about feet and hands is that they are a world unto themselves. There's a certain kind of painting rhythm you get into and the background can be done in the same sort of scale as the body. But it cannot be done in the same scale as hands or feet. They have a kind of anatomical detail that is similar to the whole body itself. It's hard to stylize hands and feet in a way that doesn't take away from the gestures of the body. It's hard to find the relationship as to how much detail or lack of detail to give them. It's an interesting painting problem.

Gornik: It would be like painting a little miniature sky in one section. It's hard to maintain the concentration.

Fischl: You go from painting with your wrist or your arm to painting with your knuckle to get that kind of detail. But the other thing about feet is that they're at the bottom of the page, which means you have to bend over to paint them. And you're not sure if you really need that detail. Sometimes some gesture towards feet is enough. It's funny. Sometimes you really need it because you want people to be standing there. You need the weight of them on that colored ground in order to have them be there.

What's a typical work day like?
Fischl: I don't get out of bed until noon!

I didn't say ideal, I said typical.
Gornik: I get to my studio late in the morning and stay till around four or five or six.

So you don't paint here at all?
Gornik: Oh, no. When we first moved to New York we both had studios in our loft. And I hated that. It's hard enough to be working on your own work. But if I'd walk through Eric's studio and he was having this great success with a painting and I was really struggling I'd think, "I hate that man!" But it's not something you need to live with. If I was working on something I was really obsessed with, it would be right in the next room. It would be very hard to let go and relax. I think my paintings have greatly improved since I got my own studio.

So when you're here it's your life together.
Gornik: Yeah.

Eric, in another interview that you both did, you talked about what would have happened if April had been successful first.
Fischl: I said I didn't know if we would have sustained the relationship. I don't think it's something that men of my generation were brought up with. It's something that's changed—that women can be more successful. So I'm not convinced that I have what it takes to accept that. I don't know if I have what it takes to accept not being successful.

Especially once you've been so successful.

Fischl: Definitely. I have a great fear that eventually they're going to find out that my work wasn't that good—it was a weird aberration and they're going to come and want their money back.

And what would you say to them?
Fischl: "Don't give me those things back. I don't want them, either!"

What about you, April? How have you been able to deal with the differences in your careers?
Gornik: I think because I really love Eric and I've been in love with him for 15 years. And I really didn't want to give him up. Even though it was very unpleasant dealing with this lack of equality in terms of response. People think it's admirable of me to stick it out. Frankly, I'd rather be known as a good painter in my own right, and not in relation to Eric.

Fischl: We've also allowed this thing in as part of the conversation. So it's not like she can't bitch and moan about being slighted, or treated a certain way.

Gornik: It used to be different. If I would complain Eric would feel like he couldn't have his own success and that he shouldn't feel happy about it.

Fischl: And also I couldn't complain.

Gornik: But we've been in therapy. It's not one of those things that works itself out like magic. I've had periods of intense unhappiness about not being as successful as Eric.

What about now?
Gornik: I still compare my success to his. I'd like to say that I don't but I still do. People will say "This is great; you were on *Art News*; you had a great show, congratulations." And I'll say, "Thanks a lot." But in the back of my mind I'm thinking, "That's nothing. Look at Eric." Maybe 25 years of therapy would make that go away. But I think, in a way, it's just real life.

❝ If you can see a character when you're reading a script, if you can visualize that character in your mind and then make yourself fit that visualization, that's primarily all you need. ❞

MORGAN FREEMAN
Actor

From the *Taming of the Shrew* at the Public Theatre, to *The Three Musketeers* with Kevin Costner in London, to a possible trip to Africa, then back to New York instead on his way to an island in the West Indies, and finally to the Academy Awards in Hollywood: This was the schedule into which Morgan Freeman was asked to fit an interview.

When that conversation finally took place nine months later, he downplayed his own part in the creative process.

Freeman started his acting career in the third grade when he was the lead in *Little Boy Blue*. Four years later he won his first acting award. "I was such a scene stealer," he once said. "The other students all wanted to give me manicures and comb my eyebrows."

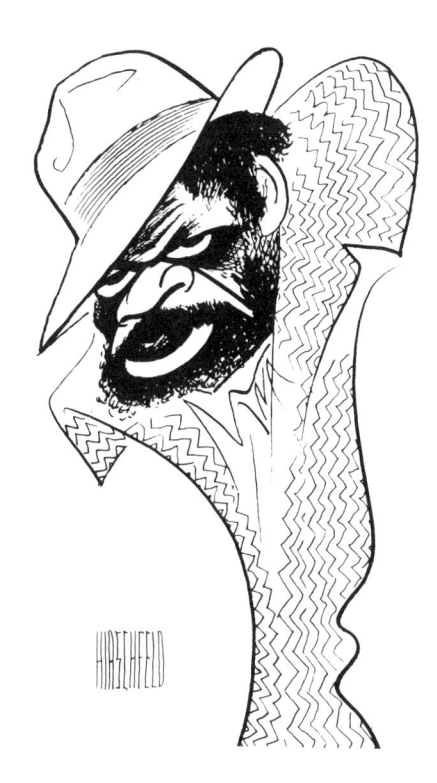

© Al Hirschfeld. Drawing reproduced by special arrangement with Hirschfeld's exclusive representative, The Margo Feiden Galleries Ltd. New York.

Morgan Freeman, drawn from *The Mighty Gents*.

His mother made him feel he could do anything. "When I see what I want, I don't see the barriers." And what he wanted was to be the first black man to win an Oscar. Though Sidney Poitier was that man, Freeman has fared quite well—three Obies, a Drama Desk award, one Tony and two Oscar nominations.

Success did not come overnight in a career that took him back and forth between California and New York. He worked with a small musical company, but when he refused to play the role of an American Indian—a role he thought was patronizing—he was fired. He took a job in the post office, then returned to New York and a job as a dancer at the 1964 World's Fair. His first real break was in 1967, in a play called *The Niggerlovers* with Stacey Keach and Viveca Lindfors. His first commercial success was *Hello Dolly* with Pearl Bailey. He then landed the title role of *Easy Rider* on a Public Television children's show. The money got better, but he didn't feel challenged. Freeman started drinking, then stopped when he fainted on the show.

In 1976 he returned to the stage and received Obies for Shakespeare's *Coriolanus* and *The Gospel at Colonus*. In 1978 he won his first Tony nomination, for *The Mighty Gents*, written by Richard Wesley. He was 40 years old and soon he hit a rough patch. After almost 10 years of not working, he landed several roles, including *Driving Miss Daisy*, *Glory*, *Lean on Me*, *Taming of the Shrew* and *Streetsmart*, which earned him his first Oscar nomination.

You once said that "changing roles is like stepping over a crack. It's not how wide it is, it's how deep it is." How did you go from an easygoing, caring chauffeur in *Driving Miss Daisy* to a volatile, sadistic pimp in *Streetsmart* without falling into the crack?

I don't know how to talk about how I make those transitions or how I do what I do. I just do it.

What attracts you to the process?

There's a joy for me. It's in doing my best to embody a character.

Edward Zwick, who directed you in *Glory*, said you don't just perform a role, you inhabit it. Do you have any sense of

how you do that?
I try to get as far away from the physical me as possible.

Away from yourself?
Just your physical self. You never really get away from the real you. The parts you play are just different aspects of the total person, of yourself.

Including the character in *Streetsmart*? Was he also a part of you?
Of course that was me. That was an aspect of my own personality that I was able to just unleash because it was safe.

Because you were acting.
Right.

So the part was not hard for you to play?
No, it was one of the easiest jobs I've ever had.

Weren't you once in a gang called the Spiders?
Way back—when I was a kid.

And you said you hated being in a gang because you found it too painful to cause pain.
That's right.

But in *Streetsmart* that's all you were doing.
I caused no pain in that movie. It all was pretend. Everything about it was pretend. One of the things that pleases me quite a lot is that actors and actresses have said they like working with me because I'm safe. I don't need to hurt you to make it look good. I believe totally in acting. It's about acting, it's not about being real.

What are some of your favorite roles?
The two that you mentioned—*Driving Miss Daisy* and *Streetsmart*.

What appealed to you about each of them?
Well, with *Miss Daisy*, I had a connection to it. I loved the character of Hoke. I knew him and I knew Miss Daisy. I knew

them because they're Southerners and I'm from the South myself.

From Mississippi.
Right. I was born in '37 and I grew up in the '40s and '50s. So the era of the movie was my era. I knew what the dance was down there, how these people acted, how the social intercourse was handled. Alfred had gotten every beat of it; it was all there.

You're talking about Alfred Uhry, the playwright?
Right. The story was very recognizable and it was clear that he was writing about somebody he cared about.

You wanted to do that part before you even read the script, didn't you?
Yes, I wanted to do it as soon as I read a synopsis at Playwrights Horizons. And they picked me.

What was the difference between working with Dana Ivey on stage and Jessica Tandy in the film?
The major difference is that Dana is from Atlanta. And like me she had a much more intimate relationship with that character in her being, in her self. She fully understood the dance, so she knew where that woman came from and where she went to in that relationship.

And that had a great impact on your work?
Absolutely.

Did you enjoy working with Jessica Tandy?
Oh heavens, yes: I just fell in love with her. She's just such a professional and gracious lady, let me tell you. And a wonderful actress.

What do you do when you're first getting ready for a role?
I just read the script. And then I use my intuition. I guess you could say that there are two things I find generally will cement a character, and that is costume and makeup. If you can see a character when you're reading a script, if you can visualize that character in your mind and then make yourself fit that visualization, that's primarily all you need.

When you talk about fitting that visualization, is that part of getting as far away from the physical you as possible?
Exactly.

And you were able to do that with both those parts—to see the characters?
Yeah. When we did *Streetsmart* the whole character hinged for me on the costume, and when I told the costume designer about that she was in full agreement. She practically spent her whole budget on what I wanted.

So you had a lot of say in designing his whole look—his gold tooth, his nails and all the rest?
Yeah, I had everything to say. They gave me that character. Jerry Schatzberg was the director, and he told everyone to give me whatever I wanted.

What about the way you walk? You had one particular walk with *Streetsmart* and a whole different walk with *Driving Miss Daisy*. Do you work on that, or does that come naturally?
No, you work on everything. It comes as a package. You put on the costume and you stand looking at yourself and you start fitting yourself into it. You know a pimp is gonna walk a certain way. A street dude, a street person—these guys have a certain hippity-dippity walk.

You did not make that role into a caricature. And that could easily have happened.
I try desperately not to do caricatures.

How do you get away from that—especially when you're doing a character like a pimp? You have a certain image of what a pimp might be like, and yet he was his own character.
You have to come back to the director. I need him to give me carte blanche so I can find the character that the writer has created.

And that's how you stay away from doing caricatures?
Yes, I try to live up to the writer's vision. Because he's the one who's really creating.

You don't feel you're creating?
No, actors are not really creating. The writer has done the creative work. There is a character already there, there is a story already there. Maybe he hasn't fleshed out the character, but if he's done the story the character is there. Or maybe he's got extra character and the story needs a little more work. But still it's the writer who has done the basic work. You're building on that—if you're doing anything at all.

What about the other actors—what do you need from them?
I think actors need actors. Let's go to *Streetsmart*. There's a scene in there with Cathy Baker when I have a scissors right under her eye. People have told me it was the most frightening scene. But you know what you were looking at? You were looking at fear, the fear on Cathy's face.

Someone wrote that originally it wasn't shot that way, with the camera on her face. That you were the one who made the suggestion.
No. The director did shoot it that way so you could see her face; but you could also see my face. So I merely said to him, "You're not gonna need this shot when you come around and look at my face because all of it is right there on her face." He agreed when he looked at it. I mean you think I hurt her, but it's really all her doing. 'Cause I didn't hurt her at all. We did that shot six, seven, eight hundred times. We just kept shooting it over and over and over.

Did she give you something that fed you or helped you in the scene?
Absolutely. That's how it gets done.

Can you describe what she gave you?
She was totally in it. She was totally believable. She was totally present. I knew that the world knew that I had her so tightly by the throat that she could hardly breathe. She feared desperately for her life and believed that I absolutely would stick that scissors in and pluck out one of her eyes. That makes you look good.

You had something to do with it, too.

Of course. I'm there. I'm offering the threat in as meaningful a way as she is responding to it. One is adding to the other. You read power to power.

It was most frightening when you told her to choose which eye she wanted you to remove. And then you took the scissors and in a playful/sadistic way pretended they were a pair of eyeglasses.
Again that comes from working with someone who is fully there. It works, there was something emotional, an electricity.

***Glory* was a whole different role for you.**
Glory was a labor of love. I was working with an entire group of people who saw it in the same light—a story that was way overdue. And everyone had the desire to do the absolute best we possibly could. Also having a production staff, a director, producer—all these people who know what they want and yet they are receptive to my input.

How important is that to you—that you have a certain input?
Very important. It makes an incredible difference. I can't stand to work with people who are not receptive to my input.

What about the part attracted you?
It wasn't the part that attracted me at all. It was the story itself. I would have done any role. I just wanted to be in it.

You've also said you wanted to do a black Western. Why?
Well, if you think about it, it's because blacks have been completely eliminated from the West. People act like none ever lived there or that no black ever crossed the Mississippi River. And in fact, one out of every three cowboys was black or Mexican. That's one bit of statistics. In different parts of the country the ratio was different. But there were an incredible number of black cowboys—from early on.

So you would do the first real black Western?
Right. But the thing about the movies is that if a moviemaker started out being black there would be no whites in the movies. It's just the way it's done. If you write a book you're not going to

write about Chinese. Unless you see some Chinese story and you're able to do research, but primarily you're gonna write about whites. There are exceptions, like the Gershwins with *Porgy and Bess*.

Do you want to write the Western in addition to acting in it?
No, I don't write. I do sit down to my word processor and bang out ideas. But I've come to the conclusion that writing is not one of my talents. I've always liked reading good writing, but I don't write.

Is directing something you've considered doing?
Oh yeah, I like directing and I'm very good at that.

How did you get into acting?
I was always an actor. I was always good at pretending. I always played full-out, you know. I think that's all I do now.

You started very young, didn't you?
Yeah, when I was around eight. But I don't know if my childhood affected my acting at all. Your childhood is your childhood. Your ups and downs are your ups and downs.

You had quite a few of those in later years when you were trying to get work in New York and Hollywood.
Yeah. The typical type of actor's struggle. Part of it was fate and part of it was just an incredible number of friends who just thought I ought to be doing this.

You have four kids and a few grandkids. Was it hard having a family and being an actor as well?
I didn't have a family.

You mean you didn't raise them?
Right.

Did that make it easier to devote yourself to your work?
I didn't have a choice. I just had to.

What about your wife? Is she in the business as well?
Yes, she's a costume designer.

How did she deal with the ups and downs?
She's a coper.

What was the toughest time?
A couple of years in '81 or '82, when I was just unemployable. And I was in my 40s when it happened.

You say you dealt with it through friends and drive...
In that situation I didn't know how to deal with it. The first year you know sooner or later the phone's gonna ring. The second year you begin to realize it doesn't have to. And then also you start to think, "OK, what am I going to do? I better go out and maybe try and get a hack license. I'm not a businessman. I can't go into business. I don't do that well at all."

So what kept you going?
I don't know. You don't cut your wrists. At least I don't. You find something else.

What did you find?
A boat. I've had it since I was 35. As long as I've got a boat it really doesn't matter.

You mean your sailboat. What about it do you love?
I don't know. I always wanted to fly. Getting in a plane turned out to be not my idea of flying. Then I discovered sailboats. And there it was—wings.

On the water.
Right.

Does it do the same thing for you as acting?
I guess it does. It does fulfill me.

What drew you to do the movie based on the high school principal, Joe Clarke?
I thought he was a man who was great. He believed strongly in what he was doing. And I believed strongly in what he was doing. I find myself sighing that it didn't work out as well as it could have or should have—or maybe it did. Sometimes you don't know. Things always happen as they should, I guess.

Wasn't Clarke often on location when you were shooting?
Yeah, and if he hadn't been around I never would have been able to do it. Because I never would have been able to figure out who, why and what. But to be around him, to study him and feel him, his energy and the power that drove him, was a great help to me.

And that's a whole different type of acting when you're portraying someone who is...
Alive and looking over your shoulder.

Was that frightening or exciting?
Both.

Pauline Kael—referring to *Streetsmart*—called you "the best actor in America." How did that make you feel?
Well, it's just a compliment. You take it and let it go.

❝ It's clear to me that the feeling of helping is really a part of creativity—like going off to Czechoslovakia as an American lawyer and helping the people write their constitution. ❞

MARTIN GARBUS
Attorney

Martin Garbus has argued free-speech cases on several continents and has represented Lenny Bruce, Cesar Chavez, Timothy Leary, Salman Rushdie, the Weather Underground, pornographers, Nazis. His against-the-grain approach almost led to disbarment by the American Bar Association.

Surprisingly, it was a very soft-spoken, mild-mannered man who introduced himself as Marty Garbus for this interview in a Greek coffee shop on Manhattan's upper West Side.

Born in the Bronx to Jewish immigrants, Garbus first met serious controversy when, as an Army private, he was almost court-martialed for giving lectures about Sacco and Vanzetti, among other topics. Garbus went on to law school and eventually became an associate director of the ACLU. It was as a civil liberties advocate that he defended the right of a Nazi group to rally in Skokie, Illinois, in 1970.

Since founding his own law firm 13 years ago, Garbus has handled numerous anti-censorship and libel cases while continuing his pro bono activist work. He sees "de facto" censorship in more conservative libel rulings of recent years.

Freedom of expression vis-a-vis novelists was foremost on Garbus's mind the morning of this interview. He had just won a case for author Terry McMillan, who was being sued by her ex-lover, who claimed that a character in her novel *Disappearing Acts* was "recognizably based on him and defames his character." Before talking over coffee, Garbus scanned the morning paper to find the article he had been looking for. It described McMillan's victory in court.

There is clearly a creative intensity in Garbus's courtroom work. Yet he longs for the "quiet" creativity of a writer's life. Soon after this interview, he had gone to Woodstock, New York, to contemplate his third book—but not yet the novel he yearns to write.

You've had an incredible range of clients, from Salman Rushdie to Lenny Bruce to Cesar Chavez. What is the most creative aspect to representing these people?

That I have to make it up every day.

Can you elaborate?

No situation is the same. Like a playwright, each situation has a totally different set of players, forces and psychology. South Africa is not like Chile, Chile is not like Kathy Boudin and Boudin is not like John Cheever. In Cheever's case, you're trying to talk about his skill as a writer and about literary concepts and the value of a sentence. You try to explain to seven judges how a sentence can be wonderful and moving.

How do you prepare for that kind of situation?

I get off the plane in Chicago the night before—let's assume on a Tuesday night. I'm about to argue the case in the highest court in the state and I know nothing about the judges. I wake up around 6 a.m. and call as many people as I can to find about these judges—in a cultural, literary and psychological sense. I speak to them at, let's say, 10 a.m. I try and establish a bond with each one of them, trying to understand what their values are. And then I figure out how to make them understand my values. [Editor's Note: A publisher was in court alleging that Cheever's widow owed them a book from the late author's unpublished work.]

How did the judges respond to you?

I won. The lower court judges treated literature like a piece of roast beef. They were trying to quantify what he wrote, ordering the estate to give 15 stories totalling 220 pages. But you can write a wonderful three words or a terrible 350,000 words.

Martin Garbus: "I grew up in the '60s and I believed you could change things through the courts, and that you could do so rapidly. I realize now that was illusory."

What happens after Cheever's case?
Let's say I argue the case at 10 a.m. and at 1 p.m. I'm flying to California because the next morning I'm representing Garry Marshall, the Hollywood writer. Then I get on a plane and I'm off to Tokyo, etc.

Two other writers you represented—Samuel Beckett and Terry McMillan, whose case you just won—were two very different cases, weren't they?
Yes. In Beckett's case the dispute was with a director, a

woman named JoAnne Akalaitis who presented his play *Endgame* at Hartford Stage. The play, as you remember, appears timeless and formless. JoAnne placed the play in something like a subway after a nuclear holocaust. So she gave a meaning to the play which Beckett claimed was not his meaning. If you know Beckett, you know there aren't many words in the play, so it's not a question of changing lines—it's changing the essence of it, the soul of the play. [See interview with JoAnne Akalaitis, Page 1.]

What happened?
We asked them to stop the production, but they refused. So we brought a lawsuit against them in Boston. The result was that they took Beckett's name off the production. The play was called *"Endgame, as adapted by JoAnne Akalaitis."* In each playbill there was a statement from Beckett saying: "I disapprove of this production." This is a complicated issue; namely, what are the rights of a director who takes a play and interprets it his own way?

In the McMillan case, the issue of who should be protected—the writer or the person upon whom the writing is based—also became complicated.
Yes. And that case involved giving maximum protection to the writer.

Didn't a former lover sue McMillan saying the main character in her book *Disappearing Acts* was based on him?
Yes. And the question is, should you be able to write about a character based on someone in real life and then say 10 things about him that are true and five things that are untrue and thought to be bad, such as he's a homosexual or a heterosexual communist? Should you be able to say those things so that people will be able to recognize him?

And you feel you should?
Well, there are two sets of values. One protects the person who is the subject of the writing; the other protects the writer so he can say whatever he wants. It becomes a balance between the two. The position we take is that once you call something fiction you should be able to say anything about your characters.

What is the courts' position?
They haven't gone that far. So through a series of cases we have tried to move them in that direction. The McMillan case, for example, says that the more stuff I write that is untrue fundamentally about a character who is based on a real person, the more I am protected.

Why is that?
Because those people who know the person upon whom the character is based will be able to identify what is untrue and realize you are not really writing about the real person. We had another case in which a college student, Robert Time, wrote about his girlfriend, Lisa Springer. In order to fictionalize her character he made her a high-priced hooker who goes off on ski trips with wealthy men. The truth is she had been attractive, she had gone skiing and she had lived, to some extent, in the international set.

What was the outcome?
The court said if you knew this woman, you'd know she was not a high-priced hooker—and therefore the character was fictionalized and the author was protected. But people who knew her could say there was enough there that was true. So the danger in any libel area is that you could ruin the reputation of a person. So it's a balance, and the question is: "Which way is the balance?"

Has there ever been a time when you felt someone shouldn't have the right to speak or to be protected?
No. I spoke recently in Czechoslovakia, where I was helping them write their constitution. I said that if you believe in free speech, then you have to believe that people should be able to say almost anything.

What was their reaction?
They thought that was wonderful. About 200 people said I was the Tom Paine of Czechoslovakia. And then, during a coffee break, they said you can't criticize government officials, because they have the power and can destroy you. One can say the same about this country, that free speech is in the hands of the very powerful. But if you really believe in free speech, then even the

Nazis should be able to speak—or someone like Douglas Hahn, who was a student at Brown.

Who is Douglas Hahn? What did he do?
In the middle of the night he started waking up Brown students yelling, "Kill the niggers." The issue became confused, because there's a difference between speech and action. Waking you up in the middle of the night can be abusive; but if I yell something about the Mets winning or losing, and that blacks are good or bad, that is free speech.

And you felt this student should be able to say, "Kill the niggers"?
Yes. But my daughter, who's a 21-year-old Brown junior, and her friends didn't feel that way. Their reaction was, "Oh you liberals, I'm tired of you. All your free speech has not worked out. Please stop it."

What did you say to them?
I told them, many of whom are liberals, "If you can keep this guy off campus because you don't like him, how about excluding women from the college on the grounds that it's a private place?"

Did they agree with you then?
No. They failed to see the connection. But I told my daughter that one of the best things that happened in her education was this Hahn incident. Because even in a narrow, protected culture like Brown, there's still racism. And one day when she goes out into the larger world she'll see that many men hate women and that many women lose jobs because they're women and that most people have racist streaks. And that there are people in this country who don't believe the Holocaust ever occurred—and if it did, it was a good thing. So I believe the Hahn case had an extraordinary therapeutic and educational benefit irrespective of what he said and what she said.

That's how you feel intellectually. But how did you feel when you defended a group of Nazis? Weren't some of your family members in a concentration camp?
Yes. My father's 10 siblings and his parents were killed in

Poland. And when I was growing up many of the Jews were from families that were decimated. They were survivors. So the Holocaust was very real to me in a way.

Did defending a group of Nazis become a problem for you?
It's always a problem. But in a way they're so different from my culture that it's not that confusing.

When does it become confusing?
When I represented Rushdie and I was negotiating with Iranian Muslims here and abroad to try and lift the death edict, so Rushdie would be safe. The Muslims were on the faculty of a major university, and many had the same cultural and intellectual interests that I had. And I would certainly approve of my daughter marrying their son. But after we're through negotiating they say, "Of course Rushdie must die." So I say, "But you were just talking about free speech and the Western culture." And they say, "We agree with all that. But Rushdie must die."

So the Muslims were more upsetting to deal with than the Nazis?
Yes, in that way, because I related to the Muslims. Another example is the American Bar Association, which filed a disbarment application against me in the late '70s.

On what grounds?
I had gone to South Africa. When I returned I wrote about it. This was before Steve Biko. People felt that South Africa was OK, and that any lawyer who writes articles criticizing judges, which I did, should be punished. So what I found was a whole set of elitist and racist biases by people in the bar association, who all day long talked about American tradition and values.

I went through a similar experience with [William] Shockley, who taught one of the most brilliant physics courses in the country, while in another course he tried to prove that blacks have smaller brains. The idea that a man could be this bright in one area and then believe utter nonsense in another area is difficult for me to comprehend emotionally. I have tried to communicate with Shockley, but I can't reach him.

How does that affect you?

It makes me furious. I can sit in a room with a group of Nazis and not get crazy. But when I deal with people like Shockley I get nuts. I'm shaking all day long. I've always believed that dialogue, or rational discourse, is a creative way of bridging the gap. Of course, that's rarely true.

What was the most difficult time you went through?
I guess the bar association, because I could have lost my license and not been able to practice again. Another difficult time was when I represented Kathy Boudin, the anti-war activist. We got an extra amount of hate mail as well as bomb and death threats.

When you say "we," are you talking about your family?
Yes. Some of the threats were directed at my daughters, Elizabeth and Cassandra, who were teenagers at the time.

Was this unusual, or was this animosity directed at your family at other times?
There were other times. Like the time I went to Israel during the uprising. It started in December 1988 and in January I came back and wrote that the Israelis were treating the Palestinians very badly. So then we got boxes of shit, literally shit, delivered to our house. Sometimes we thought they were bombs. And there were phone calls at 3 a.m. saying, "Because of people like you Auschwitz happened. You're the kind of Jew who wants to kill every Jew." And these people believed what they were saying and called us out of righteousness at three or four in the morning.

How did this affect your children?
I'll tell you a specific incident. Someone called my daughter, Elizabeth, who was then 12, and asked if I was home. She said I wasn't, and then they said, "I have something terrible to tell you but I shouldn't tell you. Something happened to your father." The kid was terrified. She hangs up and gets a similar call a half hour later, around 6:30. I finally get home around 11:30 and she's totally hysterical. This is a Jewish group against me. That's the ultimate irony.

How did this affect you on a personal level?

As a father, it made me question why I exposed my children to things like that. It made me question my values.

What was the most dangerous event you took your children to?
To Israel when the Camp David meetings occurred in the '70s. My kids were seven and 11. I felt it was an historical moment—it was when Sadat was coming to Israel. One evening my wife, daughters and Tony Lewis, from the *Times*, were having dinner in this tiny restaurant called the Blue Dolphin. The following morning we found out that the restaurant was blown up and everyone was killed. It happened at 7:30, 15 minutes after we left. The bomb was under our table. My kids would have been blown to bits.

What was your response?
The whole day I shook and cried.

Did you regret taking the trip?
At the time I felt I had been terribly wrong to have taken my family to Israel. But I also took my daughter to Czechoslovakia when I had a sense that it was going to turn. We were there before Havel was in power and when he was sworn in. We saw the Russian tanks massed out of town. So we got the best part of that period, and my daughter met Havel. If I look at where she's at now I'd say she's had an enriched life. Of course if she had been killed in that restaurant in Israel I wouldn't have said that. I don't know—she's 21 and she'll have to speak for herself.

What was the most frightening case you were involved in?
Kathy Boudin's case, which started in 1981 and went on for three to four years. In this case there was a holdup and three cops were killed. They were young guys with families in Nyack, New York. The community was furious at Kathy and her friends and they felt Kathy was so powerful that she could break out of jail and start a revolution that would wipe out the community.

What was it like in court?
Basically, the crowd wanted to rip us apart. There would be mobs on both sides. And you were protected by police who were friends of the guys who were killed. All you needed were some

sparks and we could have gotten really hurt. There were helicopters all around and marksmen on all sides. And that was terrifying. Did my kids and wife pay a price for that terror I went through? Absolutely. Did I sleep not as well? Absolutely. Was I ambivalent about whether I should be doing this? Absolutely.

Do you think the fear fed you in any way?
Yes. I'm smart enough to know that there's a reason why one gets involved in this kind of combative life, which is consistent and inconsistent with what I really want to do.

Which is?
To sit in a room and write. There's a part of me that enjoys the quietness of writing books. And yet the combative side is a way of communicating.

Has communicating always been important to you?
I've been doing it since I was a child. My mother died when I was three. My father was an immigrant who never learned English. He read Jewish newspapers. We had a candy store and I basically communicated with the world. I protected him. At least that's my vision of it.

And now you're protecting the world.
Yes. And the word "protection" has a very heavy value for me. I find it where others don't. To some extent Kathy Boudin was a woman whom I felt needed protection.

Which is a contradiction of sorts, for while you're protecting all those strangers, your own family is endangered.
Right; and there's also an economic contradiction.

Meaning?
We're talking about my ability to earn a living in a way that I want to, but it also jeopardizes my family. I want my kids to have a certain kind of education, which could be difficult if I get killed or if this disbarment business—which I've been through twice—took place. It could jeopardize me financially. It's somewhat like living on a cliff. And it seems to me that's what I want to do. What interests me is testing the limits, seeing how far I can go. And if I'm writing, I'm doing the same thing.

I was one of the first people to write an article, a short one in the *Times*, saying Nixon should be impeached—when it wasn't an acceptable thing to say. So it threw heat onto my career early on. And in a lot of my other articles I attack government officials. So I lead a combative cliff-walking type of life; but it juices me up.

Has this changed with time?
I think I have a better perspective on things. And I keep thinking that I'm never going to get into the kind of emotional passions that are totally absorbing, like the civil rights movement. And yet I just had a case where the government tried to stop a book, and I found I was functioning the same way—working 24 hours a day.

How have changes in the political climate—and the more conservative Supreme Court—affected your work?
I grew up in the '60s and I believed you could change things through the courts, and that you could do so rapidly. I realize now that was illusory. Change is far more complex, deeper and slower. At the same time I did see the enormity of the social problem and denigrated whatever contribution I was making.

Why?
Because it seemed so insignificant and so inconsequential. But in retrospect I see it as rather part of a much larger picture. So I think I feel better about some of the things we tried to do, and I realize it had more effect than I thought. So now I see things more incrementally. I would have thought that would have diluted my passion, but it hasn't. I see that the last 10 years have been much more internationally oriented as the sense of risk has diminished in the U.S.

In what sense?
I started out when Amnesty International was approximately two people. I had no budget but 30 murder cases going at one time. I was running around Alabama and Mississippi, taking on cases for no money. Now things have changed—Amnesty is foundation-funded with a staff. So in many ways the risk has gone out of it.

And working internationally gave you more of a sense of risk?
In many ways I re-created the risk there. I went to South Africa, the Soviet Union, Chile. I was thrown in jail, thrown out of countries, shot at.

Can you talk about some of the specific risks you took?
In the Soviet Union in the mid-'70s I smuggled a letter that Sakharov had written to Jimmy Carter. My wife and I were detained at the airport. We were strip-searched. They knew we were carrying something and they tried to find out where it was. They had been tailing us the whole time we were there.

What was in the letter?
A list of the prisoners who were in the various camps. Had I been caught, it would have been a severe punishment.

Were you frightened?
Terrified!

Did that experience discourage you from returning to the Soviet Union?
No, I went back five years ago. I met with another group of dissidents. This was before glasnost really started, and I told myself that I'm not going to re-create what I did last time with all that tension and jeopardy. I'm with my wife and we're going to have an easy time. But within a day and a half we were involved with a group of dissidents—not Jewish dissidents, because by then they were acceptable.

What kind of group were they?
Baptists and fundamental Christians. They were really having the hell kicked out of them. So we'd meet them at two in the morning because they were afraid of being seen. It was interesting because, where I had a bond with the Jewish dissidents, I did not have a bond with these people. Yet I felt their sense of oppression.

Were you surprised that you got involved again?
Yes. But it's clear to me that the feeling of helping is really a part of creativity—like going off to Czechoslovakia as an

American lawyer and helping the people write their constitution.

What is the most important part of how you approach a case?

Understanding the dynamics of the courtroom: the hostility, the tension, the racism and the fear. For example, when I represented Chavez in the '60s he claimed that if you squirt stuff on grapes it can be poisonous to people. That's more or less accepted now as a fact. But then it was considered insubstantial and we didn't have proof of what we were saying. There were no studies then; we were going on instinct.

So you walk into a courtroom saying that grapes are dangerous. Then what happens?

No one gives a damn about the environment, and they've never heard your argument before. On top of that, you're a New York Jew. And the bottom line is you're trying to deal with deep-seated hostility toward migrants, women and Spanish people. You have Hispanic women who look like they have just come from the fields and they're the ones who are going to challenge the law of the land.

The law is something you talk about in the courtroom. But what's going to decide the case are the dynamics amongst the people, the deep-seated sentiments, the racism and the terror that's going on in the world. Like Beckett, who has a nonsense type of language, the language you use is similar.

In what sense?

It's unrelated to the real issues, which are the racism and the fear. When you're dealing with Chavez the important point is that you're trying to stop strike-breakers. If you don't get the people to stop the goons, the people whom you're representing will get their heads bashed. You're talking about protecting their lives.

How much power does the judge have?

A lot. The law is what a judge says it is at any particular instant. So that if a judge says I'm going to let these goons go back out and the moon is made of green cheese, there's really nothing you can do about it.

So how do you get around that?
You take each case separately, and then you make it up.

In what sense?
You walk into the court at 8 a.m. and there's a judge at 9. You unfold each day like a play. At the end of a day I'll have a play written. At 8 a.m. I'll be able to tell you what will happen at 5 p.m.

How do you do that?
By understanding what each person in the courtroom needs—which includes the judge, the other side, the client and the jury. That's a total of about 20 people, and I have to be in control. If a trial runs for about three months, that can be incredibly exhausting.

How do you assume control?
Sometimes by appearing out of control and sometimes by disappearing from the scene and sometimes by just sitting back. And you have to be prepared to lose more frequently than you win. You also have to make sure the judge does not feel lectured to. He resents your being there. He thinks he's smarter than you. So you have to let him find his own way. You become like a teacher, but appear to be non-existent.

There was a case where I represented blacks in the recording business. It was purely a case about money. But because the defendants were black, the judge kept seeing them as criminal defendants. Lenny Bruce said all you have to do is walk into a courtroom, look at the color of a man's skin and you know what role he plays.

You represented Lenny Bruce. Can you talk about that case?
It was an obscenity case in New York. Lenny was being prosecuted for using certain words, which were "fuck" and "motherfucker"—with one "cunt" thrown in. Let's say there were 15 "fucks," 37 "motherfuckers" and one "cunt." So we have one witness who says, "In the Army you get up in the morning and you say, 'Where the fuck is the fuckin' knife, give me the fuckin' coffee and the fuckin' knife.'" We're talking about culture. And everybody who's been in the Army knows that you cannot hear a noun without a "fuck" adjective.

How did the judge respond?
He said, "I was in the Army for three years and I never heard the word "fuck." Now that was stunning. Here's one of the most experienced judges—who's dealt with everything, who's been sitting on the bench 15-20 years—and he says, "I never heard the word 'fuck' used in the Army."

How do you prepare for something like that?
You can only prepare to some extent, but when it comes out it's a terrific remark because at least you know what you're dealing with. You know how to shift your case, which is what I call "the switch."

Which is?
Well, we first started the case by saying that Lenny has made the most profound social comments since Jonathan Swift. And that he's using the word "fuck" as a metaphor. We brought in a professor at Columbia who states that that's what they say in *The Canterbury Tales*. And I'm thinking: "Great, he's tracing the origins of the word fuck."

But that approach didn't work?
No, because you look up and there's three judges and one of them is black. He nearly goes through the roof when he hears tapes of Lenny's performance where Lenny says, "Nigga, nigga, nigga." And you couldn't persuade him that Lenny was trying to show the value of words. He only heard "Nigga, nigga, nigga." Then you realize you have to reach him on a different level—and that's the switch.

So what did you do in his case?
We brought in Dorothy Killigan, on Lenny's behalf, who represented the Roman Catholic Church and propriety and who was a woman who would never say "fuck."

Was this one of your most difficult cases?
It was difficult, but not as difficult as walking into a courtroom in Chile or in Bangladesh and trying to learn someone else's culture totally. The ground rules are always different. In Bangladesh I represented a son of a member of the Dutch Parliament who was allegedly involved with the overthrow of

the government and was facing a death sentence. He's your witness from nine to five and then at 6:30 they beat him up. And if you don't get him out of there, the same thing's going to happen every day.

Did you win the case?
Yes.

Since you've worked with many of your clients under extreme circumstances, do you feel you have unique relationships with them?
Yes. What I feel is a sense that I can understand and touch the Lenny Bruce who sits next to me, who's totally tortured by his inability to communicate. In effect I become his translator. And what I really think I feel is a sense of love for Bruce, or let's say the 23-year-old kid in Bangladesh.

Do you think this is your strength—your ability to communicate for others—like a Bruce or a Rushdie or, as you mentioned, your father?
Yes, I think that's my strength—along with an awareness of the dynamics of the court. For instance, I seem to have a laser intensity for going after a witness; but I know how to do it in such a way where I ask the questions I think the judge wanted to ask.

When you talk about going after the witness, are you talking about breaking him down?
No. That's an easy trick, and clearly a sophisticated judge can see through that. You have to be sensitive to the judge's relationship with the witness. And the key is walking away so that the judge thinks he has arrived at his conclusions by himself.

What about your weaknesses?
I pay more attention to external events than to my internal life. If you sit and create something quietly you are enriched by it, whereas when I finish a case I am totally drained by it. Now there are also highs with respect to the people I represent, but my psychic life probably pays a high price.

You're talking about your internal life as opposed to your

personal life, aren't you?

I think so. There are a lot of things that I could have done for myself that I didn't do. I could have attempted to be creative in an internal way or to find some sense of self-expression. It's very difficult to be quiet after you've been this tumultuous.

So you've devoted your life to defending the right of self-expression for many people and yet what's suffering is your own self-expression. Had you not become a lawyer do you think you would have become a writer?

Well, look at what my children are doing. My 25-year-old decided that music was going to be her life when she was only nine and now she's going for her master's in creative writing. And my 21-year-old is probably going to be a writer.

Is it frightening to give yourself permission to be an artist?

It's terrifying. And if you're spending your time defending everyone else, it's a wonderful cop-out. It means you never have to deal with yourself. You can say, "All these external forces are keeping me from finding my own self-expression."

How do you put the voice that wants self-expression to rest?

I don't know that I have. I think this is the time of my life to see whether or not I'm entering Act Three. I've been in the legal field for 30 years. The question now is whether I can start writing. I've flirted with it. I've written two books of a certain caliber. But neither of them has been in great depth.

What is your fantasy in terms of writing?

In the last year I have started two separate book contracts. One is for a very thoughtful, ruminative talk about social values from a lawyer's perspective—all the pressure on the ability and inability to communicate. And then there's the pull of a novel which I've been plodding along with. I want to do something in quiet. And it may be that I can or can't do these things. But it's time to find out.

Are you apprehensive about finding out?

Yes, because I get so much pleasure from tension. It's like a quick hit, like chocolate. I have learned a sophisticated skill; it's probably somewhat higher than basketball and not as high as playwriting. I don't know if I have the ability or the intelligence to do something longer or more thoughtful. Do I need the chocolate, do I need the quick dessert? That's where my doubts are.

But not in terms of how good a lawyer you are.
No. That I can do. What I have done for 30 years is learn that skill. In a courtroom I am totally natural and self-expressive, but it is within the constraints of that environment.

But if you take away those constraints will you be able to express yourself?
I don't know. In that environment I am totally free. It's like acting. An actor can be totally free onstage, but offstage what else is there? It's the quiet side, that's where my doubts are.

❝ The effect of sustained hard work is unbeatable. You can overcome all faults through hard work. I've seen that happen both personally and to people all around me. ❞

PHILIP GLASS
Composer

A haunting 1988 film, *The Thin Blue Line*, made a free man of Texas death-row inmate Randall Adams. Falsely accused as a cop-killer, Adams owes his life to evidence turned up and exposed by director Errol Morris. And Morris's film owes much of its haunting quality to its musical score, by composer Philip Glass.

Glass is well known for his operas *Akhnaten*, *Satyagraha* and *Einstein on the Beach*, and for his popular concert tours with a synthesizer-dominated ensemble. Despite his vast creative output—which often is as memorable as the movie or play it accompanies—Glass credits hard work rather than talent for his success.

Having started his musical education when he was six, Glass

© Al Hirschfeld. Drawing reproduced by special arrangement with Hirschfeld's exclusive representative, The Margo Feiden Galleries Ltd. New York.

ultimately studied with Nadia Boulanger, whose students included Aaron Copland and Virgil Thomson. She was a major influence on Glass's life, as was Ravi Shankar and certain leaders in the avant-garde theater movement, including Robert Wilson and Ellen Stewart (who founded the LaMama Theatre).

It was in his early theater collaborations that Glass started pursuing what he calls "a highly reductive, repetitive style that made most of the musicians who encountered it very angry. They wanted nothing to do with it." Glass decided to perform his music himself, and in September 1968 he made his New York debut at the Film-Makers Cinematheque. "It was a very conceptual concert," consisting of visual as well as musical components, says Glass. For example, the musical scores themselves were placed in geometrical constructions to reflect their titles. One hundred and twenty people were in the audience that night, most of them artists. They responded to Glass's music, and the concert was a success. The visual artists remained the most supportive and helpful as Glass paved his controversial way in the music world.

As an interview came to an end in Glass's East Village apartment, he was asked about his collaboration with ex-wife JoAnne Akalaitis, Joseph Papp's successor as artistic director of the Public Theatre. (See profile, Page 1.)

Glass spoke with great respect and admiration for the woman he helped to launch the innovative Mabou Mines theater company in the 1960s, and with whom he continues to collaborate artistically. When asked to talk specifically about their work as artists together, Glass smiled. He looked up at a young man in his early 20s, who had been raiding Glass's refrigerator throughout the interview, and said: "He is the most creative thing we have done."

How did you get started?

I was very lucky because I discovered music as my main interest when I was only six years old. When I was eight I began studying at the conservatory for seven years and then I went off to the University of Chicago. I had a classical background in music, which was very helpful. It would have been hard for me to pick up that stuff later on. Life gets complicated as you get older and you're not as receptive. To learn a language, you have to learn it at a young age.

Was there an influence from your family?
To a degree. There are professional musicians in the family, but not in my immediate family. My father had a record store, so he was interested in music. He was not a very successful businessman, but things were different then.

How so?
Well, in the '50s the music business was not big like it is today. If you said you were going to be a musician it was like taking a vow of poverty. A lot of people go into the music business now because of the money.

Did you feel you were taking a vow of poverty?
No. I was simply doing what I wanted to do. In those days, we didn't worry about how we made a living. There are fewer jobs around now and there's less idealism around. People want a car and an apartment, and then maybe they'll talk about more meaningful things.

Do you feel your children are more materialistic than you were?
No, they're not like that at all. They're the result of the marriage that JoAnne and I had, so they grew up with people in the theater and music. They consider our life a little arty. On the other hand, they're not interested in becoming lawyers or doctors, or things that guarantee status and money.

Do you feel the impact of these materialistic times on your own work?
I have very good audiences for what I do. It's a consumer generation and my work is among the things they consume. So it's not like I am an artist in a garret somewhere. The house I live in is one that I paid for from music. I didn't inherit money from my family. For the past 12 years I've made a living in the world of music—not pop songs and jingles, but writing operas and ballets.

When did you make a professional commitment to music?

When I went to the Juilliard School of Music in New York. I didn't choose a university. I chose a trade school because I was looking to grow artistically. And I've never regretted that. I felt that I got the beginning of the techniques and equipment I needed as a professional composer. I was there four or five years and then I went on to study in Paris with Nadia Boulanger, who was my most important teacher. I was lucky enough to have a great teacher like her. Not everybody is that lucky.

Why was she your most important teacher?
Because not only did she teach you about music, but she taught three important things about how to approach it. First she said that you never get past the fundamentals of music—they're the most important thing, and if you master them you've mastered music. And then the advanced theory becomes easy. The second thing was the value of a simple, sustained effort—which is the pillar of your education. The effect of sustained hard work is unbeatable. You can overcome all faults through hard work. I've seen that happen both personally and to people all around me.

What faults do you think you can overcome?
Slowness, stupidity, lack of wit, lack of talent. In my own case I've combined consistent effort on a high level with a kind of idealism. There were a lot more talented people in music school than me, but I worked harder. On an objective level, I've accomplished more than most of the people I went to school with. I've made more records, written more operas. I could quantify it that way.

How would you define talent?
Nadia Boulanger used to call it *bien doué*. It means gifted. Those gifts come from God, they say. There were many people who had that gift in school. I was not one of them.

What was the third thing she taught you?
She was very insistent on the value of paying attention, of simply being awake to what was going on around you. And she instilled these values through a brutal regime. But she expected nothing of her students that she wasn't capable of doing herself.

I read somewhere that she didn't even go to lunch.
One year I had the 12:30 lesson, which was the worst because she never stopped to eat. Giovanni, her cook and houseperson, would bring her lunch on a plate, which she would balance on the keyboard. So you had to pay attention to the lesson, but Mme. Boulanger's lunch was falling into her lap every other minute. It was hysterically funny, but it was also very anxiety-provoking because you were always diving to catch the plate.

You talked about a brutal regime. What was that?
You got up at six in the morning and you worked hard all day long until there was a lesson. I generally didn't work at night; even today I don't. Usually I'll work until six unless there's something I can't get done in the daytime. Then I'll set aside two hours in the evening.

So you'll usually put in a 12-hour day?
Yes, when I'm writing. But when I'm in New York I also record. I do my writing in my studio until noon. The morning hours are good for me because the phone doesn't ring. I don't know too many people who will call me at 6 or 7 a.m. The other good time is in the dead of the night. The afternoon is not a good time because the phone rings. It's distracting even if I don't answer it.

What happens after you finish writing?
I go to another studio to do production work. And on Tuesdays I see people like you.

And you go to Nova Scotia, don't you?
Yes, that's one place I can work. But the best place is actually Brazil. I rent an apartment in Rio.

Why Brazil?
Because I like the country—it's physically beautiful and warm and I like the fruit juices. Also the language, Portuguese, appeals to me. I studied it for several years and I have friends there.

Do you know a lot of people there?
I have just enough friends so I can go out for dinner maybe twice a week, which is perfect. My arrangement is that no one is

supposed to know I'm there until I'm just about to leave. Then the press will find out and I'll start doing interviews.

How long do you stay?
Usually a month. And I can actually write for 12 hours a day because there's no one to bother me. I call the office in New York on Mondays, Wednesdays and Fridays, and if I need to send anything to New York I can fax it. Basically I have a two-bedroom apartment and I turn one bedroom into a studio. It's a very regimented way of life. It's a seven-day week. I can get a lot of work done.

Besides writing music, do you also perform?
I'm involved with 50 or 60 concerts a year. Then there are 30 or 40 performances I'm not in. If someone does an opera of mine I may show up for the performance or I may come to a rehearsal. Or there may be three or four productions that I want to keep track of, even though I'm not playing in them. So I have to balance my time between writing and performing.

How did you get involved with *The Thin Blue Line*?
A producer with Coppola's film company introduced me to the director, Errol Morris. I saw a rough cut of the film when Randall Adams was still in jail. I thought it was a wonderful project, so I began writing music for it.

What was it like to work with Errol Morris?
It was easy because he was very subjective. Some film people work in a very detailed way and tell you exactly what they want. But Errol doesn't know what he wants the music to sound like. He just works on a general feeling for a film.

Can you describe the process?
I wrote tons of music for him, not knowing exactly where it went. He liked to have the music so he could think about it. Then he would synchronize the music with an image or a moment. Usually I'm the one who does the syncing, like when I worked with Paul Schrader on *Mishima*. But maybe I'm being a little too self-effacing even in Errol's case. In fact I did make some particular decisions. But sometimes he came up with ideas I never would have thought of.

Such as?
Well, I said to him, "Errol, everything that is in the movie you can have, but anything you don't use is mine." When we got to the end of the movie he showed me the pieces he wanted to use. I said, "Errol, you left out the best piece"—and played it for him on the piano. He worried about that for a week and then he used it in the opening credits. I should have kept my mouth shut—because then I would have owned it! It wound up being the theme for Randall Adams, which I had tried to write eight times.

How did the ideas for those themes come to you?
A lot of it had to do with Errol's input. But there are techniques for matching an image and sound that are not taught anywhere. They come from experience. I learned that when you match an image and music, you go for a loose match, not a close one.

Can you give an example of a close match?
A TV commercial is a close match. You're told what to look at and what to think. You have to leave a space in between an image and music so that the viewer's imagination can fill in that space. That's the psychological mechanism which personalizes the material and makes it work. I also look for one place where they come together.

Can you give an example?
There's a guy in *Thin Blue Line* who talks about his wonderful memory, but he really has a lousy memory. He says, "I remember everything." And then he says, "I don't remember where that car was." As he talks you can see a nervous movement of his leg. So I wrote a cello line to underscore this nervous movement. I chose wind and string instruments over percussion because strings don't create rhythmic interference with the voice. And *Thin Blue Line* is almost all dialogue. The music had to give us a sense of character without drawing attention to itself.

How were you trying to portray Adams?
As a person who needed help. Errol discovered a musical theme which sounded like "Help me." He heard the words. It's a theme that continues to fall and finally changes key.

When most people talk about the arts it's with a certain mystique. But your examples are very precise.

Well, it's a precise business. I'll give you another example. Errol and I are working on a new project about the physicist Stephen Hawking (*A Brief History of Time*). Here we're using a harmony which has very specific emotional qualities. You can match a chord change with a feeling or a kind of emotional picture of the person. It's as precise as when you're making spaghetti sauce and deciding how much onion to put in. With experience you learn how to do that.

What specific emotional qualities does the harmony have?

It goes to an unexpected place, which is like this guy's life. Here we're talking about a life that took an unexpected turn and went in a very odd direction; so the music has to do that, too. The music mixes a lot of major and minor keys together so that the emotional quality becomes mixed, which also fits with this guy's life.

Can you give any other examples of loosely matching an image with an experience?

Yes. Did you see *Koyannisquatsi*? This is a film that has no dialogue at all, so it's all images, such as planes landing and planes floating through the air. What struck me about these huge beautiful 747s was that though they weigh thousands of tons they float in the air like clouds. I realized that I needed to pick music that was very light, so I picked a vocal sextet.

In order to show the lightness of the planes?

Yes. I wanted to bring that out, not the heaviness. It goes against the expected, and yet it connects with something we know about planes. What's so beautiful about it is that you look up and all that machinery is floating in the air. So I wrote a piece of music which sounds like a madrigal sextet—just for voices. And so when you watch these planes and you hear this music, there's a connection that happens. Music can very often create the emotional attitude that you bring to what you look at.

In contrast, a section of the movie has clouds and water. And for that one I used a brass octet. This is just the opposite. Clouds are completely immaterial. And yet they give the impression of weight and massiveness. So I emphasized the weightiness of the clouds by writing for big solid brass sounds. If I'd reversed the images and put the voices with the clouds and the brass with the planes, it would have been ordinary. But part of the art of it is the unexpectedness, and not relying on a cliche.

How have movies and theater influenced you?
I am an unusual composer in that I'm really a theater composer. I work with subject matter. A lot of composers don't, especially those who have devoted themselves to concert music. *Symphony No. 6, Quartet No. 3, Piano Sonata No. 21* don't suggest subject matter, they suggest something more abstract.

Do you think you can be interested in both?
No. I think that you have a predilection for one or the other. It's not a surprise that Brahms didn't write a lot of operas and Verdi didn't write a lot of symphonies. You need to work in a certain way. I've worked a lot in the theater and it's very natural to me. But I've done very little symphonic work. So if someone writes six or eight symphonies and at the age of 45 decides to write an opera, I'd say, "Good luck, buddy!"

When did you first start writing for the theater?
When I was 20. I wrote for dance as well, and then for film when I was 21. In 1966 I did my first theater piece for Mabou Mines. So I did theater music and other kinds of music until 1975, but after that I worked entirely in theater. By theater I also mean film, ballet, opera—music which is inspired by subject matter. People in the world of so-called concert music look down on that. To them it's a second-class art form.

Why do you think that is?
I think it's a leftover from the old days when the theater was considered a place for sinners. It's part of our Protestant morality. If you're enjoying yourself, it can't be any good. In fact, the great changes in music history have happened in the theater. Just look at Mozart, Wagner and Verdi. And the reason for that is the demands of theater are unexpected. You suddenly find yourself working with material that's new to you.

When I was doing *Einstein on the Beach* in 1976 I had to take an hour-long musical piece which had been good enough for concerts and make it work for a piece that was 4 1/2 hours long. I had to think of new ways of working to write that opera. The same thing happened with the opera I wrote about Gandhi. I found the decisions I made about its dramatic presentation required a different harmonic technique.

Such as?
Well, with *Einstein on the Beach* I was trying to combine functional harmony with overall rhythmic language. For example, I took the concept of the cadence—the formula we use to close a musical phrase. And I combined the idea of a cadence with the idea of a rhythmic variation—a rhythmic pattern that would change every four measures. I did that by an additive process. So I go from a measure of 5/8 to a measure of 6/8 to a measure of 7/8. They're all different, but each by an addition of one. I invented one that was cyclic. So you ended up on the leading tone of the note you were beginning from. I wrote a piece where I used that cyclic cadence, with an additive process in the rhythm, and to that I added scale passages in the woodwinds. That turned out to be the spaceship from *Einstein on the Beach*, which has a high energy, apocalyptic feeling. It is a piece that was based on a very specific technique.

What about the piece you wrote about Gandhi?
It has a recurring bass theme, a technique that is often associated with the music of Bach or of the church Mass. People often ask me if the pieces are religious in nature. I think that they are—unconsciously. I'm using techniques from 17th- and 18th-Century church music, which endows the opera's music with an extra kind of transcendent quality. Because in an unconscious way, you associate it with the great liturgical music of former times.

Somebody once said that Hitchcock's strength was his "articulated ambiguity," which might be used to describe your work.
In a sense that gets away from the cliche. The way I work is that I find a musical argument that goes with the dramatic argument, and usually the argument demands that I do something new.

What do you mean by an argument?

I mean a thesis or a presentation of an idea. I'm starting a new project now, based on Cocteau's movie *Orpheus*. I'm going to use that for the basis of an opera. So now I have to come up with a musical line that will fit that material. The material is unique enough to require its own musical thought.

What kind of preparation do you do to find that musical line?
I'll spend a lot of time looking at and thinking about the movie and then reading the script until something connects. Then I'll come with an idea. It doesn't happen easily. This is where talent would be helpful. If I were smarter I could probably figure it out more easily. I suspect the idea will have to do with the mirrors in the movie, which are crucial. It's just a hunch right now.

What role does the unconscious play in your work? You talk about the audience's unconscious; what about your own?
There's not much we can do about it, by definition. But I have found that when I get into these extended work periods, like I do in Brazil, that the value of doing the 12-hour days is that the work carries on into dream work and that's how I can tap into my unconscious. But to put in a 12-hour day takes about 14 hours so that there's time to eat and get a breath of air. And then you go to sleep. It takes about two or three weeks for this process to work for me. I don't know how it would be for someone else and I wouldn't dare suggest it to anyone else.

And after working this way for two weeks what happens?
I find that I'm working at night or that I'm getting up in the morning with work kind of thought through. There are ideas that are now available that weren't available the night before.

How long can you keep working that way?
After about three weeks I begin to slow down automatically. I find that my 12-hour days are becoming 10- and nine-hour days, and finally I can only work eight hours. And eight hours feels like half a day at that point. I hardly feel like I did anything. The whole process is slowed down. In order to work that intensely I have to create the conditions for that to happen.

What are the conditions?

I have to actually physically create them in terms of where I live, how I live and whom I see. I have to limit contacts with the outside. And it's worth it because of the kind of work that can happen. But it's not for everybody. I can't even do it very much myself. I can do it on several occasions a year at the most. Other people I suspect can do it more easily.

Can you talk about the use of repetition in music?

That's a structural strategy. People tend to think of it as a kind of emotional strategy. I think the emotional quality of music comes out of harmonic language, not out of structural language. And I think that repetition is part of structure and not part of emotion. That's my own experience of it. Oddly enough, I don't consider it very important—but it is useful. And you must know how to use it. There's a line in the movie *Spinal Tap* where he says, "You know there's a fine line between being clever and stupid."

How did you learn how to use it?

It's something you learn from doing. Laurie Anderson once said that the thing that amazed her most about me was that I always knew when to change. And of course that is part of the technique, but it's also experiential. When I first began writing music that was based on repetitive structures in the mid-'60s my technique was not very refined. But by the time I got into the early '70s it became very refined.

Do you feel your music has changed a great deal?

Yes. And even though the forces of success and inertia combine to make it very difficult to come up with new ideas, I'm happy to say that if you take the pieces I wrote in 1970 and compare them to the pieces I wrote in 1990, you would have trouble even knowing it was the same composer. In order to see real development and change you must look at 10, 20 or 50 years of an artist's work.

So you feel that time plays an important role in your development as an artist?

Yes; and also great effort and self-consciousness. We artists go to enormous lengths to completely change our language, and we find that we've made incremental changes, not the vast changes we had hoped for. And yet, without a great deal of effort I don't think we can make any changes at all.

Do you think there is a difference between being creative and being an artist?
Yes. We have more opportunities as an artist. No doubt there are creative bond salesmen. But they can't reinvent the language. The rules they play by are imposed by the outside and they're more stringent. Or they don't get to play the game. As artists, our ability to invent rules is only limited by the ability of people to follow our inventions. And there's a lot of that. I think we also have to distinguish between packaging and artistic creativity.

What is the difference?
The difference is that an artist can open a new window on the world. He can show us something that is unmistakably new and yet familiar. It's as if I opened a window and said, "Oh my God, I can see Second Avenue." But it was there all the time. There's an aspect to the fine arts that has to do with the spiritual side. You might find it in chess playing. Things that are closer to the idea of games. The idea that the spiritual can enter in. By that I mean the quality that suggests transcendent values.

So you can be creative but not spiritual?
Right. Real art has to do with being magical, like the water lily of Claude Monet or the flags of Jasper Johns. In India they'll tell you you have to see such and such a singer because "he was touched by God." It's hard to imagine that clothes designers were touched by God. We don't think of clothes design as being a spiritually satisfying experience.

So you feel that that type of spiritual experience is found mostly in the arts?
Yes. There are certain gray areas. But to have a vision that's transforming is usually found in the arts. That doesn't mean other fields are uncreative. You can still do new things—such as the guy who invented the steam engine. But that doesn't have the ability to transform the spiritual content of another person's life the way Beethoven's *Ninth* did. So we're talking about another level of transformation.

Have there been specific works of your own which have transformed your life?

I think *Satyagraha*, the Gandhi piece, was a pivotal work for me. Many people think *Einstein on the Beach* was, but for me it was really Gandhi because I addressed questions of social change and social issues in the context of an artwork. So it really brought together something which I hadn't done before.

Can you talk about the work you've done with JoAnne Akalaitis?

We've done lots of plays, usually a play a year. We did *Dead End Kids*, *Cascando* and a couple of Shakespeare plays.

And you worked together both married and when you were divorced?

Yeah, both.

Has it been harder or easier now that you're separated?

If it's easier it's not because we're separated. It's because we're older. It has very little to do with the marriage. We're more sure of ourselves and we know how to work. We also haven't lived together in 20 years, so it happened that we came to artistic maturity during the time we were separated, and that was something of a coincidence. I'm sure we'll go on working together.

JoAnne said that she felt you really understood her work.

I've watched it a lot. And, since we were both founding members of Mabou Mines, I was around her work a lot.

Was it hard raising a family and being an artist?

What was hard was raising a family in New York City. I think it would have been far easier in any other city, and yet I had no choice but to be in New York doing the work I was doing and having the access I needed to other artists.

But you didn't feel a split between having to be with the kids and doing your art?

No, because JoAnne and I divided up the child care pretty equally. They were with me half the time and half with her.

**JoAnne and other women in this book have expressed conflict about having a career and a family.

I think JoAnne's difficulties had a lot to do with the built-in problems of her profession, which is terribly chauvinistic. One young director I know was telling me that there are only so many slots for women directors and there are so many more women than there are slots. You don't have that kind of quota system with the male directors. So for JoAnne to become the artistic director of the Public Theatre she had to be so much better than anyone else. The ones who generally end up succeeding are stunning.

You said that you and JoAnne both raised the children?

We had them an equal amount of time. And she was back working three months after the children were born. Not even three months, because I don't think she ever really stopped being involved with the theater in some way. But the hard thing is to give up work for several years to start a family. Once you go back it's hard to get the momentum. You fall into that kind of a cliche woman who goes to art school and then becomes a mother and then people say, "It wasn't really serious."

Do you think that's true if both people are artists?

No. But sometimes you get into a family where the husband is a stockbroker and the wife is a painter and he never really thought she was a real painter to begin with, and he'd kind of pat her on the head and say, "That's all right dear, you can do it on weekends." But a person like that doesn't understand what the artistic temperament is to begin with.

Who has had the greatest influence on your work besides your teacher, Mme. Boulanger?

There are so many people. In terms of film, I learned a lot from Paul Schrader, from Errol Morris, from Godfrey Reggio. The four major people I worked with in terms of dance were Lucinda Childs, Twyla Tharp, Jerry Robbins and Melissa Finley. There are lots of dancers who've used work of mine. And I've written music for a lot of dancers. But working with dancers has to be less articulate.

In what sense?

For one thing they tend to start with the music and then they put the dance to it; so dance collaboration is not like theater collaboration, where you're actively making the piece together. But in terms of influence, the visual artists have had the greatest effect on me—though I haven't used their work directly that much.

Are there specific artists you can think of?
Well, the generation of people I grew up with, like Richard Serra; or those who are slightly older than me, like Frank Stella or Jasper Johns. The art world was very supportive financially. People like Sol LeWitt helped me do my first concert. A lot of artists helped me buy equipment. But also I think that in the '70s the intellectual leadership in the arts was really coming from the visual artists, much more than from anywhere else. It shifted a little toward theater later on.

What things most concern you in your career now?
I don't have writer's block and I don't worry about deadlines and I don't have many self-doubts. If I did I'd be paralyzed. But what I do worry about is having enough time to do what I want to do. Getting the right people to do my work, keeping the cash flow going so I can run the organization that I want to run, which involves a recording studio and a publishing company.

How many people work for you?
Eight to 10—and that's a worry. It keeps you working and gets you up early in the morning. So there are financial constraints that have very little to do with lifestyle but have more to do with the ability to exploit what talents that I have the best that I can. Someone asked me once how one person does everything that I do, and I said that one person doesn't. I have a lot of help. But all the people that help me also become an obligation. I can't take off a year because there'd be about eight people who would take out a gun and shoot me! Fortunately, I like what I'm doing.

You have a publishing company?
Actually I have an organization which presents my work. It involves a production company, a booking company, a publishing company and a performance organization.

How long has that been around?

It's evolved over 20 years. It began with an ensemble which consisted of three or four people. And then six years ago I had to start an office just to control the publishing, and by that time I got involved as a co-producer. The recording studio began as a small nightmare 18 years ago and became an enormous nightmare. Recording studios are black holes for money and time. But that employs four or five people full-time, and I have to produce other artists to keep the company going. So self-doubts for me are a luxury! I don't have them and why should I? I mean, it's not going to make life any easier. Maybe I'm just naturally a shallow, insensitive person.

That doesn't seem to be the case.
I suspect that maybe I am. I've been accused of being shallow and insensitive, but maybe it's not such a bad thing. My problems are more practical: like how to get this record finished by a deadline, or how to figure out what the harmonic language is for a new opera, and who's going to be the director, and whether I can get the right person to sing at the Met. Those are real problems. Forget the self-doubt.

Carlin Glynn and Pete Masterson: "I think the basic thing is that Pete and I are trained in the same way. So there's a basic respect for the way we each work and there's a lot of shorthand sometimes. Of course, there are also arguments."

❝ You have to find the justification for what she does. Nobody gets up in the morning and says, 'I'm going to be a sonofabitch today.' ❞

CARLIN GLYNN
Actress

❝ I used to give long lectures about the backgrounds of the characters and the situation, and now everybody is part of the discussion. The more I expose the actors and the designers and everybody else to the material and the more we discuss it, the more they come to it on their own terms and they feel like they thought of it—and maybe they did. ❞

PETE MASTERSON
Director

Carlin Glynn and Pete Masterson share a home, three children, a creative sensibility, and a great deal of success in several plays and movies. In 1979 Masterson, who developed *The Best Little Whorehouse in Texas* with Glynn at the Actors Studio, won a Drama Desk Award as best director and was nominated for a Tony Award for direction and as author of the book. Glynn, who created the role of the bordello madam, won a Tony. When the play went to London, Glynn won the Lawrence Olivier Award as best actress in a musical.

Masterson and Glynn were young apprentices when they met at the Alley Theatre in Houston. Both started out as actors. Besides winning a Tony for *Whorehouse*, Glynn won the Joseph Jefferson Award for *Pal Joey* at the Goodman Theatre in Chicago. She has worked in such films as *Three Days of the Condor, Sixteen Candles, Gardens of Stone* and *Convicts*. On TV she has co-hosted WABC's *Good Morning New York* and co-starred with George C. Scott in *Mr. President* on the Fox Network.

Masterson also has enjoyed success as an actor. He starred in *The Trial of Lee Harvey Oswald* on Broadway in 1967 and landed major roles in *The Great White Hope* and *That Championship Season*. His film acting includes roles in *The Exorcist* and *The Stepford Wives*. But Masterson began to write, as well; and he was directing at the Actors Studio when he read an article about a whorehouse that had closed in Texas. Hence the play that he co-wrote, directed and stayed with for four years.

After the successful New York and London runs of *Whorehouse*, Masterson was ready to expand once again—this time into film directing. An opportunity presented itself in a conversation with Robert Redford at the Sundance Institute, created by Redford to develop films and plays. Redford suggested that Masterson find material that was "small and meaningful" to him.

Masterson immediately thought of *The Trip to Bountiful*, a play written by a distant cousin, Horton Foote, who asked that Glynn play Jessie Mae, one of the leading roles. And so once again Masterson and Glynn were working together.

Interviewed in their Fifth Avenue apartment overlooking Central Park, Glynn and Masterson alternated leaving the room to take business and personal calls, including one from actress daughter Mary Stuart Masterson. All were awaiting release of *Convicts*, starring James Earl Jones and Robert Duvall. Once again it was a family venture: Horton Foote writing, Carlin Glynn acting and Pete Masterson, wearing one of his favorite hats, directing.

Carlin, you once said, "I have a real affinity to the characters I play"—and that you didn't want to play Jessie Mae as a shrew in *The Trip to Bountiful,* so you tried to "back-door" that role. What does that mean?

Glynn: Well, it has to do with creating a character's agenda as opposed to what the film's agenda may be. I think I was very concerned when Horton asked Pete if I would do the role, because I could see all the traps in the character—the stereotypes, the one-dimensional aspect of her. So I worked very hard to get away from that by "back-dooring it"—which means looking at the situation from this woman's eyes. I worked on an element of sexuality with John Heard, who played her husband, Ludie. They're cramped into this small house with his mother, and all they have is a clear glass door to separate them.

And you're very attracted to each other.

Glynn: Yes, and so I thought it was important to create that aspect of their relationship. I also tried to find the little girl in myself 'cause I think in a way Jessie Mae never grew up. I felt she was having a bad 36 hours but she wasn't a bad person. I wanted it to be that she wished her mother-in-law would behave, but she didn't want her to die. I think there is a feeling in all of us, certainly actors, that we want to be approved of, so you hate to be the bad guy. And for that reason I didn't go to dailies. I always go to dailies, but I just couldn't bear to see Geraldine (Page) and John being so adorable—and I was afraid I'd pull back just to get approval.

So you had to keep concentrating on what she felt.

Glynn: Right. Here she is with her husband and mother-in-law, sitting up in the middle of the night. She barely gets out of the house—even for a Coke. She can't afford anything, her husband's been sick for a year, and she's cramped up with this woman who sings hymns all day long. So back-dooring means creating a very strong agenda. And what's been most gratifying to me is that 80 percent of the people who see this movie may not like the character, but they genuinely understand her. Especially older women who are mother-in-laws and married women with mother-in-laws.

In fact, on opening night in New York somebody came up to me and said, "Miss Glynn, I really enjoyed your work, and I'm gonna go home and work things out with my mother-in-law and my mother, before it's too late." When you hear something like that you know that you've had an effect and that the film is about something that people relate to.

Pete, what do you think was the most creative aspect of your work on the film?
Masterson: I don't know if I can answer that. It all adds up to one film, so you don't know which thing you would leave out.
Glynn: I think your having the idea to do the whole thing is the most creative thing.

At Sundance Institute?
Masterson: We didn't develop it there, but that's where the idea came to us. Redford said I should pick something that was small and meaningful to me to develop, and Carlin reminded me how much I liked the play. I'd always talked about it, and so I just called Horton right then. I'd read it, and seen a revival of it around 1960. And so I was ready to do it even though I had never directed a film before.

What was your next step?
Masterson: Horton and I worked on this script, because it was only a play at first. I thought he had already written the screenplay but he hadn't. Then I called Neil Spisak, a designer whom I liked very much, and a cinematographer named Fred Murphy. He was the only guy I talked to who didn't have an attitude that he was smarter than a first-time director. Whenever I'd say that I didn't know how to do something he'd say, "You shouldn't know how to do that, that's my job. Let's talk about it." You have to be able to say you don't know. That's the number one rule, because they'll find you out. And all I knew was that we were using 24-millimeter lenses a lot.

The scenes are almost little vignettes and plays in and of themselves.

Masterson: One of the key things I did was to plan the entire shoot with the cinematographer. We went through the film saying, "Where do we start this scene, how do we make this scene different from that scene, how do we keep the interest going visually?" So we knew exactly what to do when we got to the set. We also rehearsed for two weeks, and that was tremendously valuable. We learned a lot.

I remember the first day of rehearsal I said, "I just want to get one thing straight—this is not about a sweet little old lady and a wimpy son and a mean daughter-in-law. It's about all the relationships." Geraldine said, "Thank God!" I said, "They're human beings, and they're in a situation in which they get on each other's nerves but Geraldine is not a saint." One of the first things we did was to dispel that myth. So you can see her trying different ways to irritate Jessie Mae.

I think the key thing is that they all did seem very human.
Masterson: Yes, and each of the characters learns something. In the beginning, they're cooped up in this little place and Ludie has a horror of going back to his home where he grew up. He doesn't even want to see it. Yet, what Geraldine gives him in the end is an understanding of what you get from the land, what you take away from it. You take your strength from it for the rest of your life even though you can't go back and reclaim it. Because it's not the same. But the distributors didn't like that ending. They wanted Geraldine to stay there. And I said, "What would she do? She'd starve to death."
Glynn: Then they begged you to let her die.

Why did they want her to stay?
Masterson: Because they thought the ending we had was a sad ending. Yeah, it was a sad ending. They have to go back and try to get along in this little place, and you know they won't. But at least for today, they are going to try.

Which was uplifting.
Masterson: I don't mind that. But you don't want to let 'em off too easy.

What do you think made this movie so special?
Masterson: I think we all understood it. Whenever I direct

something I like to know what made the writer write it, because sometimes it's not evident. So I asked Horton. And he said, "Well, I heard a story when I was young about this woman who was in love with this man, but her father wouldn't let him marry her, 'cause he wasn't good enough for his daughter. But the man continued to love her the rest of his life, passed by the house and greeted her every day." The man happened to be one of my ancestors, one of my cousins.

Anyway, when we got to that moment when Geraldine says that she didn't love her husband, it didn't have quite as much impact as I thought it should. Geraldine was wonderful, but it seemed like we were missing something since the whole movie was based on that moment.

So what did you do?
Masterson: I told Geraldine that even though we had the shot we wanted to try it one more time to see if we couldn't go a little deeper personally. I said, "Do anything you want, because this is an extra." Then I told the cinematographer that I was going to start the scene with a two shot and I wanted to move into a single. But I said, "I don't want you to move the camera until the emotion works. I want the emotion to motivate the camera rather than just a word, and I don't know when that's going to happen."

So you waited for that moment to happen?
Masterson: Yes, we started with a two shot and when something started to happen I tapped Fred and he started to move in. All of a sudden it exploded. I mean, the emotion took over so much that Geraldine couldn't even talk. She got through it, and she kept looking over her shoulder to see if anybody was watching her cry. When we finally ended, she said, "Well, at least that was different."

But Fred wanted to do it again because he said it was kind of messy and Rebecca [De Mornay] was bouncing in and out of the frame. That's what the operator watches, the framing. He's not really seeing the performance. At any rate, I said, "No, we're not gonna do it again, print it."

And quite honestly, I thought that that was an Academy Award-winning moment. It was different than any other moment. But Geraldine thought it was too much. And Horton thought it was too emotional. But they were both easy to talk out of their concerns.

It's interesting how you can start out with one vision and have it change into something else.
Masterson: It always does.

How long did it take to shoot that scene?
Masterson: Well, we had a grueling day of filming. We were on a bus for 18 hours. Actually we were on a sound stage. There was a guy shaking the bus and running by with lights.

Carlin, didn't you improvise the scene where Geraldine kisses you?
Glynn: It wasn't improvised; it happened while the camera was turning.
Masterson: But you didn't plan on doing it. So in a way it was improvised.
Glynn: Yeah, we didn't plan to do it. In fact, it was a stunning moment for me, because I didn't know it was going to happen. I had a hard time sitting on the emotion.

Which was?
Glynn: To not just burst into tears. The take Pete picked, you can tell she's really moved even though she's lighting a cigarette. But it would be wrong for her to bawl in front of this woman. I mean this is war. It was a beautiful moment.

And I remember another moment after we've had the fight over the recipe. She comes into my bedroom where I'm smoking and says, "I'm sorry." I say, "I accept your apology," and then I grab the recipe. This happened on camera, we didn't rehearse it. She and I never had to discuss how we worked. She's very generous and so am I, so it was like a fusion.

Masterson: You have to have actors with stage experience for Horton's stuff. He writes a lot of dialogue. Fred Murphy would say, "I've never seen such long scenes." We'd do a take and it would be eight minutes long.

Glynn: I'd like to add to that because I cannot stress strongly enough how little money Pete had to do this project. He made it for one point six million dollars and shot it in 25 days. And it wasn't that long ago, in 1985. I bring that up because he couldn't do big-bucks movie coverage, which is your master and then mediums and then two shots.

He'd design the way the entire scene moved and at what points he intended to cover it, because he didn't have time to cover the whole thing. So he needed actors that could play a 12-minute scene. That's never done in movies. You may get three pages shot if you're fast. So I really admired the way he did that.

Masterson: We had some days where we did 10 pages.

Glynn: If we didn't finish it we couldn't make the movie. There was no more money. So he had to do everything in the time allotted.

Do you think the limitation worked to your advantage?

Masterson: Sometimes it works for you and sometimes it works against you. For example, the scene Carlin mentioned, where Geraldine gives her the recipe back—I decided ahead of time to shoot that from the other room, looking in through the doors. I know that if I covered it I would have cut into it. But there are other times when I had to make a jump cut because I didn't want to wait for Geraldine and the sheriff to walk for a minute over to the other place. And everybody said, "Why did you do that?" And I said, "Because I don't have any coverage."

Glynn: He said, "Because I want the movie to move forward, I don't care if I look like a stupid director."

Can you talk about working together?

Masterson: We talk a lot off set. Actually, somebody said that after we'd been working on *Whorehouse* for awhile, they found out we were married.

What works for you professionally about knowing Pete so well and what doesn't?

Glynn: Well, his personality is such that he's a very calming influence, even when he is panicked. But I'd be aware. That's part of the positive, sensitive side of a relationship that becomes negative when you're working together. So even though I'm one of the cast, I can also see he's worried about losing the light. And it just so happened that I'd often be the last shot of the day, as the sun was going down. It would be my turn and I'd see Pete looking a little antsy, even though nobody knew that.

Masterson: Working with Carlin is very easy because she's just a very skillful actress. And she's helpful with other actors. She was with John [Heard].

Glynn: John is very confrontational. And he's like many very sensitive male artists—he has this exterior "fuck you, shock you" side. But I just ignored it and tried to get something going with him, because of the sexual aspect on the screen, which I felt had to underlie the relationship. So the first couple of weeks were really tough because he'd do dumb things, like talk dirty to try to shock me.

Masterson: John's an actor who'll eliminate everything. He'll say, "Why would I do that? Why don't I do this?" And that's the way he works, until he gets down to the only possible thing he can do, the thing he's supposed to do. We had this huge scene in the bus station in Houston, and I had planned out Ludie's and Jessie Mae's path when they come in. We got there in the morning and I even walked through it myself.

But when John got there he said, "Well, why would I do that?" I said, "Because that's where it lays out here." He said, "Yeah, but why don't I go over there first?" And I realized I'm ahead of myself. So I told him to do what he thought he should do. And he tried it out and about a half hour later he said, "I think you had it right in the first place." But he had to find it out for himself, just like all actors do. I know that, having been an actor myself. And in my haste to get this huge movie done in a short period of time I rushed things.

It sounds like you had to avoid being in an adversarial position with him.

Masterson: I never take that position with actors. There are directors who like that. Otto Preminger was famous for it. Ultimately things with John worked out. I just tried to relate to him as another human being, but it was not easy. Especially when he would say things like, "Why the fuck doesn't Jessie Mae get a job?" And I'd say, "Because in 1947 in Texas, it would be the ultimate emasculation of your character if you did not support your mother and your wife." Or one day he said, "Why can't Ludie be from Maryland instead of Texas?"

Glynn: Because John's from D.C.; he was worried about the accent.

Masterson: So I said, "Well, because people from Texas are polite, unlike people from Maryland." He started laughing.

He actually seemed very vulnerable in the movie.
Glynn: Well, that's the way he is. He's a wonderful actor. And as time passed it got easier.
Masterson: I loved working with him.

Pete, what was your favorite scene or scenes?
Masterson: The opening scene, which was not in the script. I made that up out of a monologue in the first scene, where Geraldine is telling Ludie about how she used to wake up in the night and take walks and the dogs would howl. I remember thinking, "Well, she's talking about when she was a young woman and had a little child." And I thought that would be nice —if we started the movie with some kind of romantic thing, some music. But the hard thing was that I did this all on the telephone.

Why?
Masterson: Because I was in New York and we wanted to shoot a bluebonnet field that was blooming down South. And with a small budget like we had, you couldn't afford to fly down there and back. Fortunately, the set and costume designers and cinematographer were down there. And they called me and said "You know, these bluebonnets are dying like mad."

I said, "Okay, get that girl who's going to be Geraldine's stand-in and dress her up in something that goes back 40 or 50 years." Then I told them to get a little boy to play John as a child, and I explained how they should do the scene. I told Fred to shoot it in slow motion and regular motion and different speeds and sizes and just have them run through the field. And I gave them some directing.

What was the result?
Masterson: Well, when I got down there, Fred said: "It's not any good. We got there too late and I didn't think we had enough light to shoot it in slow motion." When we got back to New York, I had some guys at the optical house take a look at it. One of them said he could blow it up in different sizes and start to pick out parts of it, and it would start to break up into little pieces. He went ahead, and it started to look like a pointillist painting.

How did you get it to look like it was in slow motion?
Masterson: You take out some frames and print each frame three to six times. Then I found this soprano to sing the hymn that Geraldine was singing in the opening. Horton didn't like it. He said, "This is not like Geraldine. She wouldn't sing like that." And I said, "Yeah, but she thinks she could. She remembers it that way."

So we went with the song. And it turned out he liked it. He also didn't want Geraldine to go into the house. That wasn't in the script. So I said, "I think that would be an interesting trip for her, if she goes in and walks around."

Why did you think of doing the opening that way?
Masterson: I kept thinking, how do we get into her mind and get the freedom of what it was before she was captured, caught in this place? So that's what I was looking for. As you segue out of that, into her singing, then you get the point. Otherwise we're in the room for 40 minutes before you get out. Then there's another musical sequence as soon as she leaves. That was all choreographed ahead of time.

We made one mistake. I was trying to get this scene to work, going from the opening sequence into the house, instead of it being a cut. I was going to have the crane move the camera closer and closer to the window until we go in the window and start the scene that way. We got out there at night, spent two hours getting everything ready and the crane wouldn't work. So I said: "Forget it. The shot's not worth it. Go home, guys."

Carlin, can you talk a little more about how you prepared for your role?
Glynn: I have a certain affinity for this character, so a lot of it was instinctual. I tried to look for the little girl in the character and therefore the little girl in myself. And I hate to say it, but it was not hard for me to do that. I have a real affinity for the sound and the language. As a young woman I was in Houston when the three movie theaters that Jessie talks about were there. So I had a sense of the place.

And though it wasn't always easy to work with John, I find him very attractive, so I could relate to him as a man. Also, there was one scene where I'm talking about my girlfriend and how she couldn't have a baby, which helped me get into my character.

In what sense?
Glynn: Well, not only was my friend childless, but so was I in the movie. That was part of Jessie Mae's subtext. It was one of the things that made her retain her childlike qualities, because she wasn't a parent. In a sense I love her because I think she's very valiant. She's an extremely unhappy woman who really refused to be so. She was going to dress up and go downtown to the movies and drugstore, and she was going to make her lists and make everything be okay. The important thing is not to create a character who has a negative impact on the audience.

So you have to get in touch with what you like about her?
Glynn: Right. And you have to find the justification for what she does. Nobody gets up in the morning and says, "I'm going to be a sonofabitch today." The women Horton writes are so rich. What he gives you and the places you have to go are so complex and fertile.

Do the props or set help you get there?
Glynn: Yes. As a matter of fact, Neil Spisak, the designer, asked us all what we wanted on the set, because every piece of furniture had personal objects in it. And I said I wanted a diaphragm put in the dresser, so that in rehearsal, when she goes to her dresser, she sees a sexual symbol. It was neat.

Did you know that, Pete? You look surprised.
Masterson: Yeah, I knew. But it was a surprise to Geraldine.
Glynn: That's why I did it. She didn't know it was in there. It was perfect. And then after she found out she just used the same reaction. We all worked using such intimate details. I had on underwear from the '40s. And I had this great walk in the movie, because I was wearing a tube girdle that costume designer Gary Jones got me.

Were the clothes made for you?
Glynn: No. They were all real clothes. They weren't built. They were found in basements out in Pennsylvania. For a period look, the hairdresser used only pin curls instead of hot rollers.

Were there any scenes that were difficult for you to play?
Glynn: Yes, the last part of the movie was really emotionally difficult for me as a person. And I wasn't aware of this until much later. I think it was because during the last period of the shooting I was the bad guy who was off in the car, or off in my honey wagon. Or I was the last one to get my hair done. I started to get paranoid and thought everybody hated me and I felt that Pete was being mean to me. But those feelings really informed the work toward the end of the movie.

How so?
Glynn: The truth is, Jessie Mae has been up all night. She's waiting in the car, while her husband and her rival are sitting on the porch of this old heap of a wreck of a house. So it paralleled the work, and there was a lesson in that. I always thought I was very good at not becoming the part I'm playing. But it taught me that I actually become very emotionally involved, even though I can leave the character and the accent behind. I remember carrying on when I had to run across the field because we were losing the light. I started screaming, "I'm never gonna forgive you again!"
Masterson: It actually was three pages of dialogue to get all the way across the field.
Glynn: So I'm feeling like everybody else got to act all day, and now that there's no time left, it's my turn! And as I'm starting this long walk across the field I see my fellow actor, John Heard, behind the camera reading a magazine. Well, I lost it! And he did not normally do this. He was usually a nice, generous actor off camera. So I just flipped out. And then I saw the daily and I said, "My God, she's such a shrew." And he said, "Yeah. It's perfect." All of that was going on so when Geraldine kissed me at the end, it just released a lot of stuff.

Were there scenes that you really enjoyed doing?
Glynn: I loved them all, and none of them was difficult technically. I liked walking down the street, or being in the beauty shop, or the drugstore, where you don't hear me say anything. Because I thought you saw another side of her—outside of that triangular relationship. You saw who she wanted to be. She wanted to have a nice day or buy a dress rather than being trapped in this situation. I love the last scene. I like walking up

to the house mad having my list of rules. I like my shoes, and feeling thirsty. There are so many turns, from coming in with a lot of anger to trying to really work this out and make sure I get the rules out, to being kissed, or trying to recover, to being left out again. I like all that a lot.

Can you each talk about the role of the unconscious in your work?

Glynn: I don't understand the question. I mean, what would you say is the unconscious?

Your intuitive side.

Masterson: I don't know what I do unconsciously. I think it affects how you make choices, why you do this project or that project. When you write you never know where it comes from. I'll write a scene sometimes and I'll think, "Well, how did I write that scene?"

Do you feel you're open to that unknown territory?

Masterson: Yes. I nurture it and I try not to make too many plans. You have ground rules, but then you allow things to happen. Like when you act, you have certain things you're trying to accomplish, but you try to leave time for the unconscious.

Do you feel like it ever gets in your way?

Masterson: You can't allow that because then you become a plot writer, which does not inform your life. And that's OK, but that's not the business I'm in.

What about your work, Carlin, in terms of the unconscious?

Glynn: Well, first I pick the externals for the character, which is what she wears, how she walks and, in this instance, the accent. But once I've done my homework I would say that my unconscious controls my work. I really listened to that voice absolutely in terms of discovering elements in Jessie Mae's character and in her relationship with her husband.

Masterson: I like to plan the shots, and then you have to leave yourself open to having a better idea—if something comes to you or something comes to one of the actors. As a director, dealing with the unconscious also has to do with allowing other people's unconscious to work. It's part of the Method work we do at the Actors Studio, which helps you get to that basic instinct. That's why the relaxation exercises are so important, because nothing can happen with tension.

Glynn: In a way this work helps you tune your instrument, which as an actor is yourself, so you can leave it totally alone. I don't think some of the moments Geraldine and I had, like with the recipe or the kiss, would have happened without the kind of training we had at the Studio.

Were most of the actors in the film members of the Studio?

Glynn: Mostly everyone except John and Rebecca. People just don't realize what it takes to be an actor. You can't just say I'm a lawyer, but often people will say: "I'm an actor." I teach a class at Columbia where I show directors how to work with actors. One of my students is a well-known documentary filmmaker who's going to direct her first feature film. She's been given to me because she's never dealt with actors before. So I am trying to teach her how an actor approaches things, and she's got four months to do it in.

We take a lifetime to hone the craft. In rehearsal once Geraldine talked about a student she had who said, "Well, Miss Page, I'm going to do this for six months and if I haven't gotten it I'm gonna quit." And she said, "Why don't you quit right now!" Acting is a way of life. It's usually not a living.

Carlin, what about playing the madam in *Best Little Whorehouse*?

Glynn: I felt very strongly that I didn't want to do anything to glorify prostitution. But I also wanted to look at this as a business and the human side of it. It was very exciting to create a part, because you had input on what they were writing. And I think we all felt the same way.

Which was what?

Glynn: It wasn't a show about whoring. It's a very funny and political show and the madam is really a very maternal figure. I remember a woman outside the stage door one day, an older woman in a print dress and that blue kind of hair. She came up to me and said "Miss Glynn, I know exactly how you feel, I'm a house mother at Rutgers." And I just thought that was perfect. So that process was very different from *Bountiful*, where I was doing a role that had already been played by Kim Stanley, Eileen Hackert and Jo Van Fleet in the play version.

Did the fact that those other actresses had played the role affect your work?
Glynn: No, I was just flattered to be in that company. I didn't want to know how they worked on it. But creating a part in a play out of a whole story was the essence of the creative experience.

Can you talk a little bit more about working together as a married couple?
Masterson: Well, we usually discuss the motivation for the characters when we get home at night.
Glynn: Or in rehearsal with other actors. I think the basic thing is that Pete and I are trained in the same way. So there's a basic respect for the way we each work and there's a lot of shorthand sometimes. Of course, there are also arguments.

Such as?
Glynn: The toughest time for me is when he knows something and I can't get it. He thinks that because I'm married to him I should get it very rapidly. And then I get my feelings hurt.
Masterson: Maybe I'm a little more impatient with you than I am with other actors.
Glynn: Yeah, he really is. And I'm very quick, too. I work with facility and speed. So I get my feelings very hurt, because sometimes I think he treats everyone else better.
Masterson: It's probably true.
Glynn: But I surprise myself at how I can scream at my husband in front of a lot of people. It happens rarely, if ever; but I don't feel like I can't yell or that if I did he'd be mad at me when I got home.

Do you bring your baggage from rehearsal home with you?
Glynn: I think so. But you know it's work and you try to sort it out in the workplace. But I remember during the last period of *Bountiful*, I told John I was mad at Pete and I said, "Am I overreacting?" and he said "You sure are." And that was very helpful. Usually we're very good together.

Because you have a similar sensibility?
Glynn: Yes, and we like the same things. I'm more interested in personal or independent films than I would ever be in TV, or commercial film. I'm not saying that a commercial film can't also be a good film, but I love theater because it provokes people, and I think that commercial film and television have stopped trying to be provocative, in the sense that *Bountiful* is.

Another thing that works for us is the way Pete runs his set. Whether it's theater or film, he has as much respect for his gaffer or his grip as he does for his stars. People are polite to each other and they respect one another.

How has your work changed over time?
Masterson: It's easier, because you get smarter, hopefully. It's not that the problems are more easily solved, but the process of directing is something I know more about. You can't take any shortcuts; but I guess one of the things I have learned is not to do all the talking. I used to give long lectures about the backgrounds of the characters and the situation, and now everybody is part of the discussion. The more I expose the actors and the designers and everybody else to the material and the more we discuss it, the more they come to it on their own terms and they feel like they thought of it—and maybe they did.

So you listen to people more.
Masterson: Yes. In a film you have a lot of departments, so you have to listen. You do in a musical, too. Working on *Whorehouse* made it easier for me to do a film, because I was used to working with a lot of different departments—the sound department or the lighting department or the music department or the choreographers. In a film it's similar. You just replace the choreographer with the cinematographer.

You get different things from each of the talents?
Masterson: Yes. I find the designers have input into things that the actors don't. The designers have their own method. I did a film called *Full Moon in Blue Water*. Gene Hackman has a house and he's looking at movies of his dead wife. And the designer said, "Who brought the furniture into this house? Was it his wife, or did he have this here before he married her? How long were they married? Is this her taste or his taste?" So we called

the writer, and we started talking about it.

Did that happen with *Bountiful*?

Masterson: Yes. *Bountiful* was supposed to take place in 1952. I changed it to 1947 because I liked the design better. The clothes were more interesting, the colors were more interesting. There was a big change after that. They had the new look, which took place around '49 when the women's skirts dropped way down. So we went back to '47 with the suits, and the spectators' shoes and hats.

Glynn: *Bountiful* was an absolute creative collaboration, with everybody pulling for the same thing, nobody being treated any differently than anyone else. But the goal was the product in every area. The crew even offered to give Pete free time on a movie. He refused, but for them to offer to work for nothing is unheard of. I guess what we've addressed pretty much is not only personal creativity but collaborative creativity. And that informed both *Bountiful* and *Whorehouse*.

Masterson: It might not seem that a big musical about a whorehouse and *Trip to Bountiful* had much in common, but they're both about place, and an invasion of space somehow by something else, and I think they're both personal stories.

❝ What happens is that there's a gradual absorption into any project. I try different things and suddenly I'm well into the project and hooked by it. And then, unfortunately for my family and friends, it takes over. ❞

SHELDON HARNICK
Lyricist

He was shy but funny, and he got a lot of attention when he wrote. So Sheldon Harnick continued to write, and found worldwide acclaim. His song lyrics have won a Tony, for *Fiddler on the Roof*; a Grammy, for *She Loves Me*, and a Pulitzer Prize, for *Fiorello*.

Born on April 30, 1924, he grew up in a non-Jewish neighborhood of Chicago. His mother wrote rhymes to mark birthdays, anniversaries and virtually any occasion. Harnick followed in her footsteps. He wrote parodies of songs, and then actual songs—none of which he took seriously until he heard the music from a Broadway hit, *Finian's Rainbow*. It was a turning point in Harnick's life, realizing that a

© Al Hirschfeld. Drawing reproduced by special arrangement with Hirschfeld's exclusive representative, The Margo Feiden Galleries Ltd. New York.

songwriter could entertain and say something meaningful.

Harnick's first break came with *New Faces of 1952*. He wrote *Body Beautiful* in '58, and in '59 *Fiorello* was produced. Several years later, after reading *Tevye's Daughters*, by Sholom Aleichem, he, Jerry Bock and Joseph Stein came up with the idea for a show that became one of the most highly acclaimed musicals in history, *Fiddler on the Roof*. In 1964, *Fiddler*—and such Harnick classics as "Sunrise, Sunset" and "Tradition"—were first performed.

Asked about his roots, Harnick spoke of his parents, an uncle who introduced him to theater, and his rabbi, who gave him a real sense of Jewish and ethical values. His mother lived through her children, pushing Harnick, his brother and his sister to succeed. Both couldn't wait to get away, but they also realized there was a value in what she was trying to do.

Harnick's father was a parlor comic, cigar maker and dentist. He came to America looking for his own father, when he was 15. He never found the object of his quest, a cause of loneliness and, Sheldon Harnick said, great compassion and generosity.

If you look today at Harnick, both the songwriter and the still-shy man, you can see traces of all these people. He is driven, compassionate and in constant search of what is meaningful and good in life and in his work. Although he has been successful in his search, writing some of the most meaningful songs on Broadway, he admitted that he approaches each project with a certain anxiety, always worrying if he'll run out of things to say and write.

You once said that when you wrote the song "Do You Love Me?", it was really about a relationship you wished your parents had.

Out of context it doesn't really make sense. But while we were in rehearsal for *Fiddler* I sensed there was a song to fit that moment. And all I could think of was the comedic notion of Tevye saying, "Do you love me?" And with those two people in that culture, that was so startling to the wife, so she just answered, "Do I what?" But I didn't know where to go from there.

What did you do?
When we got on the road, in Detroit, I went for long walks

every day and thought about what those words meant to those two characters. It was a very hard song to write, and I wrote about four lines a day after a couple of hours' work. And finally, after five or six days, I think I had a chorus, or I had the song. But the form seemed very strange. Then I showed it to Jerry Bock and said: "I don't know if you can set this so that it'll be coherent musically."

Was he able to set it fairly easily?
Yeah. And although it sounds more like a dramatic scene than it does a song, it's a nice tune. We showed it to Hal Prince and Zero Mostel and Maria Karnilova and they loved it. I think they put it in the show the night after we gave it to them, and—to my delight—it worked. I watched it for the next few nights and the actors kept getting more out of it, so the song became richer. And by the fourth time I had to leave the theater because I was sobbing.

Why?
I got outside the theater and I thought: The reason I'm weeping is that I grew up in a household that was very much affected by the Depression, so there was a great deal of fighting. And looking at these two people holding hands at the end of the song and saying, "After 25 years, it's nice to know that maybe we do love each other," affected something very deep in me. I assumed that it was the wish that my father and mother had that kind of relationship.

Can you think of other songs that expressed your wishes or feelings?
I wrote a revue number called "The Merry Minuet" which came out of reading the newspapers and growing more and more despairing with each article until I started to laugh at myself. So I wrote a song which became a type of black comedy.

Are there any songs that reflect any of your personal relationships?
There's a song in the adaptation of *It's a Wonderful Life* that I did with Joe Raposo. I needed a love song for our heroine to sing to our hero, who is extremely depressed. And she tells him, "I couldn't be with anyone but you." I tried to write it in a way so

that it was really about my wife and me. And when my wife heard one of the lines she started to laugh, because it's something that happens to her. The woman is saying, "I feel safe with you, and complete with you, I'm always finding money in the street with you." There's also another line where she says, in effect, "You even eat the steak I cook you, when I know its inedible. Your gallantry's just incredible."

And this was also based on you and your wife?
Yes, she made a steak on or right after our honeymoon. It was a little tough and she said, "How can you eat that?" I said, "It's fine." And she said, "No it isn't, you hate it, you hate me. I know when I've cooked a bad steak." And suddenly she was crying and the argument was all on her side. So I use things that have amused me or touched me, or things that I feel because it not only gives the song an authenticity, but it allows me to express myself.

You once said that after you went into therapy your work started changing.
Yes, because up until then I concealed a lot of emotion by being clever. I thought I was writing songs like [Sir William] Gilbert or Larry Hart, whom I genuinely admired. But their songs had a great deal of emotion. Mine were just clever because committing myself emotionally was just too frightening. As I got into therapy, I began to get in touch with myself. I didn't want to lose the cleverness in my work, but I also wanted to find genuine feelings. Before therapy I felt that I was too sophisticated to use a simple phrase like "I love you" in a lyric. I thought it was too corny, but actually I was afraid of those feelings.

You once said that you have a split between musical theater that entertains and theater that has a message.
There is a part of me that simply wants to write hit shows—it's sheer egotism and greed. Having had two big hits on Broadway, where there's a lot of money and a lot of publicity, you feel you're just on top of the world. I haven't had that for a long time and there's a part of me that thinks, "Oh boy, I'd like to find the commercial venture that would do that for me again." But then the next day I'll think, "I don't need the money. Basically I'm a serious person—so what is the project that will

get the best out of me?"

Do you still have that conflict?
Yes. I still have these lingering feelings that what I do should be important to other people. I read an interview with Arthur Miller, who was depressed about the fact that at one time he thought you could really change people's lives with the theater. And then he started to feel that it was meaningless. But I keep having the feeling that, no, if something that I write affects one person for the better, then it's worth doing. So I'm constantly torn between the two. And in the back of my mind I think, wouldn't it be wonderful if I could find the project that does both—like *Les Mis*, which affected a lot of people because it's a show about having sympathy for the oppressed.

Don't you feel that your work has affected people's lives?
Well, yes. I just remembered a letter I got when I did *It's a Wonderful Life*. It was from one of the older women in the company, whose mother had died. She said that one of the lyrics kept going through her head and it was of great comfort to her. Reading something like that is very moving.

There's a line from "Nine": "I want to be here, there, all things to men," which you once said meant a lot to you.
I don't want to be all things to all men, but it's true that there's so much that I would like to be able to do. But there's not enough time in the day, and the older I get, I can't understand anybody being bored.

What do you want to do that you feel you don't have time for?
Travel. There hasn't been time. The vacations have been very few and far between. One of the best ones we had was when we went to Greece for two weeks, and it was just so stimulating.

You once said that the turning point in your work was when you heard *Finian's Rainbow*.
Yes. I was either a sophomore or junior at Northwestern University when a friend of mine, Charlotte Rae, had seen the show and gave me the album. The lyrics were clever, but underneath there were serious things being discussed and I thought,

now there is a career that would be worth struggling for.

Where does the need to deal with serious issues come from in you? Were your parents like that?
My father was. My father confused us all because I think he considered himself a socialist, but he also considered himself a capitalist. He also considered himself a humanitarian, and in some ways was a racist. He wanted us all to be involved socially, because it was very important, but at the same time he would say, "Don't stick your neck out." And all this came from his own Jewish background—wanting to do things, and yet being afraid of being noticed and punished. I'm sure I inherited a lot of those feelings. Also, although he was not an observant Jew, he did have me bar mitzvahed, and the rabbi, whom I adored, imbued me with Jewish and ethical ideals. I grew up with that, which is a legacy that I'm both stuck with and delighted with.

Do you feel there are other dichotomies that you struggle with and also feed your work?
There's a dichotomy of feeling that I want to say something serious, and at the same time not believing that I'm a true poet. There's the terrible fear of being a lecturer, a bore.

Can you talk about some of the people you've collaborated with?
Undoubtedly, the most successful collaboration was with Jerry Bock. Not only did we think alike in many ways, but also I think we helped each other in certain areas where one of us might be doing something that was tasteless or not funny and the other one would catch it. Our relationship was free of any personal considerations until we split apart for reasons I can't go into. I don't know that there's anyone I've worked with after Jerry that I felt as thoroughly at ease with. I certainly have done work with other people that I'm very proud of, but I miss collaborating with him.

I remember reading that you felt intimidated by working with Richard Rodgers.
Yeah, I did. Here was a man whose songs I grew up singing. It wasn't just being intimidated by Richard Rodgers, but it was being intimidated by the ghosts of his other collaborators. Now I

was trying to write lyrics that had to compare with Oscar Hammerstein and Larry Hart at their best, and those were large shoes to fill.

And how did that impact on you creatively?
First of all, I took the show that we did for the wrong reasons. I was running away from writing problems. For all my analysis, I didn't know I was doing this. I thought I was choosing the show so that I could get the opportunity to work with Dick Rodgers.

What was the show about?
Henry the Eighth, which was a problem because I thought he was a monster. When we got on the road and the show was in trouble and I was supposed to write songs that would make the audience love and adore Henry, all I kept thinking was that he was a terrible man. I had all the sympathy in the world for his wives, and none for him. Also, although I loved meeting Dick Rodgers, it came at the wrong time. He'd been through so many physical blows and even a stroke.

How did that affect your collaboration with him?
A doctor once told me that sometimes a symptom of people who have had strokes is that they lose the ability to think abstractly. And writing music is an abstract art. So I wound up having to do all of the lyrics first. Rodgers, at this point in his life, though he didn't even know it, was incapable of writing music first, which was a big burden. Also he no longer was able to write music rhapsodically. He would turn my lyrics into little jingles that he could handle musically. In some instances, where the attempt was not to make them rhapsodic, where the lyrics were very conventional but good, he wrote wonderful melodies. And we were able to write some beautiful songs. But not enough of them, because I couldn't transcend my own antipathy for Henry.

That must be hard, to work with such a legend and then find out that he's not the same person anymore.
It was. But on the other hand, I fell in love with him. His sense of humor was delicious. Also, I was so moved and inspired by the fact that despite all his physical problems he just kept going.

During pre-production he discovered he had cancer of the larynx, which he wound up having removed. And then he immediately went to a class to learn how to use laryngeal speech. His spirit was so strong that he even used to make jokes about his operation. Once, when I was trying to imitate him, he said, "*You* can't use laryngeal speech, because *you* have a larynx. I, on the other hand, don't have one, so I can do it."

What about your other collaborators? Joe Raposo, for instance?
Joe's tape is just brilliant. I loved Joe. He was a complicated person.

In what sense?
I can say this because Jim Henson said it publicly at the memorial to Joe, which of course he said in a loving way. Joe, because of whatever his own background was, needed to be with stars. He was a name-dropper par excellence. And they were all his best friends. And that was sometimes difficult to deal with. But on the other hand, his talent, his vitality, were wonderful. I've found that I need to work with people who are buoyant and positive, because I tend to be skeptical and apprehensive about what we're doing. He was also a wonderful pianist; so to sing something you had just written with him at the piano was a glory.

What are the most important things that you look for in a collaborator?
To be excited by a melody. Jerry would give me a tape, with maybe a dozen or more musical ideas on it. There might not be more than two or three things that really excited me. But if I were excited, I couldn't wait to put a lyric down, and quite often a melody—which has its own unspoken, unarticulated emotional content—may suggest words you wouldn't have thought of.

Can you think of an example?
That happened when Jerry played "Sunrise, Sunset" for me. I listened to the music and suddenly out came that lyric. I didn't realize it was in me. So, that's one thing a composer can do. Also, Jerry and sometimes Joe Raposo would take one of my lyrics and work with a certain part of it, which excited them.

And then I'd have to change the rest of the lyric in order to accommodate what they had done.

And you were willing to do that?
Yes, because it can be very exciting. And, as one of my gods, Yip Harburg, said, "If your composer can get a better melody by altering something you've done, always be willing to change in the interest of a better melody." He said that if you take a comedy lyric, the second time somebody hears that lyric they're not going to laugh so hard. And the third time they're not going to laugh at all because they know the joke. The words will wear thin. But if it's set with a gracious and infectious melody, then you can do it over and over again, because the melody will carry that. Or the lyric will be wedded to the melody in a way that remains amusing or charming.

Can you talk about your writing process? Do you have a schedule?
No, no. Unfortunately I'm very undisciplined that way. What happens is that there's a gradual absorption into any project. I try different things, and suddenly I'm well into the project and hooked by it. And then, unfortunately for my family and my friends, it takes over.

The process begins with studying the source material, sinking into it, and trying to understand the characters and letting myself begin to explore what they might be feeling and thinking. And then I try writing lines down on paper. Does this sound like something that they might say or will it lead to an interesting song? Once in a while a song will come out very quickly. Most of the time it's trial and error, that's when the lyric is coming first. But it's a process of exploration—exploring the characters, exploring the situation, exploring myself in relation to those characters, even when they're characters I don't like. Because there are parts of myself that I certainly don't like, and I can identify with those characters.

Isn't that one of the hardest parts of writing, in a way?
Well, it was in the case of *Henry the Eighth*, because I despised him. On the other hand, the villain in *She Loves Me* was totally immoral, and that was kind of fun to write.

In what sense?

There are parts of me that have a sneaking admiration for people who can do immoral things with style and charm. And they have no effect on other people if they're strong and centered. Henry was something else. Henry had the power to kill people when they resisted, and I couldn't bear it.

What part couldn't you bear?

That he used his power. He tortured and killed people. He put his first wife, Katherine, who was a wonderful woman, in isolation. He wouldn't allow her to see her daughter, whom she loved and whom she lived for. And I thought, that's just total abuse of his power. And he tortured and killed a man whom he suspected of being Anne Boleyn's lover. Early in his career, there was a quote where Sir Thomas More said, "If the lion were to know his own power, there were no holding him." And when the young Henry discovered his own power he was just impossible.

Are there other qualities in your characters that are hard for you to write?

Yes—the people who are truly aristocratic and the very wealthy. I don't know them, so I can't genuinely write them. The people I'm most at home with generally are middle-class people, maybe upper middle class or lower middle class. The very poor and the very rich I don't identify with, so I don't know their worlds.

You said that at some point the writing takes over your life. Has that ever created a lot of problems for your family?

The only time it was a problem was when my wife and I were both working on projects.

Is she a writer also?

No, she's a painter; and she's become a very good painter. But she's a nervous painter. She's as anxious about what she does as I am about what I do. I recently did two one-act operas at Music Theater Works, called *Love in Two Countries*. They ran for a month and were extremely difficult to do. And we got two bad notices, one in the *Times* which was one of the worst notices I've ever had. But fortunately, about a week and a half into the run, it started to work and I was very proud of the show. So when we closed on April 13, I planned to be with the cast, who had all worked so hard on it. As it turned out, my wife was included in an art exhibit in South Hampton. Her paintings were in a new style, which she loved, but she was uncertain how people would react. So she said, "I need you with me."

Did you go with her?
Yes, but it was very difficult, and then finally I had to think, "I have an ongoing relationship with her, not with the people in this company." So I chose to be with her; but it was a conflict.

Has your work presented any conflicts in terms of raising a family?
I have a daughter and a son. That can be difficult, when all of my attention is going somewhere else. But luckily my wife is very understanding and at the same time very strong. She can draw me back to reality in a loving way.

What do you need most in your life to be creative?
I have to be involved in a project that I believe in and that excites me, and that I feel elicits things from me that I feel are important to say. I also need a composer who will support what I do and also inspire me to do things I didn't know I was going to do. And after it's written, then it's the attempt to get it out. And along with that, more and more, is the support and the love of my wife and family. That's harder to ascertain, to weigh, because certainly I wrote well while I was a bachelor, and didn't have those responsibilities. But along with that came a lot of wasted time, when I was just lonely and couldn't get myself to work.

So you need the stability of a family?
Yes. Then I can go off and enjoy the creative parts of my life.

What do you think your strengths are as a writer, and what do you think your limitations are?
I think my strengths as a lyricist are that I'm extremely sensitive to musical value and to music as a totality. I think I have a feeling for words. I'm able to project genuine emotion into the lyrics in a way that doesn't become sentimental, especially since

I've been in analysis. And I think that I still have humor that can make the lyrics unpredictable and sound fresh and unforced. You wouldn't believe any of this if you'd read Mel Gussow's review on the last thing I wrote.

What about your limitations?
That has to do with form. Since I had to write all the lyrics first with Dick Rodgers and Joe Raposo, it forced me to experiment with different forms because I didn't want to give the composer the same form to deal with all the time. So I'm better at it, but I still have a way to go. I mean, my mind boggles when I see what Sondheim does—his adventurousness with form and his mastery of it. I tend to be best in short forms.

How do you think your work has changed?
What interests me now are the problems of writing arias, of opera texts, rather than formal songs. I'm less interested in having the restraints of a formal song, where everything is metrically perfect. I'd rather have the freedom to explore, and then write it in such a way that a good composer can make a coherent whole out of the lyric. That's where my work has gone, which may be the result of a lot of opera translations that I've done.

Do you think musical theater has changed over the years?
Yes. There's a kind of middle ground right now. For example, take the music of Andrew Lloyd Webber and the guys who wrote *Les Mis*. They start with pop music with an undercurrent of rock and they get to the middle ground of contemporary theater music. And what Tom Shepard and I did in our operas was to try and get to that middle ground from the direction of more serious opera. And I was very pleased with what we wrote.

Have there been any events in your life, other than analysis, that have really had a strong impact on your work?
Oh sure. I was divorced twice. One was an annulment, another was a divorce.

You were married to Elaine May.
Yeah, and my marriages forced me to look at myself in ways that I wouldn't have. They caused me grief; and I recognized the grief I caused in both Elaine and my first wife, and so it created a

need for a lot of introspection, separate from the analysis. I guess the other major influence was the success of *Fiddler*. It came at a good time. If it had come earlier, I might have been paralyzed by it, the way Ed Kleban was paralyzed by the success of *A Chorus Line*. For a while he could not write. He told people, "With this kind of money I don't have to write anymore, so I'm retired." But I knew him well enough to know that he was unable to write. Then little by little he came out of it.

But you were not paralyzed by the success of *Fiddler*?
No. By the time *Fiddler* came along, I had already had hits and flops. *Fiddler* allowed me the luxury to do a lot of things that I might not have done, like the opera translations. Part of me is glad that I did them and part of me wishes that I had kept writing for the Broadway theater. *The Rothschilds* was important because it caused the break-up of Jerry and myself.

Can you talk about that?
No, I'd rather not.

Do you have any feelings of self-doubt?
I think the most important thing is how that question applies to me since I became successful. Sure, I had self-doubt before that, and I had a lot of people reassuring me that I was right to have self-doubt. But after *Fiddler*, when I was accepted as a good lyricist and capable of writing successful shows, I was confident. During the writing process itself, when I get immersed in the work, there's no room for self-doubt. The anxiety occurs when you're playing the songs for the first time for people. But that's just regular artistic anxiety.

So when does the doubt occur?
To give you an example, I did one show all by myself, called *Dragons*, based on a Russian play. I kept abandoning it, and then being drawn back to it. The composers I showed it to didn't like the play so I decided to do it myself. It was first done at Northwestern University. Audiences seemed to like it. I also could see that the second act didn't quite work. The *Chicago Tribune* critic just slaughtered it. And that's when I had self-doubts, so I let it sit for a while and I came back to it. I reread and liked what I wrote, even though I couldn't get it produced

in New York. So I had doubts, which I tried to override. And then about two years ago it was done at the University of Michigan by a director there who's a friend. The show was designed by professionals and it looked like a million dollars.

What was the response?
The audience seemed to like it. But I wondered what the local critic would say, because he can be quite acerbic. And then I saw a picture of the actors in the paper with a quote that said, "*Dragons* is pure magic." I took the newspaper and went back to my hotel room and read the whole article. And I just sobbed, because somebody had seen in it what I had seen in it. And with that review I thought, now I can get it done in New York.

Were you able to?
No. And again I'm assailed by self-doubt. Luckily, that kind of doubt has never crippled me.

Whose opinion matters to you most other than the critics?
My wife's.

Will you show her something in progress?
Generally not. Sometimes I'll try a lyric if I'm not certain of it. And that's always a strange process, because invariably when I show it to her, it's because I think it's particularly wonderful. And when she says, "I don't understand it," I realize that my real reason for showing her has to do with my own doubts. Because if I'm confident of it I wait until it's all set to music.

Have you ever changed a song because of something someone said to you?
Sure. When we did *Dragons* at the University of Michigan there was a young director named Brent Wagner who really probes, the way I do. Even though it had been done at three other colleges, Brent asked me questions that I couldn't answer. I resisted giving him answers because I knew it meant rewriting, but his questions were unanswerable. I did wind up rewriting, and out of that came a stronger show.

Is it hard having your own vision and also staying open?
Yes. You get very defensive about what you've done. But

sometimes you have to fight for something you believe in. I did that once with a whole lyric in *The Rothschilds*. The producers didn't like it because it was a downer. It was called "Never Again." But we fought to keep it in. And when it was recently done at the Circle in the Square downtown, I was very proud of that lyric, because times had changed and the audience absolutely understood what I was trying to do.

It sounds like you have a strong enough sense of your own vision that other people's opinions don't interfere that much.

If I understand what they're objection is, I leave myself open to the possibility that I was wrong. And if enough people articulate what is wrong to my satisfaction, then I'm willing to change it. There's a number in the adaptation of *It's a Wonderful Life* called "Linguini." It's strictly for entertainment. It's at the top of Act Two and gets the act off to a light start, and then the play gets dark very quickly and continues to get dark. We did it at the Papermill Playhouse in New Jersey about a year and a half ago and took a survey. Half the people said it was their favorite song and 25 percent said it was the song they hated the most. So the director wanted me to take it out of the show. But I didn't because even though 25 percent hated it, 50 percent loved it. But I did compromise by cutting it and rewriting part of it.

You once said that you preferred Herschel Bernardi's performance in *Fiddler* over Zero Mostel's. Why?

Zero was difficult. A very simple illustration was that none of us wanted any Yiddish in the show that would cause laughter in the audience—you know, cheap laughter. But we agreed to use a few Yiddish words to give some color and if they got laughter, they'd come out. And then one night, Zero was dancing in the scene in the tavern and when the Russian bumped into him, Zero let out a stream of Yiddish, ending with the word "tucchus," which means "behind." So we got exactly the kind of laughter that we did not want.

Did you talk to him about it?

Yes, and using strong obscenities, Zero said in effect, "Mind your own business." So he decided he'd leave it in for two weeks. He also did things that threw the scenes out of shape. We wrote him a note saying, "We know that your imagination is endlessly fertile and it's boring for you to do exactly the same thing every night. All we ask is that when we feel you go over the line, that you allow us to talk to you." And he chose to be indignant about that. Even though 90 percent of the audience loved what he did, I like Herschel better because he gave the same performance. He found ways to keep it fresh without having to resort to those kind of interpolations.

Wasn't there a difference between the political sensibilities of Mostel and Jerome Robbins?
Well, yes. Zero was considered an unfriendly witness by the House Un-American Activities Committee, while Jerry Robbins had been called and was a friendly witness. So they hated each other politically. But Jerry Robbins didn't make his political feeling known. He was very private about that. And I think he has very deep feelings about that episode in his life. But Zero made his feelings very well known, his abomination for anybody who had cooperated with the committee. And yet, he recognized that Robbins was the right director for the show, and did agree to work with him. In fact he said, "We on the left do not blacklist."

Did you enjoy working with Robbins?
Yes. But it was mixed. Robbins had a very strong vision, but it wasn't always clear. So he drove himself and everybody else crazy trying to achieve that vision. And that meant rewriting about nine songs while we were on the road. He drove people very hard, but he also inspired everybody to do the things that they might not have done otherwise. You work with Robbins because you know that he's looking for the best possible version of what you're doing.

Who were your greatest musical influences or mentors?
I learned more about singing, more about phrasing, from listening to Heifetz than anybody else. I'd listen to the way he would turn a phrase, or just gracefully slide into a note, and that affected the way I sing. I was also influenced by jazz musicians, like Benny Goodman. And then when I got out of the Army, Dizzy Gillespie and Charlie Parker and that whole school. I was thrilled by what they were doing. And then little by little I got into serious music and leaned towards Mozart, Bach and Ravel, particularly Ravel.

Was there a lot of music in your house?
My father and mother loved music. She would play the violin and piano by ear. The other thing I remember about my father is that he was forever buying books. He was a sucker for any glib salesman that came by. There were sets of books that I don't think more educated people would buy, the complete works of Richard Harding Davis, for instance. And he loved to take us to museums and then join the tour, and he was always the one who would ask questions of the tour guide. So we grew up with his respect for learning.

It's interesting that so many of your songs have stayed with people over the years—like "Sunrise, Sunset." Why do you think that is?
With that particular song I was trying to identify with the situation of Tevye and Golde, and having their daughter marry a man they had very mixed feelings about. But they also marveled at the fact that their daughter was not just a young girl, but a woman. When I wrote that song I was looking back at my sister, and my daughter, and Elaine May's daughter, whom I helped raise while we were married. All of those things were in my mind and in my soul and apparently got into the song. And people were affected the way I was affected.

Can you talk more about the writing of "Sunset"?
When we first wrote it, Jerry Bock was living in New Rochelle. He had a studio in his basement. He wrote the music first and the song got written very quickly because I was immersed in all the material. The rising and falling cadence of the music suggested the words sunrise, sunset—and the rest just kind of poured out. After we finished it, we sang it to his wife.

What was her reaction?
I never look directly at anybody when I'm singing. I can't. I look at the wall, or over their head. But when we finished I looked at her and she was weeping. And when I first played it for my sister she was also crying. And I thought, "My God, what have we got here?"

Was this your favorite song?
No. There are too many songs that I poured myself into. Often

my favorite is the one I'm working on right now. There's one song that's in this evening of operas that we just did. Mel Gussow hated it the most. And yet I know that he's wrong. John Kander was sitting in front of me one night, and at the end of the song, he just reached over and took my hand and squeezed it.

What's the name of the song?
It's called "Caviar," and it's sung by a man to his wife. They've been married for three years. She cannot have a child and she knows he's longing for one. She's afraid he'll ask for an annulment. And so she says, "Don't leave me." And he sings this song, in an attempt both to reassure her, and to make her laugh. He starts out by saying, "To me, you are my blintzes." And she starts to smile. And then he says, "You're my caviar..." And then he says that caviar is wonderful as it is. But it's even better with a little chopped onion, a little chopped egg, some capers—but that's all garnish. And then he says, "I can live without the garnish. If we had children, they would be the garnish. They would be the chopped egg and onion. I can live without that. I can't live without the caviar." It's a wonderfully tender song. And I just don't know why Mel Gussow said, "Well they're supposed to be talking about love, but it's a song about food."

Are there any songs that made you discover something about yourself?
"Do You Love Me?" was one of them. And I was very pleased when I wrote a song like "She Loves Me." I thought, "Oh good, the analysis is working." I'm able to say things that really come right out of me, unselfconsciously. For instance, there's a line, "My teeth ache from the urge to touch you." And that was because there have been moments when I've been with a girl and the back of my teeth hurt.

Can you talk about the nuts and bolts of writing? Do you write at home?
When I wrote with Jerry Bock, quite often I would go to his studio. Or he'd come to the apartment. Mostly it was in his studio.

And he'd write the music and then you'd write the words?

Sometimes the words came first. But when we got together, usually it was for the polishing process, or to complete something, or to rehearse it and go over and over it until we felt it was right. Because until you sing it again and again you don't know if it feels right in your mouth and in your mind.

But in terms of the nuts and bolts, these days I write the lyrics in my study. Then I give them to the composer. We'll go over them together, and then he'll go off and compose, and when he's got something we'll meet. Then I'll sing it and find out whether I have any objections to any of the setting, whether any of the accents are in the wrong places. And then we'll try to polish the song to our mutual satisfaction. But often adjustments have to be made. If I love the music and it alters the lyric, I may have to change the lyric.

What do you want to work on in the next few years?

Hopefully I will find a project that enlists both my heart and my mind and my history, and something that will affect other people.

Do you have any regrets?

Yeah, I do. During the '70s, after the rupture with Jerry Bock, and for all my analysis I wasn't able to see what was happening. I retreated into a great deal of translation, because that usually meant that the composers were dead. So I was working with composers where there were no emotional problems. And even though I've done some good translations, there's the lingering worry that translations only last about 30 or 40 years and then language tends to become a little dated and new translations are done. So I regret that I wasn't doing more work for the theater at that time. And I can't get back those years.

We talked about self-doubt before. It occurs to me that the great area of self-doubt with me is that I want to do serious pieces. I want to do important pieces. And sometimes when I start them, I suddenly feel, "Am I smart enough? Am I witty enough? Do I have command of language enough? Am I poetic enough? Am I expressive enough?" These are all the doubts. "Am I tackling the right project for me? Is this something that'll be laughable because it'll come out so ludicrous or so unsophisticated or so banal, or so juvenile?" Depending on the project I tackle, those doubts can surface at any time.

❝ My mom and dad and aunts and uncles were always talking about characters they knew, and what Old Man So-and-So did, and what his wife did. It was the ability of these people to tell a story that made the stories interesting. It was a natural proclivity for them. Maybe we picked it up. ❞

ERNIE HARWELL
Baseball Announcer

Word pictures of screeching line drives and mighty swings that hit nothing but air have flowed from Ernie Harwell's tongue for half a century. Even the blind can watch a baseball game, as long as they have a radio tuned to Harwell's voice.

A wisp of a mild-mannered man wearing a beret and a smile, Harwell has always been more than he seems to be. On the record, he is a baseball announcer who has called major league games in six decades (the '40s into the '90s), a

Ernie Harwell: "Anything can happen. That's the beauty of it."

feat equaled only by Harry Caray. He has plied his trade well enough to earn a plaque in Cooperstown, and he has written a pair of books on the game (*Tuned to Baseball* and *Ernie Harwell's Diamond Gems*).

Less quantifiably, Harwell is highly regarded wherever baseball is played in the United States and is a beloved icon anywhere the Detroit Tigers have fans. And baseball's lure and reach are such that, in diminishing concentric circles of fanaticism, Tiger freaks can be found everywhere. Tom Selleck wore a Tigers cap throughout the run of *Magnum P.I.* George C. Scott—decades after leaving his hometown—once wrote an impassioned letter to a Detroit newspaper about the fortunes of his boyhood heroes.

Harwell understands this. Like a conductor true to his Beethoven, he has always been devoted to the score. The game comes first, last and always. Using simple, declarative sentences he paints a minimalist rendering. Then, with an anecdote or two of baseball lore to etch in some perspective, the game—dreary or momentous—is revealed in lush, green simplicity.

It's a craft (Harwell would be the last to call it "art") he honed on broadcasts of the Atlanta Crackers in his native Georgia, the Brooklyn Dodgers, the New York Giants (his TV call of Bobby Thomson's 1951 "shot heard round the world" was never saved on tape), the Baltimore Orioles and—since 1960—the Tigers.

The Detroit front office, for reasons never announced, decided that 1991 would be Harwell's 32nd and last in the Tiger Stadium booth. The outcry from fans and media was immediate, intense and lasted throughout the season, but to no avail. In 1992, no foul balls were caught by "a man from Ann Arbor," or by "a young fella from Sterling Heights"—suburbs picked at random from Harwell's imagination, the only fictional aspect of a Harwell broadcast. Instead, Tigers fans settled for Ernie broadcasting from cities in both leagues on CBS radio's Game of the Week.

A change of Tigers ownership brought him back for a Last Hurrah in 1993. A true classic, in extra innings.

You've written songs, you've written books, you have a patent on a can opener. When did you realize you had a creative bent?

I guess probably when I was in high school and I started writing for the *Sporting News*. I wanted to be a ballplayer first and foremost, and I couldn't make that, so I got in the writing business. That was probably the beginning of my creativity, if you could call it that.

You don't seem to think there's much creativity in what you do.
I think a creative person creates something, makes something, develops something. He could be a bricklayer, a sculptor, a painter in oils. But, yes, anything you do to make something a little bit different than the ordinary is creativity, I guess.

Maybe it bothers you to suggest that you are creative because you are very proud of your straight reporting skills.
I try to be a reporter. I react more than I create. Some people have likened broadcasting a game to creating a picture. You start with a blank canvas and then you fill in whatever happens. You draw a picture for the listener. So I guess in that sense it's creative.

My job is to look at the pitch when the pitcher releases it and if the batter hits it or doesn't hit it to react with my mind and tongue and try, hopefully, to coordinate the two and give a picture of what's going on. I think it's creative in a sense, but it's reaction in another sense.

A lot of the action of this game is in the mind's eye of the beholder—and in the voice of the play-by-play announcer.
Sure. I think so. It's a matter of interpretation, just like a painting or a movie or a play. You have to put your own imprint on it. From the fan's standpoint, the interest goes across all kinds of barriers—social, economic and everything else.

Were you a reader as a kid?
Oh yeah. My mother read to us. My father wasn't a big reader because his eyesight wasn't too good. But my mother was a great reader. My uncles and my aunts loved literature. My uncle was city editor of the *Atlanta Constitution* way back when. So he had a literary bent, and I might have inherited something from him.

Did you read a lot of the popular adventure stories?
I read the *Rover Boys* and the *Hardy Boys* and a lot of baseball fiction, like *Baseball Joe*. I loved those books. My first novels were mysteries. I got into Agatha Christie when I was in junior high probably, and Ellery Queen, who was just getting started about that time.

In your era, a disproportionate number of fiction writers, journalists—and baseball announcers—came out of the South. What do you make of that?
I don't know. Too lazy to make a living otherwise, I guess. I think we grew up in a storytelling culture. A lot of it was maybe rural. Even if we lived in the cities our families had come from farms where people sat out on the porch and told stories. My mom and dad and aunts and uncles were always talking about characters they knew, and what Old Man So-and-So did, and what his wife did. It was the ability of these people to tell a story that made the stories interesting. It was a natural proclivity for them. Maybe we picked it up.

You were Margaret Mitchell's paperboy.
That's true.

Did this mean anything to you at the time?
No, not much. My paper route was in the early '30s, and she was just a woman on the route until she wrote *Gone with the Wind*. Then I realized it was something. I was carrying papers in '33, '34 and '35. I had a route for the *Atlanta Georgian*, which was the third paper in Atlanta—the old Hearst paper. I made about $2 a week.

What's your very first recollection of baseball, either playing it or seeing it?
Well, probably when I played it as a toddler. But the first game I ever saw was in 1926. The Atlanta Crackers played at old Ponce de Leon Park and I went out there with my dad on the Fourth of July and saw a game with New Orleans. I don't remember much about it. But I was hooked. My dad was a baseball fan and I got that from him.

More books, certainly more memorable books, have been

written about baseball than any other sport. David Halberstam and George Will have written recent baseball books. Is there something about the game that makes it more... literary?

I think so. I think there's a continuity in baseball that you don't have in other sports. It's every day and every night for six months. Because it has peaks and valleys it's more like the flow of American life than, say, getting up for one big game on Saturday. I think it has lent itself to more storytelling, more legends, more history. You have a statistical basis in baseball that you don't have in other sports, a yardstick by which you can measure people. But especially in baseball you have the stories and jokes and legends that develop through the retelling that you don't have in other sports.

Do any of the players understand all of this? Or are they too young?

I think a few do. But I don't think most of them have much of a sense of history. They know maybe a little bit about the players who were stars when they were kids, but they don't go back any further than that. A few of them don't even go back that far. They just like the idea of playing and weren't great fans when they were a kid.

But a lot of players on other teams coming into Tiger Stadium tell me they used to follow the Tigers or listen to the games, and now they're going to play against the team they rooted for. That's a fairly common situation.

Are there certain very good players, or special players, who actually have a sense of drama on the field? Is there such a thing as a guy being creative with a bat or a glove in his hand?

I think so. I think Babe Ruth had that charisma. I think Mark Fidrych had it. Reggie Jackson certainly had it. Maybe Jose Canseco. Certain guys come along and have a certain charisma about them that attracts attention, and they have a sense of the dramatic.

Many years down the road, will superstars from the age of TV saturation—with every pitch preserved on video—ever achieve the dimension of legend and myth that they did in Ruth or Cobb's era?

I don't know. There's more marketing now of the players, and people are probably more aware of them. On the other hand, Ruth and Gehrig and Cobb and those guys have the advantage of nostalgia. The passing years have polished their image a little bit. It might come out even. It may just depend on which is more effective: nostalgia or marketing. I've got a feeling that in time marketing will win out. I think fellas who can be marketed might come out in the long run as big as Ruth or Cobb, maybe without as much ability.

Do you think when Mayo Smith moved Mickey Stanley from center field to shortstop for the '68 World Series, he realized he was scripting maybe the biggest rewrite ever done on the eve of opening night? Or was he just trying to get Al Kaline's bat in the lineup?
I don't think Mayo understood the drama. He was very prosaic about it. I thought it was a bad move at the time. A lot of people agreed with me. But it turned out to be a good move. And it certainly was not characteristic of Mayo Smith because generally he was a very conservative manager. He'd just write out the guys' names and let them play. He very seldom worried about strategy or trying to outsmart anybody.

In the fifth game of that Series, when Jose Feliciano sang the anthem, it didn't seem to cause any furor at all in Tiger Stadium. But when the fans got home and turned on TV they discovered there was a huge national outcry.
I got that same feeling. I think a lot of it was manufactured after the fact. When I came off the field [after pre-game ceremonies] there were a few cheers and a little mixture of—not even a boo, just a little lull, people a little bit surprised. But then I heard later on that a couple of TV guys asked questions like, "Can you believe that guy sang the anthem that way?" It began to snowball, became a *cause celebre*.

Today, that version of the anthem would be commonplace at any sports event.
It would be very mild now. It was sort of a landmark, I guess, the first guy who sang it the way he felt it. My own feeling was that he didn't denigrate the flag, he wasn't disloyal, he didn't do anything wrong. He just sang it the way he felt the song. It was a little bit different. He was likened to the hippies because he was

playing a guitar, sitting in center field with his dog. And because he was blind he had on dark glasses—and that was another symbol of the hippies. It was a time of revolution and counter-revolution in our society, and I guess people looked at him as one of the revolters.

A friend of mine in the music business out in Hollywood recommended Jose. He said Jose had done a great national anthem at the Greek Theatre. So I contacted him and he said, yeah, he'd love to come. I also picked the singers for the other two games in Detroit—Margaret Whiting and Marvin Gaye—and they sang it just fine.

Marvin Gaye sang it straight?
Marvin Gaye sang it straight. The Tigers were very, very concerned about Marvin. They were worried he'd do a Motown version and it would bring disgrace to the ball club. So they asked me to ask him to sing it straight. And I did, and he did. And he got some criticism for that. So you can't win.

You've written many song lyrics. When did that start?
Not until the mid-'60s. I always loved pop music. But in the mid-'60s I figured that like everybody else in America I could write a song.

Do you feel more creative when you're writing a song lyric than when you're calling a game?
I think so. I think you're making something out of nothing when you write a song. You're sitting down and you're not really reacting, you're not reporting. You're bringing something out of thin air.

Are you still writing lyrics?
I've been away from it for a year or two, but I want to get back to it. The thing I like about it is you can do it any way you want to—on the back of an envelope or any piece of paper. You don't have to go to the library and look up stuff. You don't have to go to the ballpark and watch a bunch of guys hit a ball or throw it. You can just sit wherever you want to and do it.

Did you ever work on a lyric in the booth?
In the booth, on airplanes and trains and automobiles, and

everywhere else where you might get a line or two that might start you off on an idea. I think most everybody who writes lyrics has had that kind of experience.

Have you ever figured out how many big-league games you've called?
Somewhere around 7,000. We could sit down and multiply it out. It's a lot of baseball.

How many no-hitters have you called?
About eight. Never a perfect game, though. I missed that with Milt Wilcox.

Jerry Hairston.
Yeah, Hairston hit a line drive up the middle with two out in the ninth.

A lot of times you have to describe not much at all happening.
That's right. But the thing is you never know what's going to happen. You might have a no-hitter that night, or it might be a 13-12 game. Or your team might win gloriously or be beaten ingloriously. So you never know.

And unlike other sports, you might have a historic moment in a meaningless game.
Any time. Anything can happen. That's the beauty of it.

You have certain stock calls on your palette—"He stood there like the house by the side of the road," for a called third strike; or "It's looooong gone," for a home run—that are sort of like Jackie Gleason saying, "One of these days, Alice—pow, right in the kisser." We all know the line is coming, and we can't wait for it. What's that all about?
I don't know. Those things just sort of happen. I think if you contrive them, they don't work too well. The thing about the foul ball just happened one time. "The house by the side of the road," I said one time long ago, and it just sort of stuck as a trademark. "Long gone?" I don't think I did that until the mid-'80s. I don't even remember what year it started.

Do you remember what your home-run call was before that?
I just said "It's outa here," or "It's over the fence," or "It's a home run." I said a lot of different things.

Do you remember consciously trying a stock call and then tossing it out because it didn't work very well?
No. I never really did that. I just sort of reacted to what happened. I used to have one about "Pull up a Stroh and sit awhile with us." Of course I discarded that when we lost our sponsor and got another beer in there. I guess I could have substituted, but it didn't seem quite right.

You're a devout Christian. But you call 162 games a year and you only quote the Bible in the first game of spring training. Even atheists look forward to it. What does that line mean to you?
It's from "The Song of Solomon." I think it's Chapter 2, Verse 2. I can't do it all right offhand. "The rains have come and gone, the flowers are in bloom, and the winter is past, and the voice of the turtle is heard in the land." It's Solomon, you know, talking to his girlfriend or his bride. To me it's just sort of a symbol of spring coming and bringing baseball with it. The winter's gone! That's the part that appealed to me. Winter's over now, and the song of the turtle, for us, is going to be baseball. The modern translation says, "the turtle *dove*." It's not the turtle singing, of course.

Baseball is a renewal. It arrives like an equinox. The dead winter is over. Everybody starts from the beginning. Everybody starts equal. No team has lost. Every team is going to win the pennant. Every pitcher's going to top 20 games. We're all going to have a great time. It cleans the slate for everybody. And even the poorest team in the major leagues has a chance. And we found out in the last [1991] World Series that they do.

Symphony conductors don't actually write any music, or perform any music, but they're great creators. They take someone else's music and 100 musicians and make something of it. And they do this unto their 100th year. By everyone's accord they just keep getting better. Most Tiger fans seem to think of you as an Ormandy or a Toscanini.
I've always heard that conductors stay young because, num-

ber one, they have a lot of physical activity in moving their arms to lead the orchestra; and number two—and I think this applies to baseball announcers—they get a lot of feedback from their audience that feeds their ego and keeps them going. They like to hear that the people enjoy their music, or their broadcasts. I think ego is there and it has to be fed and it keeps you going. Maybe we are on a sympathetic note with conductors. I don't know how the Tiger fans felt. That would be up to them to say.

Well, they said it. How do you account for such a long, loud protest over the firing of a radio announcer in the video age?
It's amazing to me. I think it's really a tribute more to radio and baseball than it is to me. When a fella has been in an area broadcasting baseball, people begin to get used to him. He's on for three hours, 162 games a year, every day and every night. People really can't escape from him if they're interested in baseball. If they want to get the baseball score, they have to tune in and hear Ernie Harwell whether they want to or not.

In four or five seasons they get used to the announcer, because he is a conduit between the team and the public—especially in the case of the Tigers, because they weren't really public relations minded. The owners and the executives didn't go out too much. The sportswriters can't do it, because they're out there a little bit on the edge. The players can't do it—they have to play.

The announcer becomes a member of the family. I have people say, "My grandfather used to listen to you, and when I hear your voice it reminds me of my grandfather." People who are under 40 have never heard anyone else. So it's not me. It's that I was in that chair behind that microphone, connecting the team to the public.

One thing creative people seem to have in common is that they do what they love, something they would have done for nothing.
Baseball announcing would be a very dull existence and very hard for somebody who didn't really have a love for the game—the travel and the hours and all that.

There is a kind of go-go atmosphere taking over baseball. Does a player making $5 million a year still put forth full effort?

I think so. A lot of people don't think so, but I do. I think that by their nature players are very competitive. They've been in a competitive situation all their lives. They have a great deal of pride, and they don't want to put on a poor performance. I think if a guy is going to hustle, he will whether he's making $300,000 or $3 million.

Who was the most creative manager you ever saw?
Paul Richards, or maybe Gene Mauch. Richards was the guy who really brought in the slider to its fullest. He had different stratagems, like moving a pitcher and putting him in the outfield for one or two pitches. Mauch was the first to use the so-called double switch. Casey Stengel was another one. He brought the two-platoon system to its utmost.

Mauch was almost universally recognized as a first-rate manager, but he never won it all.
Yeah, when you think about it, he was a perennial loser really, in the big games. He never got the big bauble that he was looking for. He came close, but he never got it.

Is that big bauble something that announcers yearn for, too?
Oh sure. The announcer loves to get into a World Series. Even if he doesn't get there himself, he wants to see his team get there. When I was coming up, the height of our ambition was to broadcast a World Series. That was the event of our profession. It's like playing at Carnegie Hall, and that's what you want to do.

Is there any technological possibility that somewhere, somehow, someone has a recording of your TV call on Bobby Thomson's home run that won the '51 pennant for the Giants—someone who maybe had a wire recorder sitting in front of their TV set?
We've explored that, and no one's come up with one yet. There's always a possibility. Last October the Bob Costas show came up with a Red Barber tape that nobody had before from the same game. It's always a possibility, but it's very remote.

There've been quite a few modern baseball movies. *The Natural, Field of Dreams, Bull Durham.* **What did you think of them?**

They're very different. I was disappointed in *The Natural*. I had heard so many good things about it, and my anticipation was too high. *Field of Dreams* I enjoyed. It was sort of a wispy, allegorical kind of thing. Usually I like a little more realism—but I enjoyed that. *Bull Durham* was almost a little too realistic, a little too raunchy. It had some scenes in the clubhouse that I don't think ever would have happened. *Major League* was sort of fun because I didn't expect much of it.

Are we taking sports far too seriously these days?
I think we're permeated a lot more by sports now. We're bombarded with these images. You hardly get any rest from it. In the '20s it was big but it wasn't the whole thing. Most people didn't even see Babe Ruth play. They read about him in the paper the next day. People would read the *Sporting News* once a week.

Has the kind of fan who comes to the ballpark changed over the years?
I think so. I think TV is responsible to some degree. Fans are exhibitionists. They carry signs saying, "We love you NBC," and paint themselves in the color of the team, or don't wear a shirt. And people are now directed by the scoreboard. In certain cities, the board will call for more noise, as if the fan isn't smart enough to know when to cheer. Like he needs that big TelePrompTer in the sky to tell him what to do. It's a bit ridiculous.

The audience used to have to bring something to the performance.
Now they tell you. It's all cut-and-dried. At the same time, the audience is more sophisticated because of the proliferation of information.

Are people in the booth, the front office, the sportswriters in tune with fan behavior out in that corner where Canseco plays, where Reggie used to play? There's some incredible dialogue out there.
I don't think they are. It would behoove everybody in the media to go out and sit in the bleachers once in a while. The owners are pretty much in their ivory tower. Most of them are rich people who don't want to rub elbows with the hoi polloi.

they've got their drinks and sandwiches in their own private box.

What's the biggest change in the booth?
When I started we were all pretty much pioneers. We didn't have the advantage that writers have in being able to read all the writers of centuries before. We had to pretty much fly by the seat of our pants. The early announcers were guys who worked at a station. The station manager told them to go and get a scorecard and announce the game. They didn't care much about reporting, getting out there early and gathering material. Approaching it as a reporter started with Red Barber, really.

Name a couple of creative people you admire a great deal.
Shakespeare is tops with me.

Did you ever listen to Wayne and Shuster do the old Shakespeare at the ballpark routine—"So fair a foul I've never seen?"
Oh yeah. "Alas, poor Yogi; I knew him well."

In the songwriting field my hero is the late Johnny Mercer. He had such a great feel for both music and lyrics, but I regard him as an outstanding lyrics writer. His estate came to me and asked me to rewrite, of all things, a Johnny Mercer lyric. The original title was "My Harvesttime Letter of Love." It had a guy sitting on a porch writing a letter. But nobody sits on a porch anymore, and nobody writes letters anymore—certainly not about harvest. So we brought it up to date, got it out as a song called "Sing Sing Sing Every Song." It was fun.

And I finally got to do a lyric with Johnny Mercer.

❝ I believe everybody is creative, and everybody is talented. I just don't think everybody is disciplined. I think that's a rare commodity. ❞

AL HIRSCHFELD
Caricaturist

© Al Hirschfeld. Drawing reproduced by special arrangement with Hirschfeld's exclusive representative, The Margo Feiden Galleries Ltd. New York.

Al Hirschfeld has taken caricature drawing to new heights and kept it there for seven decades. He still works an eight-hour day, capturing new show-business stars and legends such as Brando, Monroe, Olivier and Chaplin in a simple line.

It all started accidentally one night in 1925, when Hirschfeld, who was attending a Broadway play with a publicist, began sketching one of the actors, Sacha Guitry, on his *Playbill*. The publicist took the sketch to the *New York Herald Tribune*, which ran it. The next year the *Times* requested his services, and in 1926 this became an enduring exclusive arrangement. Hirschfeld has made his mark on the Sunday Arts and Leisure section ever since.

The 1920s also marked the beginning of Hirschfeld's travels abroad. In 1923 his uncle gave him $500 and a ticket to Paris, which would become his temporary new home. Traveling has always been in Hirschfeld's blood. In the late 1940s, he and S.J. Perelman were hired by *Holiday* magazine to do a series about their travels around the world. They were offered a high fee and all expenses—an offer neither could refuse in the wake of *The Sweet Bye Bye*, a musical collaboration which opened and closed before it reached Broadway. Their world tour was successful and resulted in a book called *Westward Ha*.

In 1941 the traveling Hirschfeld met and married the German film star Dolly Haas, who was the ingenue in Billy Wilder's first film. On the day their only child, Nina, was born in 1945, Hirschfeld hid her name in a drawing from a play called *Are You With It?* He did not anticipate that her name would appear in all his drawings to come. He tried to remove Nina's name from his work on her wedding day, but his public was infuriated. Nina stayed, and in 1960 he began putting the number of "Ninas" next to his signature.

The 88-year-old Hirschfeld sat in his Manhattan townhouse studio and discussed his amazing Broadway run. He was dressed in black and sported the long white beard he began in Paris in 1924, when a lack of warm water discouraged shaving.

You once said that when you were in Bali the sun bleached out colors so that people became line drawings walking around. Was that a turning point?

Yes, because I'd been doing watercolors. I started out as a

sculptor and a painter, and I developed this insane passion for line when I was in Bali. The sun not only bleaches out the color but it leaves shadows. It's not accidental that painters come from Europe, where it's usually gray and cloudy.

In tropical climates graphic art has been the predominant creative force. It only works where there's sunshine, because the sun plays a very important part in eliminating color and delineating line itself. I latched onto that and tried to find out why a line communicates so much.

Why does it, do you think?

I have no idea. I don't know anymore now than when I started. It's just one of those things that you're constantly preoccupied with. It's still a mystery to me. All I know is you take a blank piece of paper and you insist on creating a problem for yourself. And then you solve it, to your own satisfaction. And that's about what it amounts to.

Can you give a specific example of a problem you might create?

Well, it's a juxtaposition of line, one against the other, and mysteriously, through your insistence and your control, you manage to get something that pleases your own senses, and hopefully the viewer's. You want the viewer to see what you see, and you do that by communicating what is in your mind into your hand and onto the paper.

You do a lot of drawings of people in theater. Can you talk about the nuts and bolts of the process?

In the theater the heroes and the villains are not mine, they're the playwright's conception; and I try to capture in line what the playwright has done in prose. But there's no editorial comment from my point of view, it's just interpreting what the playwright had in mind.

How does the process work for you? When do you go to the play?

Since my drawing has to be in about 10 days before the opening, I usually go two or three weeks before. I sit in the darkened theater, either here or out of town. There used to be more out-of-town openings. They wouldn't open cold in New York. They would go to New Haven or Chicago for Tennessee Williams.

You said you sit in a darkened theater.
Yes, I've learned to draw in the dark. And I don't necessarily make graphic drawings, they're kind of hieroglyphics because the lines don't connect. But I've learned to read them, so that I can, along with a faulty memory, put the two together and re-create what I saw.

Do you ever use photographs?
No. They wait until the week before the opening before they photograph, in case of cast changes and that sort of thing. And I can't wait that long, so I have to do mine from the thing itself — which is helpful, actually.

Is there a particular aspect of an actor or person that captures your imagination? In your drawing of Sammy Davis Jr., for instance.
He was like a rubber band, you know. He was elastic and he defied anatomy. He bent the wrong way. The way he used his body was incredible. A lot of people think that I invent those things, but I don't. I remember Ray Bolger always said that he copied my drawings, which is ridiculous. I only tried to capture what he had done. But it works both ways, I suppose. He uses my drawing of him to expand his performance. It's one of those mutual benefit things. Carol Channing, for instance, told me that she tries to look like my drawings.

What part of her?
Her face mostly, and the movement of her hands and her body.

So when you're looking at an actor like Carol Channing are you trying to capture a specific part of her?
No. I try to capture the whole personality, the thing that she communicates to the audience, so that people can recognize her. Everyone who has control of their senses has the talent to recognize. The talent of people is a drug on the market. It's that other capacity to shape it and communicate to somebody else that pays the rent. Say it's snowing, and you see someone a block away who's wearing an overcoat. You can't see their face but

you recognize this person and you know it's your friend. How do you know that? It's some mysterious thing that happens that's inexplicable. All I know is that the image that I see, I can sometimes communicate on a blank piece of paper to somebody else. Everyone sees it; they just can't articulate it.

You once said you like drawing actors because they use all of themselves, while writers are more limited.
Well, no. In the case of a writer, I'm trying to get the essence of what they're writing, you know. I've made many drawings of humorous writers, of Thurber and Benchley and Perelman and so on, and I've used a completely different approach to serious writers.

Did you ever draw Tennessee Williams?
Oh yes. He was very introverted, you know. Non-communicative, actually, in his personal relations. He seemed to be outgoing and uninhibited and freewheeling, but I thought of him as being inhibited. I don't know how you relate that in line, but you try. You try.

You also drew Woody Allen. What comes to mind when you think of him?
Like most humorists he's a sourpuss, misanthropic, sore at the world. Most humorists find a lot of things sad and depressing instead of amusing. Perelman is an example, but not that typical because he was abstract in his writing.

You were very close with him, weren't you?
Oh yes. We did about five or six books together. We went around the world together for *Holiday* magazine. But most humorists are misanthropic. They take a very dour and cynical view of life.

Were there people you drew who had a great impact on you?
Zero Mostel. He was a very creative personality, and a helluva good painter. He started out as an artist, you know. He used to come to the studio quite often when I lived in the village, and he entertained us. He'd imitate a coffee percolator, or a pregnant woman. He was marvelous as a mime.
One evening, Barney Josephson was there and he said,

"Listen, come to the cafe and do your act." Zero said, "I'm not an entertainer, for God's sakes." Barney said, "Try it." And Zero tried it, and he just tore the place apart. And from that night on he became an actor.

What about Mostel impressed you?
He had unbelievable energy. I don't now where it came from. He could go on all night long.

What did you think about when you drew him?
He was larger than life. He was an exploded ventricle. I don't know how you could exaggerate Zero and still keep it on paper.

What about singers you've done—Tony Bennett, for instance, who is also a painter.
He impressed me as being a very creative fellow, which he is, of course. And I'm a great admirer of his singing particularly. I don't know when he finds time to paint, but it's become a kind of hobby with him. He's undoubtedly a very gifted fellow.

You also did a drawing of Gloria Steinem and Shirley MacLaine.
I never had much contact with them except to draw them, and maybe see them once or twice after that. But I loved drawing Katharine Hepburn. I've drawn her all these years since she first appeared in a little play up in Connecticut.

What appealed to you about drawing Hepburn?
It's marvelous to draw her. She's invented herself, like most of these people. They know what they look like. And that has sort of gone out of style, actually, among politicians and theater people. People walking in the street look more theatrical certainly than the people in the theater. You know these girls walking around in their underwear, with makeup—it's unbelievable. I saw a girl the other night walking down the block in what looked like a bikini. People from the theater are now more conservative. They're no longer larger than life. We've tried to condense theater and make it more like the fellow next door.

How has that affected your work?
Not terribly. Except visually there is an impact.

How so?

Actors used to slam the door, not just close it. And through their voice and gestures they communicated to the last row of the balcony. But now, with electronic devices, everybody is walking around with a small radio up their rear, you know. You hear them all over, even if they whisper.

Most of the theater people never really made it in these new mediums, in TV and movies, because their gestures were so exaggerated. When you have an eyeball that's 30 feet in diameter on the Radio City screen, and you're sitting two blocks away from it, the simplest gesture is magnified so that it doesn't work unless you're very shrewd about what you're doing. A few have done that. Helen Hayes managed to do it reasonably well. Katherine Cornell never made it. The Lunts never made it, because when you saw them on the screen, their movements became grotesque.

So they are different visually?

Yes. The difference is the way they gesture and the way they look and in the way they wear makeup. Barbra Streisand and Meryl Streep came from theater, but they've learned how to be photographed and how to underplay what they normally would have expanded in the theater.

You've done quite a bit of Streisand.

Yes, yes. Ever since she first appeared in the musical, *I Can Get It for You Wholesale*, where you could hear her in the last row of the balcony and every gesture was as wide as the stage. But she's learned to calm that down in the movies. The new generation realizes that their actions must be smaller.

When you did Streisand, what was the image you had of her?

I've had many different images. I remember I did a kind of glamorous drawing of her. But I've had her on roller skates, I've had her like Fanny Brice. I was getting out a book of drawings, and I came across a lot of old movie drawings of Joan Crawford. And I noticed that the eyebrows have gone up to the top of her head and down again and up and down. It became a kind of a trademark with her.

When you drew Imogene Coca and Sid Caesar what struck you about them?

They're both wonderful comics. And what they were trying to exploit is what I tried to capture. There's a kind of zany quality they both have, and both had a wonderful sense of mimicry. They understood what they were doing, and they knew what they looked like, too. I mean that thing of Imogene with one eye half closed and the other one wide open is not accidental. She must have rehearsed that in front of a mirror for many, many hours. None of these things are accidental, by the way. They develop across a lifetime of work.

So when you think of Imogene, you think of her eyes?

Yes. Her eyes, and her mouth. Her mouth is unpredictable.

What about Sid Caesar?

He's a great mime, the closest thing to Chaplin that I can think of. I'm sorry that he's not working more. What Caesar and Coca have is the permanent material of art. It's beyond time.

You did Eli Wallach and Anne Jackson. What was striking about them?

Their closeness, really. They're so involved with each other's talents, it's unbelievable. There's no beginning and end to it. They're a real theater couple. They live it and breathe it.

What appeals to you about the work you do? What do you see as the most creative aspect of it?

I haven't thought too much about it. I haven't been introspective about my work in any way. I've never tried to do anything else. I think it's wonderful to have that kind of limitation. So that you're not tempted to do something else. I've always drawn. Whether it's sculpture or painting, it's primarily drawing that I'm interested in. Sculpture is really a drawing that you fall over in the dark. But it's a drawing, a three-dimensional drawing.

You've been drawing for 50, 60 years, right?

Oh, for 70. I've been at the *Times* since 1925, but before that I was drawing for the *World* and the *Tribune*. I enjoy what I'm doing and I can't imagine what other people do all day long.

Can you talk about how you got your first job? Weren't you at a play and you started scribbling on a program?

That's right, on the *Playbill*. And Dick Maney was with me. It was his first show, and he said, "Put that on a clean piece of paper, and let me take it around to the papers and maybe I can place it somewhere." So I did that, and the following week, big as life, there was a large drawing in the *Tribune*. And then they asked me to do a drawing on assignment. And from that time on I was doing stuff for them, and for (Alexander) Woollcott down at the old *World*. Then one day I received a telegram from the *Times* asking me to do a drawing. But these experiences are of no value to anybody, since they're so personal. They don't mean a damn thing.

Actually a lot of people are interested in how you started.

I know. But when people ask me that I say, "Well my start is so unique it doesn't make any sense to anyone." I can't tell a young person who's paying $750 for a part payment on a loft in the Village how to make a living. My early years were spent in Paris, where you could live for very little.

Didn't your uncle give you some money to go to Europe?

Yes, and I lived there off and on for many years. I originally took an eight-year lease on a studio with two English fellows. We had only met that night and we took the studio together. It was 2,500 francs a year, which was $100. That's $33 apiece. And coffee was one-fourth of a franc, which was about one penny. A *prix-fixe* dinner, with a carafe of wine, was six francs—24 cents. You could live very comfortably for about $40 a month.

Did you sell any of your art?

I managed to sell a drawing every now and then. But nobody I knew around the Quarter in those years ever made a living at it. They all were on a pension. That whole romantic era, so-called, of the arts. It was an economic freedom rather than a spiritual one, you know. I don't care who it was, from Hemingway to Stein—they all had an income. Ten, 20 dollars a week, all of them. I don't know anybody who made a living there. It was marvelous because you could take two or three years out of your life and find out what the hell you were all about.

Did that help you personally?
Oh my God, yes. Sure. That's when I realized this is the way I want to live. But the kids today don't have that opportunity. I know the young artists who come up here and share a loft in the Village with two or three other fellas, but the loft is $1,500 or $2,000 a month. There's no chance to find out what you're about. You've got to find out what the whole system is about, rather than what you are capable of doing. And since all of these things are so personal, it seems to me that you need to discover what you want. Maybe you want to be a streetcar conductor, or a shoemaker, or something else.

Was it being in Paris or having the time or both that helped you find what out what you wanted to do?
Both. Having the time to think about what you were all about is irreplaceable. I don't think it will ever come back again to that. I think from now on you have to start earning your living when you're born. And you have to worry about paying the rent, unless you come from a very wealthy background. But if you're poor, or middle-class, it's a rough row to hoe.

Has your work changed a great deal over the years?
I assume it has. I mean, I've always looked at my early work and wondered how the devil anybody ever bought it or printed it. It's so awful. I always like the last drawing I did. It seems to be an improvement over everything else I've ever done. And it's a constant learning process of trial and error. You overcome a lot of handicaps over the years.

Now that I'm getting a book together, I've had to look back at the early things. It's a terrible job, which I don't recommend. But it made me aware of starting with a kind of arid stylization that is very restricting. You get into the habit of doing things to meet a deadline instead of really thinking it through and developing a small ulcer in the process. You do the easy thing, one that's worked before. Across the years I managed to fight that tendency, which comes with stylization. I've never purposefully tried to be stylistic in my drawing, but I'm cutting it down and trying to get it down to just the purest line possible. And just the movement of the line should communicate, rather than trying to please an audience with patterns and other things that distract from my point of view.

Charlie Chaplin had a great influence on you, didn't he?
Like most comedians, he was a great mime, really marvelous. I loved to draw him, too.

Were there any other people who had a great influence on you? Or did you have any mentors?
Johnny Held had a great influence on me, not so much as an artist, but as a human being. He was very successful in those years. He had a huge estate up in Westport with his own zoo, and his own golf course. He had five adopted children, three wives he was paying alimony to, a house in Florida with a yacht. On weekends there'd be 20, 30 people up there. But he was living in a one-room penthouse on 54th Street, where he was turning out these drawings.

I remember when I first went to Europe in 1924, he saw me off at the ship, and he said: "God, I envy you." And I said Johnny, "For God's sakes, you're a multimillionaire. I've got 500 bucks in my pocket." And he said, "That's what I envy. I can't move. Never get too successful."

Johnny invented the flapper, open galoshes, slickers with writing on them—all of that is attributed to Fitzgerald, but actually it was Johnny Held. It was very much like the Gibson Girl. The flapper was Johnny's contribution to the '20s. But when the long skirt came in, Johnny's drawings became cartoons. They lost something, there was no style about them.

He took a room over Barbetta's Restaurant on 46th Street to wait for the whole thing to blow over. He was convinced that the short skirt was coming back. He had lost all of his contracts. Hearst, all of them, dropped him and took Russell Patterson, who could draw a girl in a long skirt, and get the same response Johnny got from the short skirt. In Johnny's drawings you had the feeling you were looking up a girl's skirt all the time.

Well, the short skirt never came back. And Johnny wound up living in New Jersey.

Why did he affect you so much?
He influenced my morality, my life, more than anything creative about me. I don't know how you disassociate the two.

Are there any other people who really had an influence on you?

I suppose the whole ambience of Paris, sitting around talking about art—schmoozing until 3 or 4 a.m.—had a tremendous influence, you know. And there was a conglomerate of ideas that had an effect on you.

Which kind of people inspire you the most?
I like doing comedians, of course.

Why?
They're bigger than life. And there's something funny/sad about them. The clown is a funny, pathetic character. I don't know why I'm attracted to that, but it lends itself to my limitations, somehow.

To your limitations? How does it do that, do you know?
No, except that most comedians have action, movement. I love to draw dancers for that reason. There's movement, obvious movement, rather than people just sitting in a chair talking, or on a telephone. Most theater takes place in a living room, for some odd reason. Nothing ever happened in my living room that made any sense. But comedians are beyond any room or anything of that nature. They're abstract; they're dealing with ideas. I find that stimulating.

What do you feel are your strengths and weaknesses?
I just do the best I can, and try to make a drawing that has some believability from my point of view.

So much has been said about Nina. It's hard not to ask you about her.
It's one of those facetious things. I put her name in a drawing the day she was born, and then I tried to eliminate it because I thought the joke wore thin after a couple of weeks. But I was getting mail from all over the country and I had to answer it. People were finding it where it didn't exist, and I thought it was easier to keep it in there. But Nina had a rough time as a little girl. Everybody would say, "Oh, you're the Nina!" Being that well-known for having done nothing is very tough for a little girl. It never occurred to me that there was any problem connected with it. I would never have done it. But now that's a thing of the past and she's an adult and she realizes the reason I put it in

originally was not to exploit her.

Did you ever talk to her about it?
Many times. I told her how I tried to leave it out, but she said to leave it in—but at that time it was very tough. It's a very difficult thing for a little girl to make peace with that—if she's different than her peers.

So how did she deal with it?
She grew out of it. You do. You cope with those things eventually.

Are there events in your life that have had a certain impact on your work?
No. Mine has been a kind of progressive thing. One thing leads to another, all accidental, unplanned. Being on one side of the street as opposed to the other, I suppose, changes your whole life. The first drawings I ever did for reproduction were for Goldwyn pictures. It so happened that I was walking down Fifth Avenue one day and I met a fellow who had been in art school with me. I was about 18 then. He had a job with Goldwyn pictures, in the art department, cleaning brushes and running errands. I was a sculptor, and I had no way of making a living. So I went up to Goldwyn pictures and I was interviewed by Howard Dietz—who later became a songwriter—and he gave me a job in the art department, at $4 a week. But had I not been walking on Fifth Avenue, I probably would have had a completely different career. I know I would have drawn, that's unquestionable, because I couldn't do anything else.

What's a typical day like for you as an artist?
I work 365 days a year. Even when I'm on holiday, I draw. I've never thought of it as work, really; it's what I do. Fellas work all their lives so they can retire and play golf. What happens to a fella who plays golf and gets paid for it? Is that work? I think work is something you do that you don't want to do. But if you're doing something that you want to, whether you get paid for it or not, I don't see that that's work. That's fun, that's my pleasure in life. I have no other hobbies. I don't exercise.

Do you work in the evenings as well?

No. We have people over, or we go to the theater. Once the sun goes down I become a different person. But during the day, I'm sitting here all day long.

How long does it take you to do a drawing?
Sometimes it goes very quickly. Other times it produces a small ulcer. There are no rules.

Are there things you need to be creative?
No. When I'm writing I need complete solitude. The phone annoys me. But when I'm working, people can come in or out, the phone rings, I answer it, I keep right on drawing. It doesn't bother me at all. Writing to me is hard work. I can take one week and redesign a sentence, over and over again, and I never know which is the right one. But I know when a drawing reaches the same state of unfinishedness, that's when it's finished. You add to that one little thing, and then you're in trouble, because then you've got to keep adding.

And you call it a state of unfinishedness.
But I know when that point is reached in the drawing. There's nothing I can do beyond that. That is my limitation. I don't care if I spend the next two years on that drawing, I'm not going to do anything better than that. But with writing, it's unlimited. I suppose a real writer knows. He does a sentence and that's it.

So you don't think there are rules in art?
I think the only rule is: If there is a rule, you must break it. If somebody tells you, "You can't have a line go to the corner of a drawing," as any art instructor might tell you, well that's ridiculous. Because the minute anybody says that to you, you insist upon doing a line going straight through. You just refuse to accept that limitation. You want to break that boundary and expand it.

That's part of being an artist, right?
I suppose that's the difference between that and being a teacher. A teacher has to have rules, you know. But there are some things you can't teach. You can teach anatomy. You know there are a certain number of bones in each finger. You can teach perspective. The lines do converge. And when you're at a certain

height, the horizon is farther away than when you're lower. And you know at sea level, eight miles is the horizon and as you go up it expands. These things can be taught, and they do affect your vision and your perception when you translate it into a line.

What can't you teach?
The actual drawing, or what comprises a work of art, is inexplicable. Anything you say about it is nonsense. There are no words for aesthetics. We've invented a language that communicates a little bit of what an artist is trying to do, but it's senseless, really, when it gets right down to it. The only way you can criticize a drawing is to make another drawing. The only way to criticize music is to write another symphony instead of inventing a language that describes music. It only describes it intellectually, but you have to listen to it to hear it, and you have to see the picture to appreciate it.

What do you think differentiates an artist from a non-artist?
A form of insanity, I suppose. It's no way to make a living, I'll tell you that. If you want to make a living, open a delicatessen.

Do artists have a sensibility that separates them from the rest?
I suppose if you concentrate on one thing all your life, your point of view is a little different than people who have scattered things.

Do you have a different point of view than a lot of people?
I think so. It's nothing that I've consciously tried to develop. I've always tried to be as amiable and foolish as my peers, but then I realized that my behavior is so different than everybody I know. People always seemed to say, "Well, how can you just sit in the chair all day long and draw?" And then I realized that I'm a little different.

You've never felt blocked or stuck or burnt out?
Every now and then I would get to the point where I just don't know what the person is anymore. I remember drawing a fella who used to be with Durante. They had a TV thing together, Durante and Garry Moore. I had drawn him many times

before, and when I got this assignment to do a drawing of him, I didn't even bother to meet him. I made this drawing and a girl that worked for us at the time looked at it and said, "Oh it's a wonderful drawing: Buster Keaton!" I said, "Buster Keaton!" I took the drawing downstairs and showed it to Dolly, who also thought it was Buster Keaton. So I knew I was in trouble.

What did you do?
I came back up here and worked on it for the next week, 10 hours a day. I must have had 5,000 drawings of this man, and I gave up. I was about to call and say, "Listen, whatever talent I had has disappeared. I can't do it anymore. I'm finished, forget it." And the same girl, Millie, came by, and looked at it and said, "Oh, that's uh, Moore." And I brought it downstairs and showed it to Dolly and she said the same thing. So I didn't even touch it. To me it looked the same as all the others I had done. To this day I don't understand what they saw that I couldn't see. A couple of years later, or a couple of months later, I ran into Moore, and I told him this story. He said, "That's very odd. When I started out I used to do Buster Keaton imitations."

You talked about the feeling of wanting to give it all up. How do you get over that?
By doing it. That's the only way. Otherwise you become a hospital case.

Has your wife had an influence on you?
Every drawing I do I rush downstairs with and show it to her. She's a wonderful critic, actually. She has a wonderful visual sense. I take her very seriously when she says, "Oh my God, that's not him at all," and I try to figure out what she sees that I don't see.

Do you ever make changes because of something she's said?
Yes, because sometimes you get blinded. You're convinced that you've done it, but then somebody will make a suggestion and it hits a nerve and you have a feeling, well maybe they're right. I made the mistake of writing and then I discovered that everybody is a writer. Not everybody considers themselves an artist, a graphic artist. They're much more timid in their criticism. For instance, I've seen articles by Churchill where the edi-

tor has taken a blue pencil, crossed out things, rearranged sentences. I looked at him and I said, "If you ever did that with a drawing, you'd be in trouble."

Why is that?
Because people don't use drawings if they don't like them. But they don't say "move the head a little bit to the right, and put a finger over here."

I've never thought of creativity as anything special. To me it's just normal functioning. It's just a limitation that you exploit to the best of your ability and that's about it. But I believe everybody is creative, and everybody is talented. I just don't think everybody is disciplined. I think that's a rare commodity. Most artists or writers are highly disciplined.

I remember a story Somerset Maugham told when Sid and I were traveling around the world. We ran into Maugham in a barber shop in the South of France.

Did you know him?
No, but I recognized him. I looked over at what looked like the rear end of an elephant. I'd never seen such parched skin and I said, "It's gotta be." From the photographs I'd seen no one else had skin like that. So Sid, who had a letter of introduction to Maugham, was about to get out of the chair and walk over to him, but Maugham was finished first and came over to Sid and said, "Mr. Perelman, I presume?" And then we went over to his place for lunch.

I said, "I know this is presumptuous, Mr. Maugham, but tell me, what is your work schedule?"

He said, "Are you really interested in my work schedule?" And I said, "Yes, you've done such a huge amount of work, I can't understand how you've accumulated all of these books!"

He said, "I start at about 10 o'clock in the morning. I work in that chair until about noon. At noon I go to my barber shop and I get a shave where you met me."

I said, "You go every day?" He said, "Every day. I haven't learned how to shave. I come back here about 12:30. I have lunch. And then I take a siesta at about 2:30 until about five. Then I shower, and people start arriving and we have cocktails and we sit around and schmooze."

And I said, "Now wait a minute. You mean you work from 10

until 12?"

He said, "That's right, 365 days a year, whether I like it or not, whether I'm on board ship or in hospital. I work those two hours, those are holy hours, I work them every day. At the end of the year, you suddenly discover that you have 1,000 or 2,000 pages. Now you keep that up for 50 years and you have a body of work."

Which is quite a lot of discipline.

That's the thing that's beyond talent. I take for granted that anybody who picks a profession in the arts must be talented. I mean, you have choice of all the things you can do—you can loaf, you can do anything you want to do. But I've always discouraged people from becoming artists. It's no way to make a living.

❝ When you play the situation, not the result, you're very strong and it doesn't matter what people say. ❞

ANNE JACKSON
Actress

© Al Hirschfeld. Drawing reproduced by special arrangement with Hirschfeld's exclusive representative, The Margo Feiden Galleries Ltd. New York.

❝ After a couple of movies I'm eager to find a play to go back to, so I can have my moment on stage where you say, 'Oh my God, look at his response to that.' ❞

ELI WALLACH
Actor

Amid a myriad of clocks in their upper West Side apartment in Manhattan, Anne Jackson and Eli Wallach talked about their marriage and their work together in careers spanning four decades. They have acted together in 15 plays, several films and many TV shows.

Jackson and Wallach met when they were cast opposite each other at the Equity Library Theatre in *This Property Is Condemned*, by Tennessee Williams. She played a 13-year-old prostitute. He was supposed to be 15, though he was straight out of the Army. Jackson told the director that Wallach was too old for the part, but her future husband proved otherwise.

Born in Brooklyn, Wallach was encouraged by his parents to be a teacher. In 1938, to his relief, he failed a teaching aptitude exam. He then started studies at the Neighborhood Playhouse in New York. When the Actors Studio was founded in 1948, Wallach was in the core group along with Jackson, Marlon Brando, Kevin McCarthy, Maureen Stapleton, Sidney Lumet and John Forsythe.

When the director Herbert Berghof told Jackson she should be an actress, and she agreed, her father was disappointed because he wanted her to be a biologist. He asked her to leave home. Jackson went to live with her sister, Katherine, and like Wallach, started studying at the Neighborhood Playhouse before joining the Actors Studio.

Despite their parents' negative view of their career paths, both were met with huge success. Jackson won an Obie for her role in *The Typist* and was nominated for Tonys for roles in *Oh, Men! Oh, Women!* and Tennessee Williams's *Summer and Smoke*. Wallach, known for his roles in Williams's plays, won a Tony, Theatre World and Donaldson Award for his part in *The Rose Tattoo*.

Each has different styles both professionally and personally. Wallach collects clocks and is on time; Jackson is late and loses things. But they clearly are each other's greatest support. Disagreements and mini-explosions were apparent in this interview. But moments later they were singing each other's praises.

As the interview ended with Wallach waxing poetic about Jackson, he mentioned that she frequently loses her glasses. Instantly Jackson, who was late for an appointment, cried out: "Where are my glasses?" If the scene had been staged, the timing could not have been better. After a mad search, the missing glasses were found along with two new pairs that had just been

Anne Jackson with a three-year-old future director, Ron Howard, on the set in photo by the late Yul Brynner.

delivered by the mailman. As things calmed down, Jackson and Wallach parted ways, planning to meet later in what seemed a most likely setting—a movie theater.

[Jackson and Wallach moved in and out of the room, taking questions first individually and then together.]

How would you define the process of creativity?

Wallach: A lot of it is by accident, a lot of it is the right forces coalescing at the right time.

What are those forces?
Wallach: Things that your mind has stored away. The value of the Actors Studio and the Method was not how to act, it was how to utilize what you've already stored away, and how to channel it properly into scenes.

What's happened more and more in America is that people are now aware of the financial structures of things. They know what's the number one movie, what the cost of it was. It used to be who did you sleep with? And did you wear the bottoms of your pajamas? Now it's, "That picture cost 48 million dollars, and it hasn't recovered."

Can you talk about how you prepared for a specific role?
Wallach: Well, take *The Magnificent Seven*. I was asked to play a Mexican bandit and I thought, "What am I, a man from the city, going down into Mexico to play a bandit? How do I approach it?" Then I thought, "You always see robbers holding up banks or robbing the train, but what do they do with the money?" So I decided I would be an ostentatious bandit. You know, the kinda guy who displays his clothing and his wealth. So I had them make me red silk shirts, I put two gold teeth in my mouth and I had a silver saddle. I displayed what I did with the money. So that was one answer in the creative process.

What about the movie *Baby Doll*?
Wallach: In that movie I thought, "I'm the manager of a cotton gin in the South. The local people are objecting to the fact that

the big plants are taking away from their livelihood, and one of them decides to burn down the cotton gin that I'm managing." The picture basically deals with the kind of revenge I use on people to find out who did it and why and so on. Kazan was a brilliant director, is a brilliant director. He said, "Listen, I want you to walk down the street of this town and I don't want people to say, 'Oh, there's an actor.'" So I put on a T-shirt and a hat and went for a walk. The man I was playing was Sicilian. I grew up with Italians in Little Italy, Brooklyn. And I understand their courtesies, their vengeance and motives and their attitudes and feelings about people. I've spent a lot of time in Italy in the last 25 years. So I thought I understood that aspect of the man.

Can you talk more about the feeling of wanting revenge?
Wallach: There's a scene in the movie where I turn around from the burning wreckage of the cotton gin, and I look right into the camera and say, "I want to find out who did it and why." I had to pick something private in my life that the audience is unaware of, so that when I turn around and face the camera, they connect my loss of the cotton gin and my anger with the cotton gin with the look on my face—they must see a desire for revenge.

How were you able to do that?
Wallach: Well, there's an exercise called the "Magic If." You think of a situation and you say, "What if?" You see children play the game all the time. They say, "I'm gonna go in there and bake a pie." And there's no bakery and no pie, but they imagine it. Well, as you get older that "what if" gets flattened out, it gets dull. People don't utilize it. However, if you have a technique to shake the ashes in you, then you can be creative. So when I was preparing for *Baby Doll* I said, "What if I came home and found my house burned and my wife raped and my children killed, what would that be like?" And then I turned around and faced the camera. So that's a way of getting the creative juices flowing.

So technique is crucial.
Wallach: Definitely. Creating is like trying to pick up mercury. It splinters. The more intense you are, the more you pursue it, the more it will elude you. So you have to get your instrument tuned up and leave it alone. When artists like Shostakovitch per-

form, they don't say, "My finger has to go here." They know they just have to play. Barbra Streisand used a little aspect of the Method in the song, "Happy Days Are Here Again" and thought, "What if I sing it just after learning my mother died?" If you alter the circumstances privately, nobody knows, and then you've really got something to work with.

Does the outside world ever affect your work on stage or in a film?
Wallach: Yes. Anne and I were doing a two-character play. We had a fight earlier in the afternoon and I told her to shut up! This added another factor when we got on stage which the audience wasn't aware of. So when she got to her line where she had to say, "You have kind-looking eyes," she could hardly say it that night.

You talked about the "what if" exercise. What are some of the other exercises you do to get the juices flowing?
Wallach: The most important thing you can do as an actor is take any behavior and make it look like it's not acting. That's what Method acting teaches you.

Which is why Kazan asked you to just walk down the street like a regular person.
Wallach: Exactly. But you see, if you ask most actors for a certain behavior, like remembering something, they'll raise their eyes and look at the ceiling. Now I don't know what's on the ceiling, but they're indicating to you the conventional cliche of remembering. The Method says, forget that. You can remember by staring at the other person and saying I remember, and it'll have a dynamic that's alive. It's not a cliche. If you look at an actor and you're not aware that they're acting, they're really creating. Marlon (Brando) was a perfect example of this.

He was at the Actors Studio when you were there, wasn't he?
Wallach: Oh yeah, he was at the Studio at the beginning. But he was a unique, breakthrough type of actor because he'd talk and you'd think: He's not acting, it's really happening right now. I saw him on stage, long before he was in the movies, and he was remarkable. But you see, you have to marry talent with

technique. When you get a fusion of the two, then you do well. A lot of actors imitate. You often go to museums in Europe and you see a person sitting there with a big canvas and they're painting a Goya, or they're sitting in the Prado doing different paintings. And they're saying that artist had the discipline and the insight and the know-how. Maybe if I copy it, some of it will flow into me. And so it goes.

How do you define talent? Philip Glass says he doesn't feel he has talent but that he has made up for it by working hard all his life.
Wallach: Well, you can have talent and still have to work hard. People think the equation is talent equals no work, it's just there. And that's not true. I always feel that talent is never satisfied. It's never set. It's always a curiosity. There's a relationship between age and talent and artistry.

In what sense?
Wallach: Well, if you're really an artist you're always curious. Look at conductors who are still working in their 60s, 70s or 80s. They're still up there pumping away. Athletes go through a terrible thing. In tennis an athlete is numbered. He's number two or number four, number seven. In theater, unfortunately, that almost happens too, in another way. Someone, like Julia Roberts, is hot this year—and two years from now there'll be another 16-year-old they've discovered.

But how you utilize your talent is what's important. When I talk to graduating classes I always say that you must think that what you have to offer is unique. No one else thought of it, no one else did it. You have to have that to ease the pain of rejection that you constantly get. I just read for a film and they said, "Wonderfully done. But we're looking for a man with a smashed nose and he's twice your size." So I say, what am I gonna do? To ease the pain I always say, "It's their loss."

What do you think you have that's unique?
Wallach: Well, mine is a marriage between the characters I play and my own sense of fun, no matter who I'm playing—even when I've played killers. I just finished playing a man in a movie called *Mistress* with Robert De Niro and Danny Aiello. It's a small movie but with an amusing premise. I played one of these

Hollywood types—wealthy with a young mistress. You know, the shirt is open to the belly button and they wear gold chains and they work on their arm muscles. All of that was fun, to create that kind of guy. Before, I played an old Army veteran who'd been stored and warehoused in a hospital.

What was fun about that?
Wallach: Well, I knew the situation. In the Army I was a medic. I spent five years in Army hospitals. I knew what it was like to want to stay in the hospital and not be sent back out into the lines and I knew the machinery of how to do it. And I kept thinking about my attitude toward young doctors in the Army.

What was your attitude?
Wallach: To give you an example, when a young doctor comes in and says, "Good morning. I'm here to examine you," I have a dirty line. I say, "It's a waste of time, kid. I've been examined more times than you got wrinkles on your nuts." That's my first line and I knew it would lead me somewhere. It's like Joe Heller says, "I'm asleep and I wake up and I get the first line of a book. I don't know what the book's about, but that first line pops up." Maybe the first line is something like, "And then he slammed the door, with regret." So Joe Heller begins the story with his first line, which leads into a certain maze. And that's how he writes his book.

So what you're saying is you begin with a line or an idea, like your attitude toward the young doctors in the Army.
Wallach: Right. I leave my instrument alone for an invasion of an inspirational idea or something, but I don't know when it's gonna come. We're gonna see a movie sometime soon. These two young Cohen brothers made this movie called *Barton Fink*. And what they say is this kid is hired to write a screenplay and he sits in front of a typewriter and nothing comes. It's a blank page. Sometimes you just have to wait.

Let's talk about *Nuts*, the film you did with Barbra Streisand.
Wallach: When I was on a ship recently, floating up to Alaska, they showed *Nuts*. Each cabin had a TV set and that's what they were showing. I thought *I'd* go nuts! I had one funny incident with Marty Ritt, who was directing. In the movie I was the

prison psychiatrist and I had to testify first. So I went to him and I said, "Why do I have to sit in the courtroom for the next six weeks while you do Karl Malden?" And he says, "What do you mean? You're getting paid! When I turn the camera on, I want to see you sitting in the courtroom." So after three weeks of sitting there, I went to him and I said, "I'm a prison psychiatrist. I have a lot of other patients and they need me." So he says, "You're not going anywhere. You're gonna sit right in the courtroom."

How did you work on your character?
Wallach: Well, I looked at this man as someone who thought he knew a lot. But when Barbra talked to him face-to-face, the things that she said to him always hit home. He could try and dismiss her by telling himself she's mentally unstable. However, the thing she said is, "You couldn't practice on Park Avenue, you're stuck away in this prison thing. You're down the ladder in the achievements as a psychiatrist, let's face it. Therefore you're trying to establish something which isn't true, which is saying I'm incapable of defending myself." And the more she did that, the more insecure he became. But that had to happen in the scene.

You said he thought he knew a lot.
Wallach: Yes, but he didn't.

Did you see him differently than he saw himself?
Wallach: Yes, in a way. I thought, he seems to be unsympathetic but he doesn't think he's unsympathetic. In the first scene I did with Barbra, my character laughs at her character. I ask her, "Would you like some coffee?" She says, "As long as it doesn't have medicine in it." And I say, "No, just cream and sugar." He really thinks, "I'm doing my best."

I did a movie with Candice Bergen where I played another prison psychiatrist. It was called *Murder by Reason of Insanity*. It was about a Polish lady and her husband who came to America and how she changed. They were both nuclear scientists, but she received greater recognition here than in Poland. That drove him crazy and he threatened to kill her. He said that she was molesting the children. And finally he attacked her. The judge said, "You have to stay away from her," and he said, "I'm gonna kill her, whether I'm in prison or wherever I am, I'm gonna kill her."

So they put him in a psychiatric hospital.

Is this a true story?
Wallach: Yes.

Why did you choose the role of the psychiatrist?
Wallach: Because there was a moment in it where I've given the husband permission to go out. The nurse is horrified, and I say to the nurse, "I've handled many of these cases. Don't worry, I know what I'm doing." The husband leaves and sure enough he kills his wife. And the moment I wanted was when the nurse comes into my office and throws the paper down on the counter and the headline says "So-and-so murdered by husband." I wanted that moment of realizing what I'd done.

Again here is a man who thought he knew more than he did.
Wallach: Right. And he realizes that. That moment is very revealing. It destroys that man in that one second. All his expertise has gone out the window because he made a decision and he was wrong. It's like these guys who just had this coup against Gorbachev and Yeltsin, and now they're fleeing. They're on their way to the airport and they're going to be arrested.

How did that moment play on screen?
Wallach: Unfortunately they cut it. All you see is the nurse throwing down the newspaper and the camera zooming in on the headline. There's no cut to me. In movies the actor has no say over what finally appears on the screen. That's why after a couple of movies I'm eager to find a play to go back to, so that I can have my moment on stage where you say, "Oh my God, look at his response to that."

What were some of your most memorable moments as an actor?
Wallach: A scene from *Camino Royale*. It's one of the great love scenes. It takes place between a young prostitute and Kilroy in a little house of prostitution where he wins the dance award and he says to the little girl, "You don't talk much." She says "You want me to talk?" He says, "That's the way we do it in the States—if you're in the mood for romance." She says, "OK, what do you think of the world monetary situation?"

[Anne Jackson enters]

Wallach: Why don't you talk to Anne now? You'll enjoy that. She's brighter than I am.

[Wallach leaves]

Eli was talking about some of his most memorable roles. What are some of yours?
Jackson: When I played Gertrude [in *Hamlet*]. I once asked Meg Wynn Owen, "How do I play Gertrude and make that believable?" She said, "Annie, (director) Peter Hall gave me the clue to that. He said, 'Play her with lots of rings and a silk handkerchief.'" She said, "Well, think about it, Annie. Think about it." And that's all she would tell me.

Did that help?
Jackson: Not at first, because I thought: lots of rings and a silk handkerchief? That sounds so external. And then I realized that anybody who wears lots of rings and carries a silk handkerchief doesn't blow her nose on the handkerchief, nor does she ever do anything with her hands. That's a queenly thing. Nor would she ever suckle her baby. So I started thinking about those things in realistic terms—very specific things for a fast fix, because I didn't have time to go into greater depth nor did I have to do more than one scene. But even something like perfume on my handkerchief gave me something to believe in, so that I wasn't acting out somebody else's version of a queen. At least she was my queen, whoever she was.

Can you think of any other times where someone suggested something that helped you play a scene?
Jackson: Well, I'm very receptive to help. But I'm such an egotist, it has to be that kind of help that I can fathom out. And a really good director, or somebody who knows how to talk about art, gives you that. Like Marty Fried in *The Diary of Anne Frank*.

What did he tell you?
Jackson: In one scene we had a celebration with a cake. And Marty said the cake that they had has to feed a lot of people but it's only as big as a cupcake. So he had a tiny cake on the stage

for the Frank family and the other family, and we had to divide it up. I can't tell you what that did to all of us when we saw that cake on stage—just presenting that reality on the stage. Fried kept saying, "A tiny cake. I don't want a big cake!" Everyone else thought it was comic to have a small cake on stage. But he insisted. Those things that people find to create a reality are so important.

Have there been times when you used personal moments from your own life to help you create a character?
Jackson: Yes, when I was doing *Cleopatra* at the Actors Studio. I was working with [director] Arthur Storch. I was dealing with jealousy and Storch said, "You do the lines well but what would happen if Eli went off with someone?" I said, "Don't talk to me about Eli!" He said, "No, I'm going to talk to you about Eli. What would happen if Eli went off with someone?" And at that time you know Eli was working with Marilyn Monroe and all my own jealousies were coming up. So I thought about it, and then I went home and I sat in the dark. Vivian Nathan, a wonderful actress, who taught me a lot, told me to do that. And I teach that now. I tell my students to relax and sit in the dark and understand what is going on inside, not what is out there or how am I going to look when I say this.

And sitting in the dark helped you prepare for that role?
Jackson: Yes, I used that and thought of what Arthur Storch said to me about Eli. And then I was able to reach my own inner source. And that's really all you can ask for. I must say I'm sounding as though each time I work the brainstorm comes, but it doesn't. But you try to allow your work to come from an inner source that is well-founded, an emotional logic, really, by following your own instincts and allowing yourself to be informed by the situation of the play. When you play the situation, not the result, you're very strong and it doesn't matter what people say.

Have there been times when you got a lot of criticism for a role in which you thought you did your best work?
Jackson: Yes. I remember when I did *Rhinoceros*. I got a lot of criticism and a lot of raves. And the criticism, for the first time in my life, didn't really bother me, because what I wanted to do was what was recognized by the people who mattered to me.

But the others, I said, "It's their right not to like what I do." It's like if Picasso does a face and abstracts it, and people say, "What is that? That's not art." Or he does *Guernica* and doesn't put red in the painting.

You said you did what you wanted to do. What was that?

Jackson: I made a woman into a character that I knew. The director, Joe Anthony, said to me, "I want you to play her like a cheerleader." Well, that image meant one thing to him; it meant something else to me. It meant ego, being body proud and not having too many brains in one's head. It meant being the feminine little kitten and a character that I don't respect in a woman. I want a woman to be proud of her mind, and to be proud of her body, athletically, but not cutesy-wutesy. So I played a cutesy-wutesy lady because I thought a cutesy lady would become a rhinoceros, would go with the crowd, you know, would, if you will, go with Mr. Bush, be a Republican. I mean that's what I thought. Right or wrong.

What specifically did you do in the role?

Jackson: I saw a picture in the paper of a girl kissing a sailor, you know—with the leg up. So I did that gesture from the time I came on the stage. That was my Daisy, and I took a lot of flak for it, but I also got a lot of yeas. The yeas were more important to me than the nays.

Did your director support this action?

Jackson: Yes, I had come up with this gesture in rehearsal. I was just fooling around and I thought the director would take it away. But he said, "I want you to do that gesture when you become the Rhinoceros." So he used what I was doing, and his production supported it. It's easier to talk about the process once you're done.

[Eli returns]

You said your role in *Camino Royale* was one of your favorites? Have there been times when you did parts that you really didn't care for?

Wallach: Yes, but you must compartmentalize your career so that every role that you get isn't a priceless piece of prose. There are times when you get films and you think, "Oh God, why did I do that?"

Such as?
Wallach: Well, there was one called *The People Next Door*, which I did with Julie Harris. I love Julie. But things just didn't work, they didn't gel. I didn't feel I was right for the role. I usually fight and say, "Yes, I can do that. I can play an Arctic explorer, I can play a black man, it doesn't matter." But in this case, some instinct told me, "No no no—it's wrong for you." That's one example. And just recently we finished a play in which we did three weeks of intensive rehearsals. But the author didn't see our viewpoint and wouldn't make any alterations and the play didn't work. So we felt crushed by that.

How do you deal with that?
Wallach: When we enter a project, particularly a play, we don't know what's going to happen. We did a play once called *Twice Around the Park*. The idea came to us after we had returned from a trip to China. We had just heard a lady named Dr. Ruth Westheimer and we thought there was a play there. So we spoke to our friend, Murray Schisgal, who is a playwright, and told him the idea. And he said, "Listen, I wrote about this years before I ever heard about Dr. Ruth!" So then he wrote another one-act play about a guru called Dr. Oliovsky. He put the two of them together and we decided to do them in Syracuse. We rehearsed for a month and played for a month and a half. Then we took the two plays to Washington, to Baltimore, to Wilmington, and then we opened on Broadway. We were ahead of the game but then there was a terrific snowstorm, and no money to advertise, and out we went. It was a hurtful thing. We wanted to do the second play. It was the funniest thing either one of us had ever been in. We tried to do it on TV but we couldn't sell it to Warner's or HBO. So, I don't know, a lot of it has to do with luck or instinct, or where you are at a certain moment.

What has it been like working together?
Jackson: I think it's like dancers or chess players. You learn a game and you begin to know each other's moves and you can afford to be courageous in acting or in a game because you trust

that person. You know that the other person can hit back, can go with you, can change, and there's an excitement in that.

Is there any danger in being so familiar with each other?
Wallach: Yes. For example, in one play, Annie kept bringing up certain points and I was impatient. I said, "Let's get on with it! Do the lines, get through it." But the imperfections in the scenes stuck in her craw. It wasn't until after we opened and began playing that I realized she was right. I was wrong to insist that we move on. I had the juicy part. She had a part that caused her pain because it didn't justify any of her actions. I understood that. In *Rhinoceros* she made a certain choice and I said, "Are you gonna do that in the play?" She said, "Yes, I am gonna do that in the play. That's what I feel and I'm gonna do it." Every review of the play talked about that choice.

Anne, was that the choice based on the photo of the sailor?
Jackson: Yes.
Wallach: So I thought, "I'm gonna keep my mouth shut and maybe she should have the right to express herself." After all, she's an actress, she has an ego, she has drive, she has a technique. It's hers, not mine.

Have there been times where you've done a project together where the characters didn't work well together?
Jackson: Yes, we did *Twentieth Century*. And the audience was disappointed because those two characters don't come together enough in the play.
Wallach: Or the play *Cafe Crown*.
Jackson: It was imbalanced.
Wallach: We loved the play, but Annie had basically one little scene where she came in.
Jackson: There was another time when we did a film with Michael Landon. Michael didn't like his mother, adored his father, and wrote a melodrama. In his film all of the love and all of the sentimentality went to his father. And his mother was the heavy. So when he sent the script to me, I said, "No, I don't want to do it." I had played the heavy and the man comes out the sweet hero, and I didn't want to do it again. And Michael kept saying, "Please do it. This is my mother and father and it means so much to me and I will change the mother's role." But when

we did the film the part was still tilted and it still bothered me. So I vowed that I wouldn't get into that position again.

Have you?
Jackson: Yes. And I hate to say this even in front of Eli, but I have found out what a battle women have had to fight. I've learned it the rough way, in seeing all those old films where it would be the man's film and the lady would just be a token. Her part wouldn't even be written, except if she was a big star—then they'd strengthen her part.

How does that affect your relationship with Eli—if he has the bigger role?
Jackson: Or the better role. It's hard. Unfortunately, I don't let things alone. Eli had a rough time with me on that play because I kept saying, "Wait a minute," and I would drive him crazy. It's not his fault. He's a brilliant actor who does his work and he would get impatient with me. And quite rightly so, because I was trying to make a point that the writer did not get.

And then you have to deal with it at home.
Wallach: I remember when we did a play called *Waltz of the Toreadors*.
Jackson: I adored that.
Wallach: She had one tiny scene in it. But it was a strong scene and she adored making this character...
Jackson: What tiny scene? I had a whole act! I had the second act scene. Are you joking? That's one of the greatest scenes ever written!
Wallach: I'm saying it was a smaller role.
Jackson: Yes, oh yes, except that Mastroianni was offered to do the part that Eli did. It's a brilliant play, and what a playwright! [Jean Anouilh] And Zoe Caldwell, who is one of our great actresses, was going to play the part that I played, which was the wife. And remember what Mastroianni said? He said, "That's the best part in the play. That woman comes in in one scene and wipes the man right off the stage." And so he didn't want to play that type of man!
Wallach: I want to show you an old program we have. Anne wrote an article in it called "After the Kiss." It deals with us being on the road with *Twice Around the Park*. It's a marvelous

article, it's a brilliant article and I think it will answer all the questions about how we work together and what happens in the working process.

Jackson: I'm so thrilled that you liked the article.

Eli mentioned that you were working on *The Typist* and that you had had an argument that afternoon. And that affected your work.

Jackson: Yes, but knowing each other so well can also help your work. Recently we performed in front of a group of psychiatrists. Eli did Lear and I did Cordelia. And I think we never could have done what we did that evening, if we hadn't had such a strong relationship. Eli's reading from a prompter as he's crying over my supposedly dead body. I was so proud of him, that he attempted to do King Lear in four days, without a real rehearsal because there was nobody to direct him. It was as if he went into the eye of the hurricane.

Wallach: I had a problem, because I was too far away from the TelePrompTer, so I had to memorize my role.

Jackson: And at that time Eli only had peripheral vision in one eye. I kept thinking, I don't believe I'm on the stage with this man doing what he's doing, and he was wonderful.

Wallach: Well, we'll see when we get the tape back.

Jackson: No, I know. I know what I feel inside.

Wallach: I want you to read Anne's article because in it she captures what actors go through.

Which is what?

Wallach: A certain pain and anguish. Actors are on an active current when they're in a play, that other people don't understand. You might think they're doing the same thing every night. Well, they're not. The actors are living a life that's turned up three notches on the scale.

Jackson: And anything can happen.

Does that then turn up your own personal life three notches?

Wallach: Well, yes, because you feel—well, say you're playing a gangster. Do you go home and still act like a gangster? No. But you feel fruitful and creative and then your life is richer, that's all.

What qualities do you each have that helps the other one on stage?

Jackson: Eli has a lovely innocence, and it's so infectious in a way. It's as if he's a little boy roaming around into new territory. He doesn't make decisions about how he's going to do something. Sometimes he does, sometimes he gets into what I think are posing positions, but he breaks them himself. I'm impatient with that. I learned from Geraldine Page. She broke every rule of staging there was to break. She just knew how to do that. There was no audience as far as she was concerned. She never came down front and stood and put her face out front, but when it needed to be seen, it was seen. She was just a genius at that. When I worked with her, I caught on very quickly to that thing that she had, so that I never felt upstaged by her.

What about with Eli? Have you ever felt upstaged by him?

Jackson: Yes, I think so. But once we get into the characters and once we get deeply rooted in the play, you forget all that. But it's very hard for the actor not to feel positioned or in the wrong position. It was interesting to work with Mike Nichols because he let the actors do the staging, so that they almost automatically went into the right positions. But when we did a play called *Nest of the Wood Grouse* with Joe Papp, who is a great producer but not a great director, we had very young kids on stage. And he let them loose with the professionals. It was murder because they didn't know how to stage themselves and we had to battle it out. But Eli and I don't have that kind of ego problem. The ego problem I have is that I am a stickler in a scene.

And he's not?

Jackson: No, he's willing to keep going. He's much much easier to work with than I am, I think.

You get obsessive, is that it?

Jackson: I guess obsessive would be a good word. I'm like a little mad animal.

And he's looser about the process?

Jackson: Yes. Yes. I hope that I've gotten mellower and learned somewhat from him. But when I feel that I'm being led by a chain, I get rebellious.

Has there been any competition between the two of you?
Jackson: Yes, I guess there would be. If the character that I'm playing is put in the position of being a heavy, then I get competitive. I say wait a minute! I don't call it competition, I think that it's more a sense of trying to find the right motivation for the character, so that it doesn't get into that cliched type of acting.

Eli, what qualities do you like about Anne that help you on stage?
Wallach: I'll tell you what I love about Anne is her insight, her awareness of the problems in the play or in the character, and how she sets about to solve it. It takes a longer time. We work differently. I tend to want to memorize my part right away and then fool around with colors and so on. But she says, "I don't know how you do that. I want to know why I'm saying what I'm saying before I say it."

Jackson: I truly can say that Eli's way is better because it frees you. If you have the lines down it frees you and the other actor. You're not holding up the other actor. The other way is very selfish.

Wallach: I don't think of it in terms of being selfish. I think you felt you couldn't know what stresses or accents to put on the lines unless you knew what you were doing. But in the early days of the theater, when you got your script, you didn't get a complete script. You got the last four words of the other speaker. And that made you damn sure to listen to what the other person said.

Jackson: (Laughing) Just for the last four words.

Wallach: But you began to listen. And then you'd think, "Oh my God, when are those last four words coming?"

You were saying how you loved Anne's insight and awareness of the problems in a play.
Wallach: Yes. I wrote something about her for the actor Roddy McDowell. He's also a wonderful photographer and he has a series of books with pictures of well-known people. And then he asks other people to write about them. His second book is called *Double Exposure* and in it I wrote about Richard Dreyfuss. Anne wrote about Burgess Meredith. Now he has a third book coming out which contains a picture of each of us and he asked us to

write about each other. So here's what I wrote about Anne before I saw the picture he used:

> One picture is worth a thousand words, so it is said. My knowledge of the lady in question is made up of a thousand pictures which I'll try to put into words. She cries aloud in theaters. Talks back to the movie screen. Loses 10 pairs of eyeglasses annually. Mentally tears down ugly office buildings in New York. Dreams of directing traffic, issuing summonses and parking tickets. I give her watches but she's never on time. She always surprises me. She never went to college but has a doctor's degree. Can't carry a tune, but she's musical. Her timing on stage is as perfect as a Movado watch. I love her.

Jackson: He writes beautifully.

How many years have you been working together?
Wallach: Forty-some-odd years.

And do you still feel you have very different styles of acting? Or has that changed?
Wallach: I think I'm slowly coming around to Anne's way in some ways, and she's beginning to adopt some of my ways. Maybe there's something in both of us which will coalesce and make a complete picture.

© Al Hirschfeld.
Drawing reproduced by special arrangement with Hirschfeld's exclusive representative, The Margo Feiden Galleries Ltd. New York.

❝ You don't aspire to become an artist. You learn your craft. And hopefully you are born with a gift. You come out of the womb with this gift. Then hopefully somebody else has the gift of being able to teach and bring out your creativity and make you grow and develop into an artist. ❞

JUDITH JAMISON
Dancer and Choreographer

She is 5-foot-10, with long legs and a smile that can project to the back of a 5,000-seat theater. And, Judith Jamison—legendary dancer, choreographer and now artistic director of the Alvin Ailey American Dance Theatre—seems filled with more energy than ever.

In her third-floor office on Manhattan's West Side, two things were on Jamison's mind as she sat down for this interview. She didn't want to be on the third floor anymore—she wanted to take over the entire building. And she had just spoken to Jackie O, a conversation to which Jamison reacted like a young girl who had just spoken with her favorite movie star. In fact, Jamison was the star, because it was her autobiography that Onassis would be editing.

Jamison's life will easily fill a book. At 17, she was discovered by Agnes de Mille and left her Philadelphia home to make her New York debut in de Mille's *The Four Marys* at the American Ballet Theatre. From 1965 to 1980 she was a principal dancer for the Ailey company. She then co-starred with Gregory Hines in *Sophisticated Ladies* on Broadway. In 1984 she choreographed her first work, *Divining*. In 1989 she choreographed her first opera, Boito's *Mefistofele* for the Opera Company of Philadelphia. And then, just before taking over leadership of the Ailey company, she launched her own company, the Jamison Project.

It is fitting that Jamison assumed leadership of her late mentor's company. Ailey discovered her in 1965 when she was an unknown auditioning—unsuccessfully—for *The Strolling '20s*, a Harry Belafonte TV special. Ailey, who judged Jamison to be "beautiful," decided immediately that he wanted Jamison to join his company. But he didn't call her for three days—an eternity for someone who was suffering enormous feelings of rejection after the Belafonte audition.

Ailey and Jamison seemed to be immediate soul mates. He transformed the dancer he described as the "gangly girl with no hair" into an international star, creating some of his most enduring dances for her, including *Cry* and *Pas de Duke* with Mikhail Baryshnikov.

Now, stepping into Ailey's shoes, Jamison dreams ahead. "I want my own building. We need the whole building," she repeats. But waiting does not come easily for her. "Waiting is one of the lessons I haven't yet learned. I mean, waiting patiently, so that it does not destroy me."

As the interview ended, a young man appeared with a letter in hand and a smile on his face. "Good news?" asked Jamison. He nodded. "Very good news?" she asked. He nodded more emphatically and then showed her the letter.

A very large sum of money was forthcoming from a longtime supporter of the Ailey company. Jamison raised her arms high and let out a loud cry of relief. It must have been the same exuberance that Ailey had seen in a teenage girl on the Belafonte set decades ago.

What, in your eyes, makes someone a dancer?

When they're dancing above the ground. That's what's important to me when I see a dancer. It's like they levitate, because it's coming from a whole other place. It's not about the steps they're doing. I love it when I can get a dancer like Desmond Richardson. He's 24 years old. He has a facility and he's a technical tiger. Plus, he can *dance*.

So do you believe someone can be skilled technically but not be a true dancer?

Yes. I always say there are very few dancers in the world.

There are lots of people up on stage moving around. But those people who are dancers, with a capital D, are artists. Those are the ones who are coming from that other place.

What is that place?
It's internal—it's as if they are turned inside out. And when you're in the audience you recognize yourself in that person and there is a common ground that says, "We're all human beings and I can do that." I may not be able to reach my leg up like yours. But I know you're reaching for something and I know what that feels like. And I can feel that you're trying to reach for something not just because your leg is up or your hand is stretched out, but I feel it from the very ground that you're standing on.

So when you meet a young dancer what are you looking for?
That constant aspiring ember, that's inside, that reveals them as who they really are. All of these dancers must be recognizable to you. It's an inner light that has to show. Because when the curtain goes up you're emotionally naked.

So you're looking for someone who can really reveal himself.
Exactly. Otherwise you're doing steps. Who wants to see steps? You can go to the Olympics to see steps. When I hire dancers, if I can't see a vulnerability in them, then we can't work together, because there's nothing for them to grow toward. I mean, what are we here for? Because if I can't see their vulnerable side then an audience isn't going to see it.

And that's as important as the technique.
Oh yes. Because I don't want a machine on stage. I want a whole person on stage.

You seem able to transcend the dance in your work.
It's interesting, because I was talking to someone very famous—whose name I can't mention—but he denies that there was any kind of transcendence going on when he danced. And every time I saw him dance he was so extraordinary on a technical basis that you kind of went "Whoa!" He really knew how to connect movement. But he was right—he did not transcend the

dance. And so there was something lacking in that performance for me.

His heart and soul?
Yeah. But in the kind of dancing he did it wasn't exactly necessary to give you his heart. But that is not the kind of dancing I love. To really transcend the dance you have to be a creative person.

Do you think you are born with the gift of being a dancer with a capital D?
Yes. That's why it tickles me, for instance, when young dancers who are 20, 25 years old and have just begun their careers say, "I'd like to become an artist." You don't become, you don't aspire to become an artist. You learn your craft. And hopefully you are born with a gift. You come out of the womb with this gift. Then hopefully somebody else has the gift of being able to teach and bring out your creativity and make you develop and grow into an artist.

Do you think everyone is creative in one way or another?
Yes. But many people don't have any mentors around them. We have three Ailey camps where, besides dancing, children write haiku, write poetry, write prose, because creative writing is part of what we teach. Most of these kids aren't artists; but God knows, some of them might turn out to be extraordinary, because kids write the truth. And their lives are tapped in these camps. Everybody's creative, yes—except that everybody doesn't know they have this little light on inside.

You once said that the dancer Dudley Williams had a great influence on you.
Yes. He's amazing. He has something that is called *ballon* of the arms. Ballon usually means bulliency and balance but he has this incredible *port de bras*—carriage of the arms. He looks like he has balloons under his arms and his arms just float. The upper torso is just carried so beautifully. Elegance is the key word, and he's still that way. He's been with the company for 27 out of its 33 years and he hasn't changed a bit.

What if you discover a young dancer who has this gift that

you're talking about? What do you say to him to help him cultivate this gift?

I talk to him about his or her own vulnerability. But usually the first thing a young dancer will ask is "How do I do that?" And I say, "There's no 'how.' There's no formula. Except being who you are and getting to that."

You have to be able to look in the mirror either when you first roll out of bed or when you're in a studio and realize that what you're seeing is not all of you—it's just the physical part that you're seeing. And though you have to deal with the physical part of yourself and the stage, there are other sides.

You talked about being vulnerable. Isn't that something that most people resist to avoid being hurt?

But I'm talking about when the curtain goes up.

How do you shut it out in the real world?

You married? I hope you can share that with your husband. That you can be that open. So there are situations that lend themselves to that vulnerability—allowing people to act like people, you know. Out there in the street, it's difficult. But within your circle of people, whom you trust, that's where you can be vulnerable. And on the stage. I think it's probably more difficult for a writer because you have to put those feelings into words. But I can dance mine.

But you still have to give yourself permission to be that open. How do you do that when so much of life demands that you protect yourself?

By getting in touch with how much I love this life. It's very important to me that while I'm on this Earth I say that the best way I can. Even when I'm going through traumas. Because if I'm up in an airplane and it starts bouncing around too much, that's when I really realize how much I love this life.

So when you said that a true dancer has to get to a certain place internally, is part of that place an acknowledgment of life?

Yes. I feel that when you watch a performance you should be able to see someone on that stage celebrating life. They just happen to be doing it through movement. If Isaac Stern plays the violin, I'm up there listening to music pouring out of this man and I sit there and love it with him. The only way I'm going to do that is to be able to recognize something that's coming from deep within him. I figure, what are we here for, unless we can share our commonality, in the highest sense? But we often don't do that—that to me is what tears people apart. It happens every day. People get in the elevator and don't even know their neighbors.

What happens when you are not feeling that open? Do you think the audience can always tell?
Yes. I found out that if you shut down, then it's going to show that you have shut down. And I don't want anything to cut off a communication with people who are in the audience or who are important to me in life. I hate 'em, I love 'em, and everything in between, but I still want to communicate with them.

What happens when things from the outside affect your work?
They're supposed to. The wonderful and most painful things that have happened to me, deaths or whatever, affect how I am on stage. And a light inevitably goes off in my brain when I know I'm shutting down, and I just force-feed myself.

Meaning?
I tell Pat, my assistant: "I'm going to go to five performances this week. I'm going to go to five companies I've never heard of before. I refused to go to that thing the other day? Tell 'em I'm coming." There are some things that I can automatically trigger that will get me out.

What would you do with a young dancer who has shut down?
As Alvin used to say, "Everybody doesn't respond to the same combination." It's like when you're choreographing a piece and you're doing it for 12 people and 11 of them are responding, and one person isn't. I'd say, "We've got a problem," and try to do it with as little tone of voice as possible and not imply something like, "This is your job. You are getting paid to do this so what's the problem?" And I would have the warmest conversation I possibly could, unless this person was being totally impossible.

Is there something you would say to them?
Yeah. I'd ask, "Why'd you start dancing in the first place? Do you remember?" And I always say to them, "If you can't remember why you started this, then what are you doing here? I'm talking about from when you first started. What sparked you to do what you're doing in the first place? If you can remember that, then you can go back into this rehearsal."

And if there's still a problem, I'd say, "There are many dancers in New York who are dying to dance with Alvin Ailey." However, I don't like to think of myself as that cold-hearted. Fortunately I've had to fire very few people.

Now that you're artistic director, a lot of people must turn to you. Do you have people you can go to?
The people I could go to as a dancer I can't go to now that I'm artistic director.

Why?
The dynamics have changed. When it was dancer to dancer it was OK. But now that it's dancer to artistic director, it's not OK. It just didn't dawn on me. That's when naivete doesn't work for me. That's the only thing I regret in some cases. I can't say, "OK, let's sit down and talk like we used to talk." However, the people I can still have conversations with are just my most valuable friends. I treasure them, even more than when I was dancing.

What about the different hats you've worn?
I think there's something that being a dancer, choreographer and artistic director have in common, and that goes back to the word "vulnerable." As a dancer I've always been that. As a choreographer I had to look at myself in the mirror and say, "Hey, it's the same mechanism that's working for you. The only thing that's different is that you are working with a number of people and trying not to make a fool out of yourself."

Do their opinions and reactions affect your creative process?
Yes. So you have to not worry about people saying, "What are you doing?" Otherwise it interferes with your spontaneity. That's a hurdle that a choreographer constantly overcomes. You're always facing a different set of human beings, a different set of voices. So when you walk into a room as a choreographer

you better know who you are.

What about your role as artistic director?
I have 29 personalities to deal with now and I cherish the fact that I've got 29 personalities, 'cause if they weren't all different, I'd have this homogenized kind of dull company. But instead I've got 29 characters with vulnerability and passion, which can drive you nuts. But that is part of that lineage.

You once said, "There's so much I want to know, not about dance, but about life, about people. We know so little about people, even those nearest and dearest to us. I've heard all my life that my father wanted to be a concert artist, but I don't know what turned him away from that and what made him into a sheet metal mechanic. Someday, I want to ask him, I want to know about this man who's my father. I want to know everything about everybody so that I can know everything about myself." Do you know some of those answers now?
Some of them. But not in '72 when I was gaga because of the Dance Magazine Award, and *Cry* had just happened. But now a lot of these answers have come into the light. I was so young then, I mean mentally. I was 29 or 30. And what I didn't realize is that my father had to raise the family. And he couldn't do it singing opera or playing classical piano.

Is he still alive?
Yes, he's 77 and he can still sing. I don't know if he ever really studied voice, but what a beautiful baritone he had. One of my fondest memories in my childhood is my father singing *Lullaby and Goodnight*. So what I find so fascinating about my father and his creativity is that he sacrificed pursuing that kind of career, an artistic career, and became an installer of equipment in bars. I still have malt machines from the '40s, and a Pepsi Cola Hits the Spot little thing that you push and it plays. And in our home there are kitchen stainless steel cabinets. He made those cabinets and the dining room table and the chairs. He was fantastic with his hands. And yet there was a dichotomy.

In what sense?
Well, he always had rough hands—you know, calluses from doing that kind of work—yet he taught me how to play the

piano. And I listened to his phrasing when he was playing the piano, and I said this is the way the *Moonlight Sonata* is supposed to be played, because that's the way my father played it. He played with a complete release of passion that was terribly internal, but very generous at the same time. We talked about vulnerability. Here was a man who was really willing to share his vulnerability and his passion through those notes that he played on the piano—and then work from nine to five with drills and nails and hammers.

Wasn't that hard for him?
Yes, but he loved it. And he's loving it more now because his daughter is where she is now. And I think I learned that kind of dichotomy between the hardness of steel and callused hands and the thickness in the fingers from hammering things all the time—and someone who could gently put those rough hands on the piano and play the *Moonlight Sonata.*

Did you play the piano yourself?
Yes. My first piano lessons were from my father. When I went to take my very first "real" piano lesson, I walked in knowing certain pieces with the craziest fingering you ever saw because I had learned it through his passion and not through rote or scales. That was my downfall, because they said, "You have to start here." And I was already here. "You've got to learn the scales." I didn't last long.

How do you think the dichotomy of your father—gentleness and coarseness—affected your art?
It helped me show the different sides of myself, which is what you need when the curtain goes up. There's no gray area. That's what I like so much about the stage. It's transparent in the most positive sense: you cannot lie on the stage. It's not gray. It's either black or white, period. I guess you could say harsh or gentle—both extremes.

How else did your home life affect your work?
I think the music I listened to had a great affect. There was such a range of music. There was church music and songs like "How Much Is That Doggy in the Window?" and we used to listen to Milton Croft coming from the Met on Sundays or

Saturdays. I remember hearing *Peter and the Wolf* and getting a love of Stravinsky because I saw *Fantasia*. And I loved anything by Bach. And I remember discovering the righthand side of the dial on the radio. In every city you can think of, that's where the black FM stations were. That's when I discovered Little Richard and Bo Diddley. And I always had all that going on at the same time. So I think that affected my musical choices and vocabulary, which are very eclectic. I once did a piece that combined Ray Charles with Vivaldi.

You talked about your father's influence. Did your mother influence you, too?
Yes. She was so regal, like a queen. She walked as if there was a ruler in her back. Both of my parents showed me how I should carry myself. They also taught me not to compete with people, but to compete with yourself. I think as human beings we have a tendency to compete with each other automatically, but finally you learn that you're in competition with yourself, 'cause there's only one of you.

It takes a long time, doesn't it?
Yes. I can remember being in the company and saying, "Her leg's higher than mine, her foot points better." But then coming back to the realization that my foot is my foot, my arabesque is my arabesque, and working with it. But I think my parents had a lot to do with my looking at myself. It's not that I didn't disagree with them, but they were incredible people.

Your mother almost died once, and you were quoted as saying you knew she was going to make it.
Yeah, I had no problem about that. However, she did pass at home in '88.

What appeals to you most about dancing?
I guess there's something so right to me about being able to convey your innermost thoughts without saying a word. It's very spiritual and reminds me of the church.

Did the church have a big effect on your work?
Absolutely. I went to the first black church in America, which is an historical landmark in Philadelphia. I went there every

Sunday from the age of one to the age of 18. And it would usually be at least half the day, because you had the service at 10, or 10:30, and it would go until one or two depending on whether it was the first Sunday or not. And then you had Sunday school after that. So it was a very long day. I wasn't always exactly thrilled about going every Sunday, but it was part of the ritual when I was growing up.

What specific effect did the church have on you as an artist?
I saw what the spirit could do, what something that was intangible could do and how it could change your life. But as a child I grew up being frightened of the spirit.

Why?
Have you ever been to a black church and had people get "the spirit" on you? They pop up out of their seat and then all of a sudden the Holy Spirit is upon them, and they're just totally transformed and people can jump up and start shaking. It scared me to death the first time I saw somebody do that! My mother tried to explain it to me.

So it was the reaction of other people that scared you?
Yes. Everyone reacted in different ways. Some people would just cry and all their being would be filled with spirit and the Holy Ghost.

They are filled with an understanding that you're not in this world by yourself. There is a higher being and you are where you are not just because of your hard work, but because there's somebody else there, that's making sure that you're all right. And when people come to that realization, it brings a joy that is beyond the body. The body cannot contain it, and therefore they address it by being spirit-filled.

I was in church the other day, this Episcopal church, hearing this choir sing a cappella. They're called the Royal Priesthood. And all of sudden my face is wet and it's not just because of the music being so beautiful, but also because of its spirituality. You're surrounded by people who are thinking the exact same way you're thinking. So I've had that spiritual experience from the time I was a little kid.

Which explains why your work is so spiritual.

It's a pageant. A complete, utter, pageant—with costumers, sets, you name it. The church is the set, the costumes are the robes of the choir, the characters are the choir, the nurses, the congregation, and the elders. And the most extraordinary speakers are the ministers.

They're unbelievably dramatic, aren't they?
Yes. We had a minister named Reverend Stewart and another minister named Reverend Dandridge, and they were complete opposites, but they did the exact same thing to the congregation. Reverend Stewart was about six-foot-six, with silver hair cropped close to his head. He was very distinguished but he was also very scary. Musical notes would slip out of his mouth like air. And all of a sudden you'd be on your feet, not believing that he took you to that wonderful place that you wanted to be.

Which is what you do with your work.
Well I hope so. I try. There was also Reverend Dandridge, who would have his black robes on with those marvelous velvet things. And in the middle of the sermon his voice would be way up here someplace and he'd put his hands on his hips and there'd be red suspenders under there. And he'd walk like a peacock back and forth, preaching. It was just incredible. So there were two extremes and I didn't care about anybody in between. Yes, that has affected the way I work. It's the same kind of passion that was in my family.

Do you feel guided in a way?
Absolutely. And that's from my background. You learn that the rewards are not necessarily on this Earth, but that the best you can do is to keep challenging yourself and be well-prepared for whatever is guided into your path. You know what I'm saying? And in a way there's a certain naivete about it, but it's a smart kind of naivete. It's not blind faith.

You need it though, don't you, that naivete?
Absolutely.

It's been said that you had a love/hate relationship with Alvin Ailey.
I think that came from him first.

But you didn't feel that way?
No. When I think of him I think of his genius. He was a man who knew about the theater. He also understood human beings. He was terribly generous. Five thousand people showed up at St. John the Divine for his funeral, which gives you a sense of his generosity. Some of these people I never saw before in my life, but they knew Alvin. He had touched so many lives. Not just in the New York area but all over the world. And I think my absolute passion, there's that word again, is to make his family bigger. Because of his vision, we're here, and I think it's very important for everybody to understand that.

Then why was your relationship described as love/hate?
I think what Alvin was talking about was what everybody has when they get close to each other. Do you hate your husband sometimes? I mean if you live with someone, you know them, all the different sides of them. And when I say live with someone, I actually did live with Alvin and James Truitte for about six or seven months. And he became my spiritual walker. That's what I called him at the memorial service, because we were walking side by side spiritually. We didn't have to say anything. We were not that verbal. The conversations we had over 15 years were so few you could put them in a cup. But we exchanged some pretty profound things. We were so close that we were able to do *Cry* in five days in '72.

Do you miss him?
Yeah. Alvin died in '89 and my mother died in '88. And I haven't had time to really mourn either of them because everything is just going so fast. They were both very major forces in my life. But their spirits are still with me, so that keeps me glued together and propels me forward. Sometimes I expect Alvin to come walking through the door any minute. On stage we expect him to come walking out of the wings. Because he was such a presence, he was so there. But his presence is still with us, and what gives me happiness is that when the curtain goes up, or when I'm around the dancers, or when I'm in the building, then he's all over. I mean his spirit is all through the place. So it's enough—at least it is for now.

❝ Basically I'm a very shy person. I have great respect for privacy. Maybe I'm a little bit Victorian. But when I'm taking pictures of a tree, or the woods or a building, it's very easy to be alone. ❞

BALTHAZAR KORAB
Architectural Photographer

"Within an hour you know if something is good..."

"I decided I am not going to prepare anything because I said, 'Let the interviewer do her thing!' But a couple of hours ago I started to panic. 'How on earth can I justify myself as an outstanding talent?' So I started to dig through my things and I found an old publication which was written by one of my students at the University of Michigan many years ago. It's filled with many quotable things and it sums up a lot of what I still stand for."

So began an interview with Balthazar Korab in his two-floor studio next to his home in Troy, Michigan, on a rainy winter day. A few moments after his interviewer arrived, Korab emerged—bearing two glasses of wine. Korab, born in Budapest in 1926, was still the charming European host.

He began his career as an architect, working with Eero Saarinen and Le Corbusier and graduating from the Paris Ecole des Beaux Arts in 1955. But he soon made a transition into photography and began working professionally in the late 1950s as an architectural photographer, combining his two loves. He went on to win numerous awards for his work, including the Medal for Photography from the American Institute of Architects in 1964. He has researched and photographed buildings in France, Italy, Russia, China, Yemen, Saudi Arabia, Egypt, Mexico and Australia. *Time*, *Life*, *National Geographic*, *Fortune*, *House and Garden*, *Domus* and *Architectural Digest* are among the publications graced by his photographs.

Though Korab has had an illustrious career, it has not been without its fallow periods. "In the '60s," he said, "I was very hot and really dominated the scene. They gave me the Gold Medal only five years after I was in the business. But then I went to Italy, and when I came back I was quasi-forgotten." To make a living, he started working in more commercial areas of photography, shooting pictures for hotel brochures.

Slightly bitter about doing that kind of work, he said: "You are happy enough that your name is not associated with it." But Korab has now returned to his art. Offering his interviewer the photograph of her choice, he seemed at peace with himself and well aware of what he stands for. "My heart is really with architecture—with a capital A," he said.

It's been said that buildings express the character of builders. Which photographs do you think express your character?

That is the Catch-22 in architectural photography. I am not the artist. I am the interpreter of the art. The major artwork is the architecture, the building. So when I photograph a building I should really eat humble pie and interpret it with artistry, under-

Mosque in Yemen; 1978

standing and insight. I must make sure that my vision does not dominate or obliterate the meaning or the essence of the building itself.

Isn't that an art in itself?
That's right. If your photograph is so beautiful that people are willing to hang it on the wall regardless of the subject matter,

then you have transcended your mission, which is to illustrate this building. The prime concern of the photographer should not be to create an independent work of art. The prime concern is to interpret the building, to understand its soul or purpose.

Say you are building a gothic structure today. No matter how expressive it is of the 13th-Century religious fervor, if it does not correspond to modern ideas it's a fake. It doesn't matter how beautiful it is.

What would make it authentic?
It has to reflect the spirit of the time—which is known as *Zeitgeist*—not just the creative spirit of the architect.

You once said, "I was searching to make something out of my freedom." Can you talk about that?
I ran away from Hungary, which had turned Communist. When you leave your home and all the things that come with your upbringing—religion, manners, education—and you enter a different world, that is the true challenge of freedom. Because you can be anything—you can be a bum, a millionaire or an adventurer.

So how did you get involved with architecture?
I studied in Hungary for 3 1/2 years, then I went to Paris and completed my studies.

What were you trying to do with your freedom?
To create an existence and bring my artistic talents to fruition.

Why did you change from architecture to photography?
That's a sore point. I worked for a very famous architect, Eero Saarinen, who was on the jury for the Sydney Opera House. That was in 1956. They had an international competition, which I wanted to enter, but since he was on the jury I was not qualified.

What did you do?
I quit, and I started to take pictures in order to survive. I came very close to winning that competition. Instead of that beautiful thing that sits in Sydney Harbor it would have been my building. But it didn't happen, and I stayed with photography. I

entered a few more major competitions, but I always was the runner-up in one way or another.

What happened to your career as a photographer?
I became quite successful almost overnight in 1958. I kept promising myself that I would return to architecture, but I never found an effective way to do so. Photography became my livelihood.

Does photography give you something artistically that architecture didn't?
It gives an instant satisfaction. Within an hour you know if something is good or just a rotten experiment. In architecture it may be two or three years until you see the result. And there are a lot of potential problems. It's a very complex kind of an art.

Do you prefer photographing one kind of building over another?
I prefer photographing native architecture, like American farm complexes or nameless little towns; character buildings that were designed by or built by people without an architect. Or beautiful Italian hill towns. Or Yemen. I spent a lot of time in Yemen. Or Transylvania, where there is wild and beautiful native architecture.

What appeals to you about these kinds of buildings?
You can feel the soul of the whole population, a collective soul. This is the kind of photography that I truly love to do—ancient, timeless architecture. I have very little sympathy or patience with the post-moderns because they are extremely superficial. They are decorators, rather than architects.

What makes them shallow or superficial?
I think it's the mentality of the '80s that you can only affect people by playing on certain sensations rather than searching for depth and meaning and meaningful permanence. It's an ever-accelerating pace. It's like fashion design: you have to come up with a new trick every year or every two years.

Do you have a favorite period of time or a favorite city that makes you feel connected to the soul of the people?

Yes. I lived for two years in Florence, which is small enough so you can grasp it. It is so much a Renaissance city. It has hardly changed since the 1600s. There is an extraordinary spirit to that place. I respond to it.

You pointed out an article that said, "Architects can improve the human condition."

That is one of the major callings of architecture. The modernists gave up that high calling. They were kind of elitist and were going to solve the misery of humanity, so that each building became a difficult task. I don't really believe that they failed, they just chipped away at the hard task. Now the post-moderns simply say that since it didn't work, to hell with it, we are just going to do our little stage-setting architecture.

In what ways do you think architecture can improve or affect the human condition?

That's not a simple thing to answer. There is one case that they called the end of modern architecture. A housing project in St. Louis was blown up. It was built 20 years ago. It was supposed to have been based on the theories of Le Corbusier, which said that if we build a certain way we can improve the misery of urban life and urban condition, but the project didn't work. It became a crime-infested spot. But I have seen many projects that worked beautifully.

What did they do specifically?

Part of the theory of Le Corbusier was that if you build high-rise apartments, you liberate the soil—you leave more land for air, for sun, for parks. He didn't mean New York-type high-rises where they're all jammed in on top of each other, but the kind of high-rise developments you see just about everywhere in America. You have a lot of land and high-rises. That's a pretty complex deal.

Can you talk about using color as opposed to black and white?

There is a tremendous amount of abuse with color, because nowadays everything is color. If you go out on a regular commercial assignment, whatever the subject, you have to deliver color material. The color becomes incidental. It is not necessarily

Michigan vernacular, Frankenmuth; 1960.

a subject that should be photographed in color. If you look at a painting of Matisse, it's color. It really doesn't matter what the subject is—it's conceived in color. Black and white inherently have some abstraction in them which lends itself to composition and image values much better than color. I much prefer working in black and white.

Do you work in color?
Of course. All my commercial work is color.

When you use people in your work does that take away from the building you're photographing?
It depends really on the circumstances. Very often I use people to give a scale to the image, but that's an easy trick. I have a number of photographs where the people play a major role.

What is the ideal picture?
The ideal picture is when you capture the timeless quality of

the environment—the architecture itself without the person. Because sometimes people take away from that timelessness.

How so?
Some of my clients say that we don't want people in our pictures because fashion changes the timeless quality of the images. Also, if the person's facial expression and presence is dominant, the surroundings become secondary. Sometimes a person truly contributes to the spirit of the place, and other times the person overwhelms it. I could pull examples of both. Some of my favorite school pictures, where the kids are absolutely overwhelming the picture, are wonderful.

Do you usually finish what you've started or do you often abandon projects?
Da Vinci once said, "If anything ever fits me as a genius, it's that I never finished anything!" I personally tend to jump from one thing to another.

What stops you from finishing projects?
Probably striving for perfection and being terribly concerned with making a statement. Of course it's different if I'm trying to make a deadline; but if I'm not, I keep taking the same picture over and over again.

What are you looking for?
True greatness. That's when you know when to stop. But it's tricky in photography because you have only a split second to capture a particular situation. You have to zero in on the perfect frame and expression quite fast. Cartier-Bresson calls it the "moment decisive." But when you photograph architecture, as opposed to people, the basic subject stands still and the light and the atmosphere change. So you must manage to zero in on it with authority.

When have you lacked the authority?
Probably the answer to this is that when you are shooting beyond your native capabilities and talents, then it's very hard. It brings one back to Leonardo. His mind was so fertile, but his means to carry his ideas out were very limited—even when he had princes sponsoring him.

So in many ways photography is a very satisfying medium for me. I conceive it at the moment when I click the shutter, what the image will be once it's worked over in the darkroom and eventually printed. There is a wonderful quote from Ansel Adams, with whom I have quite a bit of affinity: "The negative is the score and the print is the interpretation." The true creative work is done when you create the score. Then in the darkroom you allow for interpretation, the way certain interpreters play identical music in a different way according to their mood of the moment or their own personal talents. That's why in many ways black and white is a very immediate medium because everybody can work in the darkroom.

How has your work changed over time?
I say what I want to say in much simpler terms. When I was younger there was more flurry to my work. But I've gotten away from that. And part of why my art has changed is because I've simplified my life.

Are there any moments or incidents that had a major impact on your art?
Music has a tremendous emotional power that we as visual artists do not command over our audience or even ourself.

Do you know why it has so much power?
I have a little theory of my own. Vision is tied directly to the brain cells, to recognition, to reason. While ear, nose and taste is more a kind of emotional experience. How do you know that you really know something? By seeing it. Seeing it is believing it. The other senses, other than vision, particularly odors and sound, can really connect directly to the nerves, to the emotion. It creates an emotional up or down. Memories come back if you smell something that reminds you of someone or some time past.

So in a sense our visual experience is very much a rational experience and not so much an emotional one. That's why I never saw anyone go into ecstasy in front of a Picasso painting or even a Rembrandt painting. It's a very quiet experience. It's a complex experience.

What moods do you work best in?

Hunger is a good state. Your sensitivity is heightened when you're hungry. One outstanding memory I have is being in Salzburg, Austria, in 1949. I was hungry because I didn't have money for food. We had just left the Russian zone and had crossed the border with great difficulties through snowy mountains. My brother's ears were frozen, so it was quite an adventure. We were 22 when we arrived. First we had to go to Vienna, which was divided into four zones, and then we arrived in this beautiful town, Salzburg, Mozart's birthplace. I probably hadn't had a square meal for three days. I was almost fainting but it was so beautiful that it really didn't matter that I was so hungry. The sense of beauty of this place came through so clearly, almost like a vision. It was really wonderful.

What about fatigue? Does that also heighten your sensitivity?
In architecture that was often the case because we had to work long hours to complete a project. You'd forget about sleep and you would be heightened by the creative process.

Are there certain moods or circumstances in which you can't work?
Yes. People disturb me a lot. I work much better alone than with assistants, for instance. Basically I'm a very shy person. I have great respect for privacy. Maybe I'm a little bit Victorian. But when I'm taking pictures of a tree, or the woods or a building, it's very easy to be alone.

Have you ever thought of doing other types of photography?
Well, I'm in great awe of portrait photography.

How so?
I'm fascinated by people who have this urge to zero in on what's missing in a human being. I have done some portraits myself. In fact, I'm thinking of making a show of them. I've collected a lot of images I'm very proud of. But they were often stolen images, where I shot the picture when the person didn't pose.

What's a typical workday like for you?
Ten years ago a typical day would be my catching a flight to

somewhere and trying to perform on a hit-and-run basis. The day would start at daybreak and would end well after sunset. I read buildings through the changing light like a sundial. Some of the best effects were in morning's changing light. In Minnesota in the summer you shoot at 5 o'clock in the morning and in the evening, so it's a very long day. And in the tropics it's 12 hours sharp, from six in the morning to six in the evening.

Do you have a favorite season?
Autumn is really my favorite.

Why?
Maybe my decadent soul. The feeling of passing and rot. It's also very rich in colors. That's when I pull out my watercolors and let it run.

Do you like to shoot a lot in autumn?
Yes I do. Even black and white.

What's a typical day like now?
Now I spend maybe only one-fourth of my time behind the camera because I am involved with getting shows together.

What do you think your strengths are as an artist?
The reinterpretation of the mood of a place, responding to the spirit of a place. I respond to the mood of man-made places, primarily. My prime interest is in what man created, whether it's a building or a garden or a city or a road.

And what about your weaknesses?
Talk to my wife! Inconsistency. I can be easily diverted, derailed from a project.

Is there something in particular that will do that to you?
No, it's just that I must have a clear slate before I start a project, and there is never such a thing as a clear slate in life. There will be always some slight influence, temptation, disturbance.

What would the clear slate give you?
It would help me to concentrate on a particular project. It's very popular these days to say "make a list of your priorities and

stick to it." Right? Well I never mastered that. That is a very serious problem because I am 65 and in order to make my statement public, to have my life's work crystalized in a sort of legacy, it's now or never.

Do you still regret making the transition from architecture to photography?
No, I am pretty well at peace with the fact that I am not an architect and did not create that opera house in Sydney. But the burden to confirm my worth in photography remains. There is a quote from Frank Lloyd Wright. He said that early in his life he had to opt for sincere arrogance as opposed to hypocritical modesty. Such confidence—and his talent, of course—paved his way to success.

And you feel the same way?
No, actually with me it is probably the contrary. I never thought that my talents would really be recognized by the world at large. So, combined with a lack of burning ambition, I have gained a certain amount of recognition almost by accident. People have responded to my work, but I have never really tried to promote myself.

When you look back upon your career how do you feel about your work?
As time passes I realize that I am quite good. And I am now trying to show my work through exhibits and books. I am also trying to finish things. For example there's an unanswered letter hanging in my study. I looked at it recently and it was dated in 1988, from a curator at the Metropolitan Museum of Art who was interested in my work. I have to answer it one day. Slowly I am getting things out of my way.

When did you decide you had to promote yourself more?
When I got older. It's a kind of an attitude when you get older that playtime is over, a pee-or-get-off-the-pot attitude. For Christ's sake, Mozart died at 35, and look what he left behind!

Do you have any regrets?
Yes, that I have not worked on enough great buildings. I have

photographed so many mediocre buildings with forgettable results.

Do people's opinions affect you a great deal?
You see, when you don't have such high expectations of the public understanding the quality of your work, you are actually quite immune to rejection. What really disturbs me a lot is when people in whom I invested faith and talent and whom I trusted did not appreciate that input. There again it's not as an artist, but as a human being.

So you haven't had to deal with a lot of feelings of rejection?
Not too much—not too much in my art and not too much in my personal life. But we had some crisis a few years back and so I decided to go to a shrink—just once. He was one of the last Freud disciples, and after two sessions he kicked me out and said go to hell!

Why?
Because, he said, "You have absolutely no need of my services. He called me "Goettersliebling"—God's favorite. "You are gifted with all the talent, looks and intelligence and your behavior pattern is perfectly normal." So I considered myself in a way a rather lucky person and in many ways this is my problem: that I am not a very hard-driving, ambitious, single-minded character, like Van Gogh or Michelangelo—archetypes of another kind.

Do you have self-doubts?
I have recriminations, such as having wasted a lot of my talents and time on trivial things. As an architect I tried to push the work towards an ideal perfection. Do I go this way with the design or that way? Or measuring the alternatives. That's the extraordinary nature of the creative process. Non-creative people have role models or a pattern of process that they can follow, or a teacher's indoctrination or a magazine that shows how others are doing things.

What do creative people have?
The creative process comes from inner or outer experiences.

Do you sometimes have to give up projects when you have not been able to realize your vision?

Yes. Sometimes you lay things aside because you feel there is a dead end. I have not cut up canvases or tore up things or burned negatives, nothing that dramatic. I have set aside things and hoped that something would come of it. But I don't think that I would have buried anything forever, no. It is probably a time element and the wish to be drawn away to something else.

One article you pointed out said something about "in the past it was easier to harmonize with the environment."

Yes. The conditions were so much more defined in a place or in time. This is probably one reason I am so fond of folk architecture. It follows a very strong tradition that was defined by local conditions. Today, and particularly in America, there is no real solid cultural base or tradition. We are creating our own tradition day after day. The speed of technology has affected things, too. And even the materials we use. Steel and glass are much more perishable than brick and stone. We are no longer creating works that are permanent, like a marble sculpture.

Some photographers have trouble taking pictures of buildings that they feel aren't ethical, or that go against what they believe politically. Do you ever have that problem?

Let me tell you a story. In 1970 I got a call from an architect to fly up to northern Michigan on a UAW plane to photograph a resort he designed. We were just back from two lovely years in Italy, broke and hard up for work. He was a questionable architect and I strongly disapproved of the union's ways. I turned the job down. The plane, with my empty seat, the architect and Walter Reuther on it, crashed.

What did that tell you?

God knows what it told me. I guess that certain principled responses have paid off somehow, which is not to say that I didn't photograph a lot of bad architecture. But I can't let that upset me. But if I was too selective I could easily have starved or gone into selling insurance. So I'm not really an absolute hothead purist in that sense.

What makes for a beautiful building? What moves you?

When the form and source of inspiration become one. When the form really expresses the metaphysical function of the building, such as the great gothic cathedrals of France. Most of those were built in the 13th Century. They had an unusual beauty and expressed the aspiration of their builders, which was highly religious. It's very difficult to find that kind of overwhelming spiritual strength in the modern era.

Are there any modern buildings that come to mind?
Offhand, no. I have great admiration for all three of those great architects they call the trinity: Le Corbusier, Wright and Mies van der Rohe. If I tried to look at what my architecture was, it was much closer to Le Corbusier than any of the others.

What do the three of them share?
They have managed to leave a very personal mark on their creation, which is quite different in appearance. If you see an F.L. Wright building, a knowledgeable person can immediately spot it. Even with Mies, whose architecture seems so impersonal, you can very easily distinguish his work from the imitators.

And that personal statement is what they share?
That's right. In many ways, that is the mark of the 20th Century—that your work is an individual statement rather than expressing a unity or soul.

What do you want people to think of when they think of your work and you?
I'd like to be thought of as the poet of man's creation. Through my vision people would respond to beauty or poignancy. Sometimes many of my images show the jarring presence of man, the spoiled environment, the destruction, the dissonance. So to come back to Ansel Adams, who became the poet of the grand American wilderness: his images stand for the great disappearing wilderness; I hope that my images will show how man affects his environment.

In a sentence, how would you characterize your work?
Soft-spoken with a bite.

❝ I don't like looking at myself on TV. Frankly, I don't know anyone in TV who sits and looks at himself adoringly. So when I have to look at myself in the edit booth, I refer to the person up there as 'Robert' or 'him.' ❞

ROBERT KRULWICH
Broadcast Journalist

Known for turning obtuse economic theories and ideas into compelling dramatic vignettes, Robert Krulwich had switched hats for the week and was hosting CBS-TV's *Nightwatch* in Washington, D.C. In the Green Room, waiting to interview Krulwich after the show, we watched a fascinating cast of characters waiting to be interviewed *by* this man who had once composed an opera simply to illustrate interest rate differences between Germany and the United States.

The characters included a 60ish, gray-

Robert Krulwich: "There are fires from all over the world on the 5 o'clock news because they're so mesmerizing on TV."

haired silversmith from California, whose clients included Frank Sinatra, was showing an odd-shaped teapot to a young producer with wild black hair. A pin-striped conservative smirked when he heard that a woman from the ACLU had arrived. A 40-something liberal kept picking up the phone to dial out, with much the compulsiveness of a chain smoker. And the makeup person did a double-take as she watched a clip on TV from the film *Tie Me Up Tie Me Down*, in which a small toy man travels between the legs of a woman in a bathtub.

Most watched Krulwich on a monitor. Then, one by one, they disappeared from this holding pen and reappeared on the same screen they had been staring at. There they joined Krulwich, who seemed completely relaxed—or in a state of what he calls "calculated relaxation." Slim and in his early 40s, he seemed to thoroughly enjoy himself as he told a country and western singer about a song title he had thought of: "I've Never Met the Governor of Arkansas But I Think I'd Rather Be With You." And he was not the least bit fazed when panelists tore into each other over censorship and the Robert Mapplethorpe photography controversy.

In the flesh after his show, the easygoing Krulwich seemed harried. His first words were, "I can't do this interview now. I'm running late. Can we do it on the way back to New York?" So the interview began in the lobby of his hotel, continued in a cab on the way to the airport, and was completed on a plane.

Chaotic as the trip was, Krulwich did not seem to be affected. When the pilot announced a flight delay, Krulwich talked about shifting his style to keep up with the changing times. He discussed the difficulty of juggling a career and a family as he attempted several times—with increasing exasperation—to call his wife on the airplane phone. And, as another passenger used the phone with complete ease, Krulwich talked openly about his self-doubts.

You started out in law school. So how did you end up in broadcast journalism?

The summer after I graduated from Columbia Law School I had a job at a law firm. I'd actually wanted that job. But I could see that I wouldn't be happy there.

Why not?

I found myself really jealous of the clients and not terribly interested in my own job. So one day I went and sat on top of a hill and took an inventory of what I could do. I decided that I could tell stories and that I was curious about things and that maybe someone would pay me to do both—be curious and tell stories.

Which is what you do now.

Right. Explaining things always seemed to suit me, but I can get carried away or take my work too seriously. Sometimes I actually think I'm on a mission to provide information that people can use to keep the tyrants and oppressors at bay. Then I get letters like, "What is your foot size?" and "I don't think Kathleen really likes you." And I get very sad that the Thomas Jefferson or Peter Zenger I believe I am is actually somewhere closer to Danny Kaye.

Have any of your ideas made the kind of impact you wanted them to? Or have you ever really offended someone?

I hope so. Sometimes when an idea doesn't work, the risk you take shows so much—you wind up looking indulgent. Occasionally when you do something different you get pretty wild applause. But that's less common. So you live with the downside always being much more of a problem than the upside.

Can you give an example?

I did a piece where I was trying to explain Margaret Thatcher's view of the post-Cold War. It involved a rather intricate map with peel-off sections that revealed various scenes underneath. The whole thing was too complicated and too clever and people lost all sense of what I was doing. Plus the fact that one of the scenes looked to some people like a caricature of Asians. It could have been seen as racist.

How did people react?

Quite badly. My wife and my producer's mother in particular were very upset and angry.

How did you feel?

Desperately sad and deeply depressed. It was the end of the world.

How do you deal with this kind of rejection and self-doubt?
By silently screaming. I have a tremendous amount of self-doubt. It comes in great buckets. Usually I take things so much to heart that I believe I am probably not worth much. I get hurt when people don't like what I do. And sometimes I get mad if I think they're wrong. But often I think they're right and that's the poisonous part of it.

When you're in these moods do you think about changing your style or doing things a different way?
No—and that's probably why on some level I don't care about what people think. Because what I do is a form of self-expression rather than a kind of tactical choice. So it's not like I can run off and be Ted Koppel. I couldn't. Period.

What is the biggest mistake you could make on TV?
To not try as hard as you can to say something. That's why people like Koppel—because he has an agenda and he knows why he's gathered certain people together. So he'll take a topic and concentrate it into little kernels by repeating or rephrasing certain words. Or he'll take people's faces and compress them into several thoughts. Sometimes I think he's a bit cocky. But there's no mistaking his attitude and he's able to orchestrate it.

How would you describe your attitude?
It's a little bit cynical and a little bit excited—a mixture of "I've seen it all" and "I've never seen this before" which I realize is a paradox. But then, that's the fun of it.

Did anyone influence your attitude or your way of approaching things? Have you had any mentors or role models?
Not really. And I haven't been anyone else's model. The people I hire, like when I worked at National Public Radio, had their own voices.

What kind of people do you hire?
Smart people. But I don't like people who like economics.

"There's no breathing space. Every day you have to meet an intense demand for spontaneous solutions to very difficult problems."

That is, I don't like to *work* with them.

Why not?
Because I like normal people. And normal people have no interest in economics.

But you do.
Exactly, which is why I need a staff who is normal. So they can argue with me about whether an idea is interesting. Because sometimes I find the oddest things interesting.

Can you give me an example?
Like the fact that the price of salmon went up one tenth of a percent. Most people say, "Who cares?" And I love things like design—even package design. Not many people think it's all that interesting that Kellogg's has changed the color of their box.

I do. I'm also interested in processes—how something gets done. While other people find interesting questions like: Is something good or bad?

So you're saying your curiosity sometimes follows some pretty offbeat paths?
Yes, which means I need people to second-guess me; I need intellectual give and take. It's deathly to be a prisoner of other people's routine. But it's equally deathly to be a prisoner of your own routine.

When you're preparing for a TV segment do you do your own writing?
Yes, all of it.

When do you write?
All the time. It's the hardest part because it's the final part and therefore so much is riding on your words. It's when you find out whether you've done a good job. You can feel so stupid when you spend so much time on an idea and it finally adds up to, "If there's a lot of rice the price of rice goes down."

When you're writing do you rely on quirky rituals that help you get into a creative mood?
No, it comes pretty naturally. I write in longhand on yellow pads. Then I run the copy through an IBM Selectric, using only half the page for the script. The stage directions and lighting cues are written on the other half. Then my staff and I pore over it. And then I stand up and perform it because I like to hear how it sounds. There was a time when I would go to a bunch of actors on a soap opera, *As The World Turns*, and I would read it to them.

What are the hardest conditions for you to work under?
Noise. I have a lot of trouble writing with the radio or TV on. I need quiet.

What about when you're on TV? Is there anything that can throw you off?
I don't like looking at myself. Frankly, I don't know anyone in TV who sits and looks at himself adoringly. So when I have to

look at myself in the edit booth I refer to the person up there as "Robert" or "him." I never refer to myself in the first person. Robert takes 29 minutes to say something that I could say in one.

Are there certain moods that you work best in?
Probably if I'm a little hungry. Or if I'm stimulated by breaking a news story or if I have a device that perfectly fits an idea and it just sort of comes together.

Many of your most compelling on-screen explorations are built around some brilliant and unexpected visual metaphor. Like the time you scattered dollar bills all around, then sucked them up with a vacuum cleaner to illustrate how the deficit works. How do you match an idea with a way to talk about it?
It's hard to understand how it works. Sometimes I just walk down the street and I make a marriage between the two, just like that. They come together perfectly and it's just so wonderful.

What if they don't come together?
Well, that's a problem because I have deadlines. So then I just force it down my throat and onto the TV set. But unlike a poet or a playwright, I do have an out.

Which is?
Something is always happening in the world that I can describe floridly or quietly. In other words, there is always news for me to fall back on. A poet or a playwright, on the other hand, has to create something from nothing.

So whether you have an idea or not you can make it work either way?
If you know how to relax into your personality and enjoy yourself. TV cameras understand that and it's translated to the audience. The main message that gets delivered is, "This looks like a friendly face." The emotion comes through way ahead of the thoughts and it's the only thing that lingers.

So relaxing is key to what you do?
Relaxing into the role you've been assigned. But it's *calculated* relaxation. The idea is to give people the room to listen to what's going on.

Is that more important than the way you transmit your ideas?

They go together like yin and yang. The reason for working creatively, for the highly produced devices I use, is what's called making it stick. But to make things stick there are things you must learn about TV.

Such as?

That it's a relentlessly visual medium. It loves fires. It loves light moving on water. There are fires from all over the world on the 5 o'clock news because they're so mesmerizing on TV. It also likes emotion, like sadness and happiness, and especially faces that reflect emotion. And it loves big noisy scenes. So it likes wars and demonstrations.

Can you talk about what TV doesn't like?

Anything that's not visual, like leveraged buyouts or a whole host of ideas like why am I not getting richer. Almost anything to do with law, economics and science.

How do you make those things stick?

By making your ideas simple and active. The problem is that those two things don't always come together. The challenge in TV is that you're working with ideas and language, in a medium where the overriding thing is to see something. There's a space and you have to fill that space. Words are fragile on TV. So if the image you put up on the screen contradicts the words—which it's bound to do in some way—it's the words that will slip through the cracks. The viewer won't think about what you're talking about. So it's really a design problem and it takes a while to figure all kinds of things out.

What kinds of things?

I did a piece about the money that everyone's been paying into Social Security. I created a nest and filled it with cash. A bald eagle flies off with the cash which is replaced by IOUs. We had to decide what kind of birds to use—two- or three-dimensional? What kinds of flight—straight up and down, slow motion or real motion? Do I do this live? Precisely what words would support this action? When do I bring in Senator Moynihan, when do I cut to the economic analyst? It's very easy, in the midst of all these production details, for the idea to get lost.

How much time do you typically have to put these pieces together?
Not long. I did one on the savings and loan bailout in about 48 hours.

That seems very fast.
It is, considering the idea had to be conceived, scripted, and taken to the artist who had to render and animate it. Then it had to be lit, staged, scripted, rehearsed, and performed. As it turned out, it was very effective.

What was the idea?
President Bush wanted to raise 50 million dollars but he didn't want to include it in the budget. He wanted to hide it. So I Pinnochioed him. I had his nose grow as I read his statement and I had the Capitol dome's nose grow with a piece of animation.

What happens when an idea isn't working?
It can be a disaster. You may finish work on a piece and you come home, sit down to dinner and suddenly you realize, "Oh, my God, we've screwed up here." But it's too late. And then you're on TV the next morning. All you can do is try and cut your losses.

Can you give an example?
A poll had appeared in a Japanese paper in which a lot of Japanese suggested that their society was structured against consumers and in favor of companies. In other words, they felt that American criticism of Japan might be right. At the same time, CBS had taken a poll in which Americans admitted that *Japanese* criticism of American business had merit. In the increasing hostile environment between these two cultures, a substrata of agreement seemed to reveal itself between the broad adult population of both societies.

What was the problem with your idea?
The problem was we didn't have a problem. We decided to

build an American and a Japanese politician and strip off their clothing, revealing them as emperors without clothes. Strange idea. The night before it aired, it seemed kind of funny. But we weren't sure exactly what it meant or even if we should go forward with it. We were stuck basically with a design that we couldn't give up and couldn't accept. In the end we did run it and probably shouldn't have. But we did the best job we could.

Have you ever discovered a problem while you were on the air?

Yes. Once while we were trying to explain how Gramm/Rudman operates I used a large slice of Edam cheese which was soft and didn't cut very well. Now if you treat this simply as an illustrated device, it's no problem. But if you spend a lot of time treating it as cheese it can get in your way. We realized this on the set. Then the question was, should we dump the cheese? Those are fairly tense decisions to make on camera. So there's a certain amount of edginess to this whole process.

Is that kind of problem unique to TV?

Yes, anything can happen. Truly anything can go wrong. Like once the TelePrompTer person didn't start the script at the right time. So my words didn't match the image on the screen.

What did you do?

I was a novice then—so I crumbled! If I'd been a more practiced person, I would have glided out of it knowing sadly that not many people were paying attention to what I was saying. My wife said everything was going along well until I started apologizing. She had no idea there was a mistake. She only noticed when I got uncomfortable and tried to correct it.

It's awful. It's like a nightmare. So the lesson is, don't disturb the surface—the surface is all that counts. Live TV is only for a personality that enjoys that particular form of risk-taking and a good sense of balance.

Do you enjoy that kind of risk-taking—having two days to come up with some great metaphor?

I must say it's getting harder. There's no breathing space. Every day you have to meet an intense demand for spontaneous solutions to very difficult problems. And one day this demand may become too hard.

What do you find most satisfying about working on TV?
That you're paid to be curious and that every day is different. And I like meeting all kinds of people. There is something wonderful about working for a big company that's globalizing before your very eyes. You rush off to the Soviet Union to cover a story, and then you meet Chris Everson, this wonderful cameraman who's just been covering street violence in Soweto. And there's Mario, the sound engineer from Manila, who's usually posted in Hong Kong. And your translator's from Stockholm but she's been at the Pushkin Institute for two years. You have this crazy smorgasbord of people who come together on a project.

What is the most difficult thing about TV?
The relentlessness. The "what-have-you-done-for-me-lately?" attitude. Journalism isn't like writing novels or movies. The broadcasting business has no tangible form whatever, so there's no real memory of what you've done. It's not about making things that last. It's about making things that don't last.

Whose opinion do you take most to heart?
My wife's—she's a very smart person who doesn't particularly like TV. So when she offers an opinion on my work, I have to allow for the chip that's on her shoulders at all times. But when she doesn't like something she usually knows why and she's almost always right. And then I feel terrible, because whatever it is that I failed at has invariably cost her three hours solo child care and a less-than-sleepful night—while I was tossing and turning and sweating it out.

Is that an issue—juggling a family with work?
Yes, it's very hard. Since my wife's a reporter for the *New York Times*, it's always an issue of getting off and staying late. And it's very hard to accommodate everybody at the same time.

What's a typical day like?
I take my son to school by 9. At 9:30 I'm at the office. I'm home by 6:30 or 6:45 which is 15 minutes late—irritating my wife and the babysitter. So I try to calm everyone down for my

being bad. It's a tremendously difficult set of circumstances.

What about your spare time? What do you do to relax?
I don't have any spare time. I used to pal around with my wife. Now I raise children, go to work, raise children and go to work. And on my vacation I just raise children more often. I'm not saying this in any complaining way. It's sort of neat. I know that it's a time of life I'm going to miss. But while it's going on there are long hours that I resent—actually not that much. Having kids is wonderful.

You talked about letting your wife down if you don't do a good show. Is there anyone else you feel that way about?
It's funny, my wife is much more important than almost anybody else. After that, I think—I never thought about this before. I guess I need the people I work with to feel like they're getting good feedback. Especially when you take smart people and put them to work buying thumbtacks and cowboy hats.

So you feel responsible to them, too?
Yes. I feel this responsibility a lot and sometimes painfully. I feel responsible to my wife for the time I'm taking; to the people I work with for the mundane things, the stupid things, the *nonjournalistic* things I'm putting them through; and to CBS because I'm out there doing this kind of weird stuff and it better be good.

Do you think it's usually good?
Yes, but it's not what you'd call normal journalism. So I feel I'm putting my employers and everybody at risk. I may be overstating it. Because they do get the benefits and attention and the sense of something different. And in any business, if you offer people something different, they tune into you or buy your service. So I shouldn't be so hard on myself. But I seem to be.

When your work is good how do you feel?
I can get extremely elated. I have no idea what I've done until the first person tells me. I believe the first person, the second person, and the third person. I always believe the last person I talk to. One day I was standing outside the Treasury Department and somebody said, "Aren't you that guy on TV? I learned more about what I'm doing in this building from you than I have from

anyone in this building." That's nice. Of course, that kind of thing is more common on radio where you already have a well-informed, highly motivated audience.

What's the most surprising thing someone has said to you?
No one in particular comes to mind. I guess because I beat up on myself a lot I'm always a little surprised whenever the phone rings and somebody I admire says something kind and informed. They'll say, "That was interesting when . . .," indicating that they actually got it and liked what they got. That always amazes me and fills me with rich, sweeping and wild feelings of joy. I feel like superman. I don't have a middle-of-the-road way of handling feedback. It's all wonderful or all terrible.

What do you think your strengths are?
Writing clearly about complicated stuff and explaining what it is I'm explaining. If it comes in two parts, the "Here's the news" and "Here's what it means," I'm certainly not the "Here's the news" guy. I'm more of the "I'll explain to you what it means" type. Like backup journalism.

What about your weaknesses?
I work too slowly. It drives me crazy and the people around me crazy. And I'm not an even performer—what I do well is much, much better than what I do not so well. And the fact that I overlook the moral elements presented by a story and try to concentrate on the morally neutral elements might be a fault.

But isn't it better to stay neutral as a reporter?
There are many reporters who are good at doing exactly the opposite, of ignoring "how did this work?" or "how did this punishment get inflicted?" or "how did this money move from A to B?" They'll say, "Look at this oppressor, isn't he terrible?" But this is a function of personality and I am very diffident about going into a public space and calling someone a name, even subtly. I'd rather their opinions and deeds speak for themselves.

Do you every feel your politics get in the way of your work?
No. I make no pretense about my politics, that I'm a standard Democrat-type. But that shouldn't interfere professionally. A

reporter wouldn't be able to see things if he were just looking to condemn non-liberals.

What if you feel very strongly about something?
That doesn't mean I'm clear about it. In the case of freedom of expression I can understand that it might be a community's interest not to have giant sexually excited naked men and women plastered up on the street for everybody to see. It's degrading. On the other hand, I don't have even a scintilla of objection to consensual sex among anybody as long as they're adults and everybody's equal party to it.

So you can often see both sides of a volatile issue.
Let's just say I subscribe to the philosophy that what is most frightening is a point of view that can't imagine its opposite. To have both the capacity to doubt my position and the energy to carry it forward in the face of doubt is the posture I assume.

Have you always assumed that posture or have you changed?
I've been reporting since '78 and there's no difference between then and now. I'm probably much more sophisticated about things now. But no, I'm not. I wish I could say that I've grown, developed, deepened. I probably have but not that I can feel. It was hard then, it's hard now. It was fun then, it's fun now. But I do feel it's time for a change. I don't think I'll become like Ingmar Bergman. I don't see the world as a desperate and a lonely place. I think Bergman does. I never will.

How do you see it?
Much more benignly—and, at the same time, much more hysterical and unsettled. I think, "Oh joy" or "Oh dear." My vision is much more cartoony, unfortunately.

How do you view the '90s—as "Oh dear" or "Oh joy?"
My sense is that the important issues of the '90s may turn out to have less to do with business and the creation of wealth than the equitable distribution of wealth. I'm talking about social justice, men vs. women, issues raised by artists. It's not insignificant to me that the tone has turned so ugly, so angry. I think it's a warning sign.

What does it tell you?
It tells me there are going to be explosions in a society that's not used to staying on an even keel or getting a little poorer. Explosions can often tip you off. This is a thesis, not a prediction yet. But it seems that instead of the '90s being a lively time, where communism is dead and we can concentrate on getting rich together, I have a feeling it might turn sour.

Can you say why?
There are people who feel really left out. And certainly along the race lines. When Tawana Brawley can stand on the steps of the jogger trial, and people can think of her and her attorney as representatives of truth and justice, when they can swallow that, they must be coming from such a desperate corner, such an angry place. It's all screaming in various forms. We'll be hearing more of this.

Is there an area you'll stay away from in terms of your work?
That's up to my personality. I probably don't mesh too well with Spike Lee. I tend to be sweeter and wry. But if you see a kind of noise coming at you and it doesn't fit your form of story-telling, then you have to shift the way you tell stories.

What kind of shift or change do you envision in your career?
Well, I won't go too far off my personal map; I plan to stay in this business. So I'll change my style or the subject or the point of view or the location. But I'm not going back to being a lawyer.

Any regrets when you look back over your career?
No, I have no regrets at all. I don't regret not being a lawyer, or any of the jobs I've had. The one I could have regretted I got out of quickly. And I've been extremely lucky. I've managed to go for a very long run doing exactly what I've wanted to do on my own terms, in little places and in big places, and everyone has agreed to let me so far. They've swallowed the failures and admired the successes. I've not been burned yet. I'm sure my day will come. But it hasn't yet.

> The minute I start thinking of writing as writing, I fall right on my face. If I have a style, you could say it's the absence of style.

ELMORE LEONARD
Novelist

Elmore Leonard: "I don't want to get in the way of the reader and the story."

Contrary to popular belief, success did not come late to Elmore Leonard. It's true that when Travis McGee creator John D. MacDonald was asked to provide a cover blurb for Leonard's 1980 novel, *City Primeval*, MacDonald hadn't heard of him. A lot of people hadn't. But Leonard had been writing for a long time—books, screenplays, short stories. His following was small but growing, and he had no trouble selling what he wrote. *City Primeval* was his 18th novel.

With his 23rd—*Glitz*, published in 1985—Leonard hit the best-seller charts; he has never left. Leonard recalls a TV reporter asking, "Do you resent success coming at your age?" Says Leonard: "I was 59 at the time, going on 60, but what I resented was the implication that I'd been unsuccessful until then. I thought I'd always been successful, especially since nearly everything I wrote was optioned or bought outright in Hollywood."

Elmore Leonard is, by most accounts, the best crime fiction writer alive—maybe the best ever. He's also among the most popular. Nearly every airport newsstand or drugstore paperback rack in America carries at least a few Leonard titles, and nine of his books, including *Fifty-Two Pickup*, *Stick* and *Hombre*, as well as two short stories, have been made into films. Since *Glitz*, Leonard typically has earned seven-figure advances for blockbusters like *Freaky Deaky*, *Bandits* and *Killshot*. His novels consistently sell more than 100,000 copies in hardcover and about a million in paperback, and remain best-sellers for at least two months. His 30th, *Rum Punch*, was published in the summer of 1992.

No two Leonard books are alike, but all bear characteristic markings—a plot as fast and unpredictable as any movie chase scene, characters you can reach out and touch (on both sides of the law), and an uncanny ear for human speech. "I'm not a great prose stylist, and I can't do metaphors and similes," says Leonard, who has raised unpretentiousness to high art. "What I can do is tell a story through the eyes of its characters. I write to entertain."

Born in New Orleans, but raised mostly in Detroit, Leonard served in the Pacific with the Seabees during World War II, afterward studying at the University of Detroit. He joined Campbell-Ewald, a Detroit ad agency, in 1949.

Even his approach to copywriting reflects his extraordinary ear for human speech. "In talking to Chevrolet truck owners, I had to prompt them to get colloquial," he says. "Finally one owner told me, 'You don't wear that sonofabitch out. You just get tired of looking at it and buy a new one.'" It was a great line, but it never made it into an ad.

Leonard got into the habit of rising each day at 5 a.m. and writing fiction for two hours. "I wouldn't be here if I hadn't done that," he says today. "I think that's half of it—the discipline. Not waiting for inspiration. You sit down and you do it. Because that's what you do."

What he wrote was Westerns. His first published short story, "Trail of the Apache," ran in *Argosy* in 1951; he sold his first novel, *The Bounty Hunters*, two years later. In 1961, with five novels and some 30 short stories behind him, Leonard quit Campbell-Ewald to write full-time. But the market for Westerns had collapsed, and Leonard found himself a man without a genre. To earn a living, he wrote educational and industrial films and freelance ad copy. The 1965 sale of *Hombre* gave him the income to write crime fiction full-time.

Leonard lives in Bloomfield Village, a Detroit suburb. Until the death of his wife, Joan, in early 1993, she was his first and best critic. He writes at a 200-year-old desk, scribbling out a page at a time on unlined yellow paper, then running it through an old Olympia manual.

Looking relaxed in a pale blue denim workshirt, Levi's and sneakers, he talked about his life and work.

You write crime fiction, yet you shrink from comparison with Raymond Chandler and Dashiell Hammett. How come?

Well, yeah, I'm a crime writer, but with guys like Chandler and Hammett, I think of a certain school of writing whose main fixture seems to be the slick private eye talking glib similes out of the side of his mouth. I don't write out of that tradition and never have.

Yet a lot of people would describe you as a writer of "hard-boiled" crime fiction.

That's true, unfortunately. Banana Republic once asked me to write a squib for their catalogue—maybe 100-120 words. You know their clothes—safari shirts, bush jumpsuits, expedition shorts. I wrote a squib and sent it in. It read, "I can see a character of mine named Chris Mankowski wearing a naturalist shirt every day on the job. Chris is with the Detroit Police Bomb Squad. He knows that in a naturalist shirt he can poke through the scorched debris of a blown-up car and come away confident of his appearance. This is a shirt that keeps its looks."

I got a letter from the editorial director. She said, "Well, I'm not sure I see our gentle naturalist shirt on a representative of the Detroit Police Bomb Squad. It seems a trifle out of character from our point of view. Too bad we don't have a hard-boiled shirt for you to write about." I wrote back and said, "I don't think you've read any of my work. Of course, it's out of character for the guy to wear the naturalist shirt. That's the whole idea. Everything I do is out of character, a little off-center." But, then, she's stuck this label on me—a hard-boiled writer. I don't think there is anything hard-boiled about my work at all.

How would you characterize your work?
I write from what's going on. I write from what I see and hear at a police headquarters or on the street. There's always been a particular sound that interests me. It's the sound of savvy people, or people who *think* they're savvy and talk that way. It's the way street people talk. I grew up on Woodward Avenue in Detroit, listening to my friends, who were all blue-collar kids. I listened to my buddies in the Navy, who were all enlisted men. Listening is hard work—but it's the major part of my preparation for writing. Talking to judges, probation officers, prisoners—listening to their rhythms and cadences, and the things they leave out.

Is there anyone in your own genre you especially like?
Ed McBain and Donald Westlake come immediately to mind. But I really don't read much crime and then only when I'm between novels—never while I'm working. Reading someone else's stuff throws me off.

Any writers you can point to as having influenced your work?
Hemingway, for one. I started reading him in college in the late '40s and studying the way he did things. He was easy to imitate, which is what you do when you're starting out as a writer—you pick out someone you can imitate, and then work to develop your own style. I learned a lot from Hemingway about point of view, how to reveal character through speech, how to make every word count. I spent a lot of time studying *For Whom the Bell Tolls*. I'd open it at random, and start reading, just to get the feel of it. I saw it as a kind of Western. But I began to borrow from other writers when I realized I didn't share Hemingway's attitude about life.

How so?
I think I like people more—and that Hemingway lacked a

sense of the absurd. He was so serious and he always had to have the right gun when his hero shot a cape buffalo. My characters are not the usual, very capable thriller-novel heroes who know how to fly helicopters and handle exotic weapons. Mine tend to drive the wrong kind of car. They're not unlike Donald Westlake's characters, the type he says go to rob a bank and can't find a place to park. My people in law enforcement tend to cut corners. They run into a lot of "gray areas," where you can't always go by the book.

Do you still read Hemingway?
I do, from time to time—especially the short stories. I've stolen, copied and picked up ideas from dozens of other writers, too. Raymond Carver has been an important influence. I've picked up ideas on how to move the story, how to get in and out of a scene. I also admire writers like Mark Harris, John O'Hara and Richard Bissell, who was an early model. He's most famous for his book *7 1/2 Cents*, from which the musical *Pajama Game* was made, and for his novels set on the Mississippi River. When I reread him again a couple of years ago, when I was researching *Killshot*, setting scenes on the Mississippi, I saw all over again what a profound effect he'd had on me. The idea I got from Bissell is to just let the characters carry the action forward. Write it from their point of view and in their voice. The reader should never be aware of me writing, or of my voice.

Why not?
I don't want to get in the way of the reader and the story. Spencer Tracy once said the worst thing an actor can do is look like he's acting. The worst thing I can do is look like I'm writing. Whenever I'm having trouble with a scene, a chapter, a paragraph, it's because I'm trying to *write* it. I'm trying to show the reader what a clever writer I am. The minute I start thinking of writing as writing, I fall right on my face. If I have a style, you could say it's the absence of style.

Do you see this as a limitation?
I do, but I think I've made something positive out of it. I learned early on what I can and can't do as a writer. I don't have the narrative style of a John Fowles or an Anita Brookner; I'm not good at metaphors and similes. So I don't try. Nor do I have

any illusions about wanting to be a "literary writer." I write to entertain. The best thing I have going for me is my ear for the way people sound—and my ability to tell the story through them.

Not all your characters are especially likeable. Is it difficult to tell a story from the point of view of a character you don't like?

No. Take Richie Nix in *Killshot*, or August Murray, the right-wing zealot in *Touch*. They're hard to like, but I have an *affection* for them, same as I do for all my characters. I accept them, and I let them speak for themselves—even if they're despicable or dumb. One reviewer in England called me "the poet laureate of wild assholes with revolvers." I liked that. When I create a bad guy, I still need to see all his sides—not just the bad parts. He gets up on the morning he's going out to commit a crime, and the first thing he thinks is, "What should I wear?" It's a human reaction.

Few people would label you an especially political writer, yet *Bandits*, in which the Contras are cast as the bad guys, clearly betrays your political views. Was this deliberate?

I didn't go into it with the idea of making it political. A producer had told me he would love to do the big caper kind of movie, where the old pros get together and plan a heist, like *The Asphalt Jungle*. I said, "Yeah, I'd like to try that. It's been done before, but I haven't done it." But first, I had to figure out something for these guys to steal. I was reading at the time in the paper about funds being raised for the Contras, and I thought, yeah—that would make a pretty good score.

Here in the States, the critics didn't make much of the book's political slant, but in Europe, it was widely perceived as a political novel. And it really wasn't—I was just looking for something different for these guys to steal.

But if you were a Reagan Republican, you would have written the book differently.

Yeah. OK. I suppose if Tom Clancy were telling the story, he'd have gone easy on the Contras and maybe played up the excesses of the Sandinistas. But just because a book reflects who I am and how I think, that doesn't make it a political tract.

You've never worked in law enforcement, yet your books reflect an intimate knowledge of police workings and the way criminals think and behave. Where do you go for background?

I never lived out West either, but I wrote what I consider fairly authentic Western novels for over 10 years. I read *Arizona Highways* for my descriptions, found out about the guns my characters wore, the kind of coffee and whiskey they drank—and the rest I made up. In 1978, the *Detroit News* asked me to do a piece on the Detroit Police Homicide Section. It was the first time I had ever gone one-on-one or had any direct contact with police. It was the kind of assignment a professional journalist would spend three or four days on. I spent weeks with the cops before I wrote a word. This was all new to me and I saw no end to the possibilities. As a result I spent most of the next three months with the homicide cops.

Did you go out with them on calls?

I did. I'd get a call in the middle of the night about a murder that had just happened. I'd get dressed and drive down to the crime scene and follow the investigation right from the blood and the body on the floor. But I got my best material just sitting around the squad room, listening to the cops and the guys they brought in, taking notes and not even asking questions. Just listening.

Do you typically do that level of research before you're comfortable writing about something?

Not always. There's a funeral director in *Bandits*, and I knew that, to make him believable, I'd have to learn something about his business. So I spent an afternoon with a friend of mine who's a funeral director. He took me to the Oakland County Morgue [in suburban Detroit], where he picked up a young woman who'd committed suicide, and brought her to the funeral home, and I followed the whole process—stood right by his side as he worked on the body. The embalming machine was called a Porti-Boy. And he filled the veins with Permaglo.

Permaglo?

That's the name of the embalming fluid he used. Permaglo. I remember thinking, gee, this is too good.

So, sometimes, you can get whatever background you need in just an afternoon.

Or less. Sometimes I just make things up. In *Swag*, I had a couple of thieves knock over Hudson's, at one time the big downtown department store in Detroit. But first I had to figure out how their daily cash intake would be picked up. I asked the store's publicity department for help, didn't get it, and wrote the scene anyway. It turned out I got the procedure right.

In *Stick*, there's a drug dealer—Chucky Gorman—who was diagnosed hyperactive as a child. He just couldn't sit still. So I had to guess how he'd behave as an adult. After the book came out, I got a letter from a psychiatrist who said Chucky was suffering from minimal brain dysfunction, and that he was the authority on the condition. Since I had Chucky's behavior down just right, he wanted to know where I'd gotten my information. I told him I made it up.

Are you one of these writers who walks around with a notebook in his pocket and jots down ideas wherever and whenever they occur to you?

Not really. But I often play out scenes in my mind, and I may walk around with them for years before I figure out a way to use them in a book. In one, a guy in a wheelchair is working as a street photographer, taking candids of people. A hustler comes up, and says, "Hey, nice camera—let me see it," and when the photographer hands it to him, the hustler says, "Yeah, I think I'll take it," and walks off, not knowing the guy in the chair isn't crippled. When the hustler is about 20 feet away, the guy in the chair gets up and tackles him.

Then I found a way to use it in *LaBrava*. I thought the wheelchair bit might be a good way for someone to do surveillance work. Only now, the photographer—LaBrava—sees the hustler take about three steps and he doesn't say a word. The hustler stops, turns around and says, "Can you walk?" And LaBrava says, "Yeah, I can walk." Now the guy comes edging back carefully, and hands him back the camera. It's a different scene—and it works much better than the way I'd originally envisioned it.

Did you know, as you began work on *LaBrava*, that you'd be using this scene?

Not only did I not know I'd be using the scene, I had no idea where the story would go or how it would turn out. I never do. I go in with an idea, maybe a scene in mind—but nothing like a plan or outline. I don't *want* to know what it's about. I'd rather let the characters lead me along. When I was writing *Maximum Bob* I showed Joan the first 50 pages, and the first thing she said was, "What's it about?" I said, "I don't know—I'm still writing it." I've learned it's OK to say that. You write the book to find out what it's about.

I was at a ski lodge in Aspen, at the bottom of the run, when an absolutely gorgeous woman with flowing blonde hair came flying down the slope, stopped, put her foot up on the bench, loosened her boot and said, "I don't know what's more satisfying—taking your boots off or getting laid." All I could think to say was, "Uh-huh," and sort of laugh. That was about 10 years ago, and ever since, I've been trying to think of a good response. Not a topper, necessarily, but something appropriate. Something clever.

And that's the wonderful thing about writing. You've always got time—not just all day, but months—to go back to page 30, even if you're 200 pages into your manuscript, and write in that perfect line when it hits you. You don't need to work sequentially.

When you're writing, do you often find the story taking turns you couldn't have foreseen?

All the time. I start with a situation, a character, an idea, or a setting—but I never know where the story will go. A character may show up I'd never figured on and turn the book into something different from what I'd had in mind. I didn't know how *Bandits* was going to end till three days before I finished it. It was Joan who came up with the ending for *LaBrava*. After writing 40 years, I don't worry about the ending or the beginning—they're easy. It's the middle that's hardest to keep going.

In *Glitz*, a character named Nancy was supposed to be the female lead. The first time you see her with Vincent Mora, the ex-Miami Beach cop, their eyes meet and you have a feeling something's going to happen between them. So did I when I was writing it. Then, about 20 or 30 pages later, I introduced Linda Moon. She's an entertainer—does a lounge act in a casino. I found I liked Linda better than Nancy, so I decided I'd go with

Linda, except that I'd already set up Nancy making the moves on Vincent. I thought, "Well, that's good. She can continue to make the moves on Vincent, while Vincent makes the moves on Linda."

You mentioned showing the first 50 pages of *Maximum Bob* to Joan. Do you often show her work in progress?
Absolutely. I'll show Joan stuff as it comes out of the typewriter, a chapter at a time. She's very good at spotting when someone is speaking out of character or when I'm using too many words. She keeps me honest and right on the line I want to be on, with the sound I want to maintain.

Has she influenced the way you portray women?
Yes. I think it's at least partly because of Joan that I've tried consciously to make the women in my books more human. When I was writing Westerns, most of the female characters were incidental to the story. After I switched to crime fiction, I started thinking about my female characters more seriously. I'd show Joan a scene or some dialogue spoken by a woman, and she'd shake her head and say, "She wouldn't say that, or she wouldn't act that way—she'd act differently. She'd be angrier. She'd be more direct."

But your following is still principally male, isn't it?
I'm not sure anymore. Nowadays, I receive many more letters from women than I do from men. But then, women are more likely than men to write letters.

One woman wrote me soon after *Split Images* came out. She said, "The language was so filthy I had to throw it right in the trash. I wouldn't even let my husband read it. All I can say to you is that you're a fucking shitty ass." I wrote back and thanked her for her interest in my work.

Do bad reviews bother you?
Sure they do. A bad review hurts. Sometimes it'll take me a couple of days to get over it. But it can also help. Back in the late 1970s, a reviewer wrote that my attitude toward women was about on par with Mickey Spillane's. I resented that. But I also allowed that if I was coming across that way, then I wasn't doing it right and I'd need to work harder on my women.

And I did. Another time, a reviewer said that *Unknown Man No. 89* was "tiresome," and that even though the action was set in Detroit, I didn't really take advantage of the setting and local color. That bothered me too—but I started paying closer attention to the mood of the setting.

What about good reviews—do you pay much attention to them?

I can't afford to—or, at least I can't afford to take them too seriously. If I read that Elmore Leonard is a wonderful writer, that he has transcended his genre and is writing truly serious fiction and so on—and I start taking that too seriously, I'm going to wind up getting in the way of the story. It's going to sound like *writing*.

How active are your editors in shaping or influencing your work?

Less than they used to be, certainly. I think editors have a role to play in the creative process, although I find that some editors are less comfortable about criticizing my work or suggesting changes than they once would have been. When an editor suggests cutting a chapter down to half its length, or moving a scene further back in the action, I may balk—but I'll back off if I can be convinced it should be changed.

The original manuscript of *Freaky Deaky* contained no reference to freaky deaky. My editor at Warner Books said, "Don't you think you should mention 'freaky deaky?' I mean, what is it?" I said, "It's a dance." He said, "Well, nobody knows that." I said, "What difference does it make? It's a sound." He said, "Why don't you put it in?" So I did. It was a simple thing to do—took maybe an hour. And it worked. But the last time I was really edited was in 1974, when Jackie Farber, at Delacorte, said that *Fifty-Two Pickup* moved too fast. She said, "Take this scene back on page 220 and move it up to 170 and fix the transitions," and that was it.

Do you ever talk shop with other writers about your work—share ideas, swap stories, critique each others' work?

Not often. Living here in the Detroit suburbs, it's not possible for me to have daily contact with other writers. Not that I'm interested in spending a lot of time writing letters and discussing writing. I don't particularly like to talk about it. I was asked to write a chapter on dialogue for a writers' workshop publication. I turned it down. I don't know how you write dialogue—or how I write dialogue—I just do it.

What's a typical day like?
I'll get up around seven, shower, have breakfast with Joan, and at nine o'clock, start to get ready—read over the previous day's work. By 9:30 I'm writing, and I'll stick with it till six. Evenings, we watch movies on the VCR.

When I think back to the '50s and my days at Campbell-Ewald, I don't know how I did it: I'd get up every morning at five and do two pages before leaving for work. I'd write on a yellow pad, and I'd bring it to the office and keep it in the desk drawer. When things were slow, I'd work on it. As soon as someone walked in, I'd put the pad back in the drawer.

These days, do you disconnect the phone, lock the door and generally make yourself inaccessible when you write?
No. Interruptions don't bother me. If the phone rings, I'll answer it; if I need to run out to the post office, I'll take a break and go. I can get into the work easily enough. If I find by the end of the day I've lost a lot of time through interruptions, I may keep going a bit past six—but if I find I'm rushing it, it's better to quit.

How fussy are you about where you work?
Not very. Obviously, I prefer working in my study, which I've set up just how I like it—pens and pencils where I want them, my typewriter to the left, facing the window. But I can work anywhere—in hotel rooms, on airplanes. I once actually wrote while I was being photographed by Annie Leibovitz for an American Express ad. Someone handed me a pad and a pen and said, "Look like you're writing." So I wrote.

Is that how you write—in longhand?
I'll write a page or two in longhand and then type it up on a manual. I cross out more than I keep, and it gets pretty messy; I'll write five pages to get one clean page and usually wind up with four clean pages on a good day. At that rate, it typically takes me five months to finish a 400-page manuscript. I can do a

book a year—which is all I want to do.

What do you do when you're angry or depressed, and writing is the last thing you want to do?
Well, I have a pretty even disposition, so that my moods don't affect my productivity. Sure, there are times when I'm really eager to write and times when I'm not. But I always sit down and do it, even if I'm not eager. In time, I usually can get into it and lose myself in it. For me, the important thing is to remember to just swing with it and have fun with the characters. When I do that and don't worry, the writing goes well.

You make it sound easy.
It's not easy, but the secret is to relax and not take things so seriously. Earlier in my career, I didn't think that way. I was serious. There was no humor in my stories. I didn't start to relax till the mid-'70s. These days, everything I write tends to be a little ironic. It's sort of on the edge of satire, but not quite.

How did you wind up writing crime fiction? Did you just fall into it or was it a conscious decision?
Back in the early 1950s, when I was first starting out as a professional writer, I made up my mind to work in a specific genre. A genre has a form and that's great when you're starting. It was almost a flip of the coin that decided me on Westerns, and I wrote nothing but Westerns for the next 10 years or so. Then the market for Westerns dried up, and I needed to find another niche. Science fiction had never interested me and neither did mysteries, except for Sherlock Holmes. I made a conscious decision to go with crime. My first book in that genre—*The Big Bounce*—was rejected 84 times. But it's a switch I've never regretted.

There are loads of irrepressible children, general troublemakers who run around and climb into everything and don't listen to their parents and so on. Thank goodness for them; they're our hope. And then we do erode their creativity a bit. So it's not so much how do you help people become creative but how do you keep from mucking it up.

PAUL MacCREADY
Inventor

The maitre d' at a posh Manhattan hotel told Dr. Paul MacCready he could not be seated for breakfast, and an interview, because he was not wearing a jacket and tie. MacCready's acceptance of this rejection was as casual as his attire. Toting a worn bag with a campus look, MacCready led his interviewer off to the hotel coffee shop. In these less elegant surroundings, the conversation got off the ground easily on its own power, just like the Gossamer Condor.

The Gossamer Condor was the featherweight, human-powered plane for which MacCready, in 1977, won a $95,000 prize from

Paul MacCready: "The most powerful force on Earth is the human mind, individually and collectively."

British industrialist Henry Kremer. It skimmed above the ground for more than the prescribed mile around a figure-eight course, propelled by the legs of a bicyclist-pilot. Many others had competed for this prize, but it was MacCready who figured out how to create a functioning plane—with a wingspan of 96 feet and weighing 55 pounds—from aluminum tubes, piano wire, Mylar film, a propeller and bicycle parts. Two of MacCready's sons, Parker and Tyler, were the original pilots. After 10 months of fine-tuning, MacCready turned it over to Bryan Allen, a bicycle racer and hang-glider specialist, who flew the Condor in Kremer's competition.

The Condor now has a permanent home in the Smithsonian Institution's Air and Space Museum, adjacent to the Wright brothers' first airplane. Another MacCready plane, the Gossamer Albatross, also sits in the Smithsonian, along with his Sunraycer solar-powered car.

The Gossamer Albatross, also piloted and pedalled by Bryan Allen, flew the English Channel two years after the Condor's prize flight. The Channel crossing won MacCready a $213,000 prize from Kremer, and presaged MacCready's dubbing as "Engineer of the Century" by the American Society of Mechanical Engineers.

Not all of MacCready's inventions have been airborne, but many of his flying creations have been spectacular. The Solar Challenger, for example. It flew 163 miles from France to a Royal Air Force base at an altitude of 11,000 feet, driven by an electric motor with power derived solely from 16,128 wing-mounted solar cells. Or MacCready's replica of the pterodactyl, the largest creature ever to take flight. In 1986, MacCready's radio-controlled pre-historic creature flew over Death Valley as it was photographed for the Smithsonian's film *On the Wing*.

On the ground, MacCready was responsible for GM's 1987 Sunraycer, a solar-powered electric car that beat 23 other vehicles in a 1,867-mile race across Australia—besting the second-place finisher by two days. MacCready also was responsible for GM's Impact, a battery-operated electric car that can go from zero to 60 m.p.h. in eight seconds.

He earned his master's degree in physics at Yale and a doctorate in aeronautics at the California Institute of Technology. While still in school, he won three U.S. National Soaring championships. Later, he won 1956's International Soaring

"If you need to move mountains you just *do it*. So the things I've described don't have anything to do with my ability or brains."

Championship in France. In 1971 he founded his current company, AeroVironment Inc., with Caltech aeronautical engineers Yvar Tombach and Peter Lissaman. Though MacCready continues to develop innovative aircraft, projects involving the environment are a major concern to him and to AeroVironment. Controlling air pollution and hazardous wastes account for most of the company's $17 million annual revenue.

MacCready answered questions for several hours over breakfast, then found conversation nooks and crannies throughout the hotel as staff chased us from one spot and then another to make room for various activities.

Let's start by talking about some of your inventions and about what you have called "mental blinders."

Let me volunteer one little perspective. The things that I'm known for tend to be some aircraft and ground vehicles which have some inherent newsworthiness just because they're large and unusual. They've also been sponsored by major corporations for the purpose of publicity and public relations. Also, the things that I do plunge into unexplored areas. It's like being an explorer who's the first one to go into some territory, and finds the river or the mountain first. In my kind of work, you may find some answers; and because you happen to be there first you get the acknowledgment.

So you're saying the success of certain projects has to do with circumstances.

That's right—being at the right place at the right time. And it's also having some publicity associated with the project. There are other things that go on in my company that may be more important and more ingenious, but nobody hears about them. The last point that I wanted to make is that all of these projects have been associated with my name, and it gets sort of embarrassing.

Why?

They're all very much team efforts. Sometimes I'm intimately involved with the design and other times I'm off doing something else. What I've done is to create a company, a culture with a certain type of people, and then empower them to do these sorts of things. They're all a part of the team and it is that which is important rather than the individual.

So part of your creativity has to do with picking the right people.
Right. There's a group at Lockheed under a person named Kelly Johnson who built the U2 spy pane. They did the first American jet airplane around the end of World War II in something like 10 weeks. Johnson could do these things with a tenth the number of engineers and a tenth of the time and money that it took anybody else. You see, big companies with all their overhead and swarms of people stumbling on each other, look longingly at companies who have a small number of people.

And it's the small company that works best for you.
Yes. And having a group of people who are isolated from the outside world so they can really focus on a specific project. We have short lines of communication, where everybody is talking to everybody and they know clearly what their goal is. The engineer's desk will only be 50 feet from the machinist's.

But I'd like to finish up this thought on Kelly Johnson. The president of Lockheed once asked him if the reason he could get so much done in such a short period was because he had top engineers. And Johnson said no, that's not why. He said he'd take "average" engineers for the next project. But they immediately became better because they were put in a circumstance where a lot was demanded of them. They had responsibility and authority. They were kept away from distractions. The circumstance made the person. And they would then be viewed as terrific engineers because they were empowered with this greater opportunity.

You've used the word "empowered" a few times. Are there ways that you specifically empower your people?
Maybe it's a case of semantics. I'm not a brilliant user of the English language so I'm not sure if that's the correct word. If you provide a culture where the answer is never "No" but "When do we start?"—it rubs off on people.

Do you believe that everyone is creative?
Yes. And everybody can be made more creative. You just need to get rid of the negatives that thwart it. It's sort of a circum-

stance that surrounds you that lets you bring that out.

You once said that we all have mental blinders in some way. How do you think that relates to you?
To put it in a broader perspective, at first, the most powerful force on Earth is the human mind, individually and collectively. It's the mind that's going to determine whether civilization is going to exist, whether the ecosystem keeps going. The human mind now is going to determine the future, can move mountains, can move the ozone, the atmosphere, whatever. We're not dealing with some interesting little topic here. We're dealing with something that's much stronger than all nuclear power plants and nuclear bombs and political systems and so on—the human mind, which requires some breadth, some wisdom, which we're in pretty short supply of, unfortunately. You probably detect I'm a pessimist for the future.

What's the solution?
We have to get tens of millions, eventually hundreds of millions of youngsters thinking more clearly, being able to perceive reality better, seeing that there are four sides to this issue instead of one side. Or if they hear a charismatic politician, then they should really worry because they'll realize how a charismatic politician can have so much more sway over their thoughts and emotions than an inarticulate politician. And so people will think more instinctively about the future, about consequences of what goes on, and they'll understand how their mind works, and how other people's minds work. And therefore when they talk to someone who's different they'll understand where that person's coming from, they'll have more respect for that person and will be able to interact with them in a different way.

So the way one thinks is really one of the most important components of creativity.
Yes. But what's disturbing is that none of these thinking skills are taught in school. People usually pick these things up from the gutter, unless you have some very good teacher in school who's sort of inspiring and sort of opens you up. For instance, if in seventh grade your science teacher says, "I'm going to give you at least one piece of bum dope every class period, but I'm not going to tell you what it is," then the kids start to listen and

reason. Whereas the ordinary teacher just instructs.

The human mind, which has a certain narrowness and gullibility, I'm sure had great survival value as far back as 400,000 years ago. And so we are left with a mind that was very good for eking out a reasonable living on, say, the savannas of Africa, gathering and hunting and escaping the lion and so on, in little groups of 10 people or 20 people, living in equilibrium with their environment.

But you're saying that the mind has to change.

Yes. If you were a teenager in the '30s in Germany and had been a good Hitler youth you realize that in those circumstances, with that surrounding culture, that's what I would be now. Or if you had been brought up in Iran and you're now 20 or 25, you'd be out there with placards against the U.S. And as you perceive things in this way you realize the commonality between what people are, but also how the culture determines so much of the way we think. Racial prejudice is the same way. If you just worked with blacks all the time and had mixed races all around you, pretty quickly that kind of prejudice disappears. But if you're brought up in a very segregated little back community in the South where there's huge segregation, then that's the way you think.

How do you change that?

You go through some thinking-skills training. Or some people are instinctively more open, which is fairly rare. They see five sides to an issue instead of one. Thinking skills don't tell you what to see, or what to do with what you see. They just make it so that you can see, and you realize that as soon as you've formed a quick opinion on a subject, usually you've stopped thinking. Whereas if before you've made that opinion, you've danced around the subject, looked at it in nine different ways, then you see many things that are denied to the brighter person who focuses in more narrow ways. The mind is like a Swiss Army knife that has all these tools. If you want to take a cork out of a bottle you use a corkscrew, and if you want to trim or whittle a piece of wood, you use the little knife. The awl is for making a hole. And so on.

How do you teach people to think creatively?

There are loads of irrepressible children, general troublemakers who run around and climb into everything and don't listen to their parents and so on. Thank goodness for them; they're our hope. And then we do erode their creativity a bit. So it's not so much how do you help people become creative but how do you keep from mucking it up.

How did you keep from mucking it up in yourself? Who and what influenced you?
I can concoct some reasonable answer to your question, but you should not take it all that seriously, because it may be completely wrong. I don't consider myself especially gifted. I do recognize that I have a couple of capabilities. One is that I don't feel threatened working with people brighter than I am. Instead I'm sort of pragmatic and interested in getting the job done. I don't care who does it or how it gets done as long as there is some worthy goal.

What prompted you to start your own company?
I couldn't find the big company that was in the field that I wanted to be in. And when you start a company with zero employees and then you have one and then two and then five and finally a hundred, it gives you the confidence that you can do it. Then I did it a second time, and again with zero employees and I built that up. If you want to do a job, you just go do it. So if I had been part of Douglas or Lockheed or some big aerospace firm, my skills as an aerodynamicist would have been strengthened, but my thinking would have been narrower. Because I had my own company I wound up dealing with many different subjects, which forces you to make connections between this and that. So you get to be more of a systems person and a connector of ideas than a specialist in a big company.

Being in a certain environment and having a determined attitude is what helped you to think creatively.
Right. If you need to move mountains you just *do it*. So the things I've described don't have anything to do with my ability or brains. The important thing is that the circumstances you're in get you into the habit of responding with "of course," or "yes." It's an attitude change, and it doesn't have to do with your technical training or brains.

What does the word "deeper" mean to you—in terms of working in a deeper, narrower way?
In the context I was using it, it was the depth of the specialty—that you knew everything. In our company, people give thought to the kinds of things we were talking about. We found that people who were trained in schools—aerodynamicists, engineers, designers of airplanes, were not very good. If you gave them a challenge, they immediately had to get out their calculators instead of sitting back and thinking: what do we really need here, what's the goal? Incidentally, they've found that the attitude of a student is much more important than his or her grade point average. It's the drive, enthusiasm, versatility that makes them good.

Can you talk about some of your specific creations—the process, the obstacles, how you personally approached your work?
Well, as I look back at the Gossamer Condor prize and I try and examine the roots of it, I realize I had very special training in my hobby of model airplanes from the age of 12 to 16. I thought I was just sort of playing with toys. But I look back now and realize what a wonderful education it was. And then when I got older I became very active in sailplane flying.

When was that?
Between '46 and '56. It was a hobby, but a very scientific hobby. So even if you're a mailman or a fire fighter, if you get involved in that particular sport you become a scientist.

Why?
Because you're interested in the efficiency of the vehicle and how you extract energy from the atmosphere, and you learn more about meteorology so it gives you an approach to problems that's a little different from stamp collecting. When I first started getting interested in sailplanes, I remember reading one article called "Soaring Over the Open Ocean," in *Soaring Magazine*. It must have been in '45 or '46 and was written by a man named Woodcock. He described how an oceanographer had gone out on an expedition in the North Atlantic. He would watch soaring birds from the ship and he would see that sometimes they would soar in circles and sometimes in straight lines

parallel to the winds and sometimes in straight lines perpendicular to the wind. And sometimes they couldn't soar at all. He realized that the birds were illuminating the various atmospheric motions by the way they were flying.

How so?
When he'd notice a bird flying a certain way, he'd measure the temperature difference between air and water and the wind speed. Then he put together a scatter diagram and he began seeing the real picture and he realized that the picture was identical to the convective motions that are called Bennard Cells in a laboratory, where you have fluid in a dish that's heated from below. He found that the kinds of motions that happened in a laboratory from the turbulent transfer of heat was exactly analogous to what was going on in the atmosphere.

I thought this was the most elegant possible type of experiment. He didn't need a cyclotron or a government grant. He just had some sort of educated eyeballs and did some thinking and connected these scales of motion using birds, which was a lovely way of illuminating motion.

How did that experiment affect your own work?
I never forgot that one article. And then when I was on vacation in '76 I became interested in the Kremer Prize for Human Powered Flight because I recognized that the amount of the prize was exactly the same as the amount of debt that I had accumulated. But also, just for the fun of it, I found that I'd always been looking for some study analogous to the "Soaring Over the Open Ocean" study, a study that also had a simple elegance. And I realized that if you watched a bird soaring in circles, by just measuring the time to do a 360-degree turn and estimating the bank angle you could immediately calculate the flight speed and the turning radius at which it was operating. And here, without any tools, just driving along in a car, you could be getting this information. So I began doing that, and I found that birds are much more interesting because now you're comparing the flight characteristics of the turkey vulture, with the black vulture, with the red-tail hawk, etc.

And you did all that on your vacation?
Yes, well, it was a fun thing to do on vacation, stimulated by

the elegance of Woodcock's approach. And as I said, I'd been grappling with "OK, it'd be nice to win the Kremer prize" because it would take care of a good part of a debt, but I couldn't think of a way to do it. But when I started to watch soaring birds and comparing this bird and that, I started doing the scaling laws of size, weight, speed and so on between different birds and wondering how it compared with a hang glider and a sailplane. Suddenly I began thinking about human-powered flight and realized that there was a very different approach to solving the problem, so simple that you should have figured it out in 10 minutes but you didn't.

What was the approach?
You could make it very large and light. Because you didn't need any structural safety margin. It could be very fragile and therefore you could make it huge, just about ready to break, but not break, because nobody would get hurt if it broke at such a low altitude and slow flight.

But I didn't actually plunge into anything until the problem had all been solved by having stumbled onto it because of this lateral way of thinking. Your mind may be so steeped in the details of the project that you are not able to find the solution. So you give up, go off and do something else, and then suddenly you get a flash of insight from some new thing you might happen to be thinking about that tells you how to do it.

And your flash of insight came from studying the flight of birds.
Actually, the Gossamer Condor project had two occasions when the light bulb suddenly glowed over my head. The first was when I realized that the amount of the prize was the same as my debt—that was the important part. The other one was doing these scaling laws stimulated by the hobby of just studying bird flight. There was one minor light bulb flicker and that was the realization that you could make something that large and that light by using an adaptation of hang gliding construction—very tiny wires—and that you didn't need a structural safety margin. After that, there was a lot of grunt work, where you had to solve all kinds of problems and you dealt with some fundamental issues of stability and control and so on. But they were sort of straightforward if you started with the right basic

concept. The only question was, was it going to be a lot of work or a little amount of work?

Were there any major obstacles that you remember?
As I look back, the project was really well done, not because we figured it out so carefully, but because we had the right attitude. Assuming that every little technical challenge along the way had a very simple solution, you just take the first obvious approach to it and try that. And most of the time, to your surprise, it actually worked. We did find a couple of very sticky technical challenges.

Such as?
One had to do with stability and control, which related to vehicle efficiency a little bit, and it was a phenomenon that is called "apparent mass." The airplane weighed virtually nothing, but because it is so large, it coupled to a large mass of air. So any time you're accelerating it, getting it from straightened level flight, doing a turn or something, you're having to accelerate this huge mass of air that it couples to. And it's the energy that you have to put in that mass of air that causes the drag, rather than the energy that you have to put in this lightweight airplane which didn't weigh more than a heavy bicycle. So, it was a new realm of flight, this apparent mass phenomenon, and no one had any experience with it. You knew it was there, in the equation one understood the concept, but you couldn't see it or feel it and so you couldn't have any real feel for how it affected the airplane. So that was a toughie. We had entered a new realm of flight—the first ones who truly encountered this phenomenon.

What was different about this airplane?
In an ordinary airplane, the plane is heavy and the surrounding fluids are light. But in this case the airplane is light and it's the surrounding fluid that tends to dominate things. So, to illuminate that, we made, and I think this is one of the more creative aspects of the project, a little three-foot balsa model—just a few slabs of wood—and pushed it around in the swimming pool where you could feel the forces with your hand. But now the surrounding fluid was about a thousand times heavier than air, and the vehicle weighed nothing. In fact it weighed less than the water it would have floated on, so that exaggerated this phe-

nomenon that we were looking at, and very quickly we had some real knowledge about it.

Also, we had done some computer analyses, which said that if the measurements we'd made in the field were correct, that's just what would happen. So this little experiment in the swimming pool did start giving some reasoning and helped us interpret what the computers were trying to say. Then we came up with the next version of the Gossamer Condor and then the rest was just a lot of detail work, making it a little lighter, a little more streamlined, a little more accurately contoured.

And that became very successful.
After a while the plane kept getting a little more successful and we had a good pilot and a good bicyclist and it all came together. Each flight was getting longer and longer and finally we were able to do it. The Gossamer Albatross that followed about six months later was done so much more efficiently. It was just a steady improvement of the Condor. It's a much more elegant plane, so that even I could have gotten the Albatross around the Kremer course. But, of course, the goal was just to win the prize as quickly and cheaply as we could. We didn't care who the pilot was, who the designer was, we just wanted to win. And so we did it.

And then you went on to the Solar Challenger?
After a while we were sponsored by DuPont. They found that the Albatross was a magnificent project which dealt with the whole soul of DuPont. They figured they got about $50 million worth of benefit out of the project. So when I came to them with the idea of doing a solar-powered airplane, they were softened up and they said OK eventually.

Were there any major obstacles that you encountered with the Solar Challenger?
Just that it was a very demanding technological project. You don't get much more power from solar cells than you do out of a person pedaling. However, this vehicle—in order to do a long flight—had to fly at a high altitude and in turbulence and had to have good stability and good structure so it would never come apart. The human-powered airplanes were just designed to win the prize and wouldn't fly higher than 10 or 15 feet, where it was

safe to fall. This new one had to be designed much more elegantly; and it was. I got a good person named Ray Morgan to run the project. It was just a lot of hard work. Again we were pioneers in a new area. We used a 95-pound woman or a 125-pound man as the pilot to make sure the plane would fly. The power was so low that it couldn't handle too much weight.

And then you went on to the Sunraycer?
There were several other things in between, but the most significant was the pterodactyl project.

Can you describe that project?
I made a flying replica of the largest flying creature for a film called *On the Wing*, which shows the evolution of natural flight, and the evolution of mankind's technological flight. It was a film that I felt was consistent with the heart of the Lindbergh Fund, where I happened to be director. It was consistent with what Lindbergh devoted the last half of his life to.

How would you define that?
Seeking a balance between nature and technology, which is so much more important than just technology. So we got going on that project, which was technologically very difficult, but it did succeed. There was another human-powered airplane for some speed prizes that Kremer put up, but the prizes were now very tiny and so in this case we were not motivated by the prize. But it was a good stepping stone in technology for some other things that we had in mind. By then this division was doing a lot of other projects, mostly government projects. Then we got into the Sunraycer project.

How did that come about?
General Motors had recently acquired Hughes Aircraft. They wanted to make the point that they were a high-technology company, which they already were, but by buying Hughes Aircraft they were even more so. So when the solar car race came up they wondered if they should do it. Someone over there knew me and got in touch with me, and we eventually became the program managers and chief assistant engineers and the builders.

I think the reason the project worked out so well was that we had this very unusual background of making the only solar-powered airplane that had ever been built that actually carried a person. We'd done the other pioneering work on ultra-low power, high-efficiency light construction aircraft. And also I'm the president of the International Human Powered Vehicle Association, a group that stimulates the development of land vehicles to go as fast as possible using just human power. So to put it together, we had the best background experience and insights for attacking the solar car project of any group in the world, because we combined all these background capabilities and interests. We were not brighter than anybody else. Just odd circumstances let us be the ones.

So you wound up doing the Sunraycer project with GM.

Yes, and that established our credentials with GM. And then GM bought 15 percent of AeroVironment to form a closer cultural connection because that project had worked so well. It was kind of a nice thing that it happened with GM in the last five years. It was using the best of the big corporation with the best capabilities of a small company. In a big company you're always worried about how to become entrepreneurial, how to get things done quickly. We did several other projects with them, but the key project was the Impact, the battery-powered car.

There was no transmission and no clutch, is that right?

Yes. We had enough knowledge and a systems engineering approach to things that we were able to come up with the basic idea. We knew how far you could go in tire drag, in weight, construction, in aerodynamic drag, in power electronic efficiency, in battery efficiency. And we could do the calculations that showed that when you had 10 percent improvement there, and three percent there and 35 there, and you put all these numbers together, you eventually realize that you would be able to concoct a reasonable battery-powered car. Even though you have to take into consideration that out of a battery you only get one percent of the energy per pound that you get out of gasoline. So that's a hundred-to-one hit that you're taking. But still, by having a vehicle that takes practically no energy to operate, you can get by with it. So when we put all the numbers together it worked out, and we were able to get the sponsors interested in battery-powered cars.

What do you think your strengths and weaknesses are in terms of the work you do?

Because of our position and reputation we have a lot of opportunities to do good things. Some other group that may be stronger, but not as well known, just doesn't get the opportunity. The team really is a competent one of good people, but also the structure that connects them—the management style—is very effective. And since I am interested in the pragmatic aspect of getting a job done, I don't care who does it. I only care the job gets done.

How do you define team?

Well, it's not just the people within AeroVironment. We use consultants and we also feel that the customer is part of the team. For example, when we do some air quality study for somebody who wants to get their new plant licensed to operate while meeting the stipulations of the new Clean Air Act, we have to be very creative when it comes to developing some new gadget. We try and work out new techniques for them, new ways of interpreting the rules, or new technologies adapted to their purpose and try and get a win-win situation where the air pollution is not just conceived of as a miserable thing that you have to pay a lot of money to cope with. We really don't think of ourselves as "we do this, and the customer just shoves money under the barbed wire." They are part of the whole process.

What do you think *your* strengths are as opposed to the strengths of the company?

Different people have different strengths and weaknesses. As I look back at my youth, I think being somewhat dyslexic let me know there are some loose cogs there someplace. All three of our boys have dyslexia, but it helped us get acquainted with the phenomenon and I think it helps explain why I was dismal in history and not good in languages. The math and physics that dealt with concepts were very simple and fun. But whenever I'd try to read a paragraph in history, by the second sentence my mind would be a thousand miles away. You tend to have a shorter attention span, and your mind darts here and there and makes a lot of connections; but it is not so good at focusing or concentrating on details. It's not that one kind of mind is good and the other's bad. People are different, and mine happens to be this way, and it involves looking at connections and broad issues and underlying meanings. Sure, I get involved in a lot of details, but that's not what my mind first gravitates to.

Do you have any qualities that may have seemed like a strength or a weakness that you view differently now?
I was always the smallest kid in high school and not very coordinated. And since I was not a very gifted athlete type and I was somewhat shy, I obviously wasn't the social lion and baseball hero, which no doubt I would like to have been. So I probably got more psychological rewards and reinforcement doing model airplanes. Maybe I was upset at the time, but like so many things in life, something that you considered to be a real problem seems different years later and you're delighted that you had it. I mean, I could be an over-age football jock now, or still an active scientist and engineer, and I much prefer the latter.

So what you'd call your shortcomings actually contributed to who you are now.
Yes. And as you can gather, I'm quite aware of my intellectual strengths and weaknesses. It's not an especially flattering picture, but I don't give a darn. You deal with what you've got. You always wish you had a better memory, or better analytical skills or better anything, but if you don't, you just deal with what you've got.

What do you wish you had more of?
Oh, everything. I deal with Murray Gell-Mann across the street, the Nobel Prize-winning physicist and certainly one of the 10 intellects of the 20th Century. You see his prowess for all sorts of different things. It would be great to have a mind like that, a mind that can remember most everything, but you don't. Maybe you wish you were a seven-foot basketball player, but you're not. I really don't care. You just always wish you had more money, more time, more mental skills, more acquaintances, more everything, but if you don't...

How have you changed over the years?
I feel that anything you want to do you can charge ahead and do. And there is one big difference. After the Gossamer Condor project, I got on the lecture circuit in 1977 and so I was forced to

think about the project in different ways. I had to figure out what it meant, what value it had, and where it was leading. I had to look at the bigger perspective and I had to answer questions from the floor, like, "Why did you guys win and all these teams in England with many more resources didn't come close to it?"

So that project was a turning point for you.
Yes, because I really had to start grappling with all kinds of issues. I've had unique opportunities in the last 13 years or so because of that project and subsequent projects. I've interacted with a lot of competent, dynamic people and had to do a lot of homework. I've had to focus my thoughts, and that has been very worthwhile. If you *have* to write an article, and you're only permitted 1,200 words and you're really trying to fit it together, boy does it help your thinking process. In fact, I once heard that they had a 15-minute audio tape of the Great Books, and all you needed was that one tape. I thought that was elegant, so I put together the history of the universe, the meaning of life and the future of civilization and I got it down to six sentences and now I don't have to worry about any of that stuff anymore. I can do things like that now, but I would not have addressed such issues in the past, nor would I have had the skills to deal with them in this way. Another difference is that now I use humor.

How so?
There's a Woody Allen quote, something like, "Civilizations have crossroads. One road leads to misery and devastation, the other to total destruction. We must choose wisely." There really is a lot of meat to that. It's another example of how you can use humor to deal with some very serious subjects.

I do find that with some high school kids, you can talk about serious subjects that adults just instinctively don't even look at. If you start asking questions like, "What is the population going to be on earth in 40 years?" or "If we don't do anything it's going to be over 10 billion, and do we want that?"—kids will get very involved in the conversation. They'll also have better ideas than grown-ups.

Do you have self doubt, and if so, what is the form or shape that it takes? What are the things that plague you?

I don't think I have self-doubt, but it is because I don't have any high expectations of myself. I'm quite aware of my inadequacies, and they are annoyances, not catastrophes. I can still do whatever I need to do.

So there are no voices that plague your life?
Maybe I just don't understand the question. I don't know.

You're lucky. Most people seem plagued by inner voices.
I say, I'm not this and I'm not that, but who cares? What you are is what you are. You've been dealt a particular hand and you can only play the hand you've got.

E.G. Marshall in Sean O'Casey's *Red Roses for Me*: "It gets easier in one way. You have your technique and you've learned some things. And what's harder is now that you know more you have to do more."

❝ You can't enter thinking of your first line. You come on stage and you see the situation and you say, 'Who left the door open?' It has to happen as if you are saying it for the first time. ❞

E.G. MARSHALL
Actor

E.G. Marshall is most easily associated with television's classic *The Defenders* or with the 1957 film *Twelve Angry Men*. But his acting skills have graced a remarkably diverse series of productions, from the New York stage premiere of Samuel Beckett's *Waiting for Godot* with Bert Lahr to Woody Allen's *Interiors*.

The Minnesota native began acting in 1932. In 1933 he joined the Oxford Players, which specialized in classics. His New York debut came in 1938 in the WPA's *Prologue to Glory*. And in 1942 he made his Broadway debut in Samson Raphaelson's *Jason*.

Marshall tired of character roles and continuous typecasting as "the funny little man who comes in with a bucket of beer." His turning point came when he did *The Iceman Cometh* in 1946. It also was the beginning of a close relationship with Eugene O'Neill, whom Marshall considers his mentor.

In 1961, *The Defenders* presented Marshall with the role that made him familiar to everyone. Thirty years later, as a dapper 76-year-old in a sports jacket and slacks, he was still difficult to separate from that courtroom classic.

He was interviewed in a small New York theater—the perfect environment, for he seemed to take in everything in the room within a moment as if he were about to perform. Which, in a way, he did in a two-hour discussion of creativity on stage or before a camera.

In *Twelve Angry Men* there's a line about your character sweating.
Yeah. Jack Klugman says to me, "Don't you ever sweat?"

And at the end you finally do. Do you relate to that character? Or are you a sweater?
No, I'm not a sweater. If I'm working in the garden and it's a hot day, I sweat. But just like that character I don't sweat from mental or emotional stress. That's not to say I don't ponder choices deeply.

What about the choices you make as an actor? How do you choose a play, and how do you prepare for it?
I read the script and I get a kind of feeling about it, an image about it. Then I go back to see if I can be more specific. And then I say yes or no.

You've said that when you were in *Waiting for Godot* you used an image to get started.
Yes. I saw two clowns in a space; and then they act out what's in their imagination. They're in this terrible situation, so they play games to see if they can get that terrible image out of their minds. But it keeps coming back. Who is it? Why does it come back? So then they play another game just to keep life going. To keep the mind going. And then that image comes back again.

What is it?
It's whatever it reminds you of. And I'm not going to tell you what it reminds me of. You've got to make up your own mind. Was it God? "You tell me"—that's what Beckett said.

Weren't you in the play's first New York production?
Yes, but what people don't know is that Herbert Berghof had sent me the play years before it was ever produced. I said, "This is so beautiful—who would let us do it?" He offered his studio, but I couldn't do it because I was busy. But eventually Berghof did wind up directing the New York production.

It got mixed responses, right?
Yes. It was very controversial. Some people hated it and others would come back weeping. And then Bert Lahr, who played

opposite me, was beginning to act up, doing some of his burlesque shtick. The producer, Mike Myerbeg, thought we were doing fine and wanted to extend the run. But I had signed into a movie and had to leave the cast. The truth is I didn't want to stay because of Bert. He just couldn't hold onto the part. He'd be doing shtick and it disgusted me. So it closed.

What attracted you to the play in the first place?

The language. And the mystery, the ambiguity. The wait.

In *The Gin Game*: "I can't say that I ever played anything that was myself."

Getting back to the images you see—do you close your eyes when you see them?

You don't have to close your eyes, you just see it. But sometimes you can see things incorrectly. There was a scene in *The Master Builder* where we were talking about the death of the child and I was supposed to get very emotional about it. But I thought, "This happened 20 years ago. If he gets emotional about it now, that means he's nuts. Or he's trying to manipulate the young lady he's talking to."

So how did you play it?

Without a great deal of emotion. I told Aline Solness, who played the wife, that the child had died. And that was it. And then I started thinking, "These people in Norway lead bleak, dreary lives. So what did they have? Emotions—which would probably explode." So when I did *John Gabriel Borkman*, another Ibsen play, I enjoyed the emotion, brought it up like a fond memory. And then it would dramatize itself. I may go back to *The Master Builder* some time.

Do you often go back to parts you have played?
Very rarely. Some actors like to take a part and make it their own. There's a phrase we have, "You hear the old music and it's different." I did *The Crucible* twice because Arthur Miller wanted to put in a new scene. And I'd want to do *The Master Builder* differently. On the other hand, there's nothing different I'd want to do with *Godot*.

So if you did *The Master Builder* again you'd play it more emotionally?
Yes. The way we played it was all repressed. To repress something you have to have something to repress. You feel the emotion and then you hold it down. It's that tension that moves the audience. So with *The Master Builder* you can hold it down so long and then it's got to come out.

What was the most difficult role you played?
Reverend Hale in *The Crucible*, because I thought it wasn't well written. I said to Arthur, "This character just sits there. He doesn't disagree. He doesn't debate." And Arthur said, "Because they didn't have any of that then." But finally he wrote a line and it was a dumb line. It was something about, "All souls walk out." But I did it. I thought, "What the hell."

Was *The Iceman Cometh* a turning point for you?
Yeah. When *The Iceman* opened they had a big audition room in the Theatre Guild and there was O'Neill, his wife, Carlotta, and a few others. And they wouldn't let you take the script away. You had to read it right there. So I did. Then I met O'Neill and we became friends right away.

What do you remember about your first talks with him?
I could talk freely with him and he with me. I could ask anything. He'd explain what he felt, and I identified with that.

Did he talk about his writing?
Oh yes. He'd say, "Oh (*The Iceman*) is so long, so dour." And I think it was opening night—the lights were dim and I was play-

ing the lawyer then. And someone in the audience shouted, "Turn up the lights so we can see that pile of shit on stage." That's a great introduction, isn't it?

What did you do after the play?
Well, he wanted me to play all his parts. We were working on *Desire Under the Elms* and *Mourning Becomes Electra*. But his physical condition was deteriorating, so he returned to Boston.

Did you keep in touch?
Sure. He even said to another writer that I was the best actor in the country—which wasn't true, of course. But I would have played all those parts had he been in better physical condition.

Can you talk a little bit more about how *The Iceman* was a turning point for you?
Well, I had done a lot of funny little parts. But after doing such good theater I learned to say "no" the way O'Neill did, to plays that weren't of the same quality.

So O'Neill was also very selective about his choices.
Yes, and that was in response to his father, who was an actor. He felt his father had ruined his life by doing the same thing—*The Count of Monte Cristo*—over and over again. He used to imitate how his father at the end of his career would say, "I pissed it away. Just for what? For money?" He felt his father could have been a great actor. He could have played *Hamlet*, *Macbeth* and *King Lear*, but he never did because he was making this cushy, easy living repeating his role in *The Count*. So O'Neill determined that he would be very strict about his own career.

Do you have your own Monte Cristo?
TV. I don't mean to look down on TV or movies. But you don't put your name on it. You're just getting your check.

But what about something like *The Defenders*, which received so much acclaim? Did you enjoy doing that show?
Actually it turned out to be three of the happiest years in my life. But, you know, I wasn't the first choice. First there was Fredric March and Ralph Bellamy. They both said no.

What did you like about the show?
Well, it kept me in New York. I hate L.A. And we had good writers and actors on the show. And we introduced subjects like blacklisting, abortion, white-collar crime, race relations.

Did you influence the scripts in any way?
Yes. Reggie Rose, who was the original writer and story editor, was very open. I rewrote a scene with Arthur Hill. Reggie trusted me because he knew I wasn't going to screw it up.

You're very active politically, and *The Defenders* was fairly consistent with your beliefs. But were there roles you wouldn't play because they were contrary to your politics?
A journalist once asked, "How can you play that part?" And I said, "I don't believe in regicide but I played Macbeth." I don't like crooked lawyers or politicians but I would play them. But I wouldn't do propaganda for an ideology that was alien to me or that I didn't approve of.

You've worked with so many different directors. Are there any you work best with—or that you had particular problems with?
Well, I worked with George Roy Hill on a TV show, with Joanne Woodward and Barbara Barrie. And in *The Gang's All Here* George wanted Pat O'Brien for the part. He said to me, "I've never seen you lose control."

I said, "You bet your sweet ass you haven't. The whole point is control." So I had a difficult time with him on the show because he really didn't want me and I wasn't about to take crap from him or any other director.

Meaning what, exactly?
Meaning when I work with a director he has to be honest and open with me and not expect me to do phony stuff just because that's what he has in his mind. It's got to be organic with me. If I can't see it, then you have to explain it to me. Like in Woody Allen's *Interiors*—I wanted to play the scene where I tell Geraldine Page I'm leaving one way, and Woody wanted me to do it another way.

How did you want to do it?

Like I was presenting a very rational way to get ourselves out of the situation, to make it look attractive. But Woody said, "Just tell it. Say, 'I'm leaving and that's it.'" I thought that wasn't dramatic enough, but I did it his way because it was his idea. Ironically, it turned out that Ingmar Bergman praised that scene and praised me for doing it that way. That's why I always say I shouldn't put myself into the part. I should put the part into myself.

How so?
If I were talking to my wife and children in real life, I'd say, "We're not in a very good situation. So why don't we have a separation and then we'll see how it works, OK?" I'd want to soften the blow, but Woody wanted me to present it as a fait accompli. Bergman, the Swede, liked that better. So did Woody. But I didn't want to hurt anybody. Because that's me.

What qualities in a director bring out your most creative side?
Insight into people. What makes people do what they do? Mike Nichols has a way of saying short things like, "Like her a little more. It's not hard."

And that helps?
It does if I'm being too distant. It helps me reach out more. After a rehearsal Mike will say, "Just two little things." So when I was in China, I had a pair of chopsticks made with "Just two little things" in Chinese. The supplier asked "You mean 'two' or 'too' or 'to' little things?" I said, "Just two little things." Later I asked a fellow at the U.S. Embassy what was written on the chopsticks. And he said, "Two little pieces of things."

What did Mike say when you gave them to him?
He said, "I've changed all that. It's, 'Just two little things of great importance.'"

What were the differences between working with someone like Woody Allen and some of the other directors you've worked with?
Once I said to Woody about a line, "That's all so literary." And it never appeared in the picture. But I think you shouldn't be like

a puppet. It shows when you see actors who are doing just what the director said.

Which actors have brought out the best in you?
Maureen Stapleton, Colleen Dewhurst.

Why?
They look at you. You see a real person there. I try to think what will help the other actor, so it's nice when I get that back. The trouble is that many actors want to play by themselves. One time at the Actors Studio, Berghof was saying how he couldn't get Eva Le Gallienne to look at him. Bobby Lewis said, "Just go up on your lines and you'll get more attention than you can handle! Just pause when she's waiting for you to respond. Then she'll look at you."

Who was the most difficult actor to work with?
Bert Lahr. He had this need to do his shtick and that made him very difficult. He was the comic, and I was the straight man, and a straight man isn't supposed to be funny. He walked out on rehearsal once because he thought I was too funny. And on opening night of *Waiting for Godot* I got an enormous laugh on my line, "That passed the time," when it was Bert's line, "It would have passed in any case," that was supposed to get the laugh.

What did he do?
He turned red. But then he got a bigger laugh when he said his line. And I thought, "Thank God." He was terribly competitive. So I had to get him to like me personally. I had to seduce him—have lunch with him, see his family—just be his lover.

So there's a romance to the business of acting.
Yes. Directors court actors, too. I asked a director once, "How the hell did you get that performance out of that guy?"
He said, "I took him to lunch; I bought him ties."

There was a movie you were in with Orson Welles...
Yes, *Compulsion*. He was such a pompous person. And he acted like he was king of the world. At that time he was so deep in debt to the IRS. He should have been easier to work with. He

never wanted you to look at him. There was a scene where he was supposed to be telling me something. So I'm sitting there and he said, "Would you mind not looking at me when I'm talking? I don't want to fight your look." So he's talking and I take my glasses off and put them down, keeping my eyes closed as he goes on and on. He finishes the scene and they say, "Cut." And he says, "You were a good soldier."

Maybe it's your penetrating look that got to him.
Yes, my piercing eyes. But we parted friends. And then I read in an interview that he said, "There are three actors who really think when they're acting: Greta Garbo, Charlie Chaplin and E.G. Marshall."

You talked about being free on stage. How do you do that?
You can't enter thinking of your first line. You come on stage and you see the situation and you say, "Who left the door open?" It has to happen as if you are saying it for the first time.

What do you do to help create that freshness?
I warm my voice up, have some hot tea and make sure I don't have to go to the toilet when I get on stage. And then I clear my mind so I'm not worrying.

Do you identify with the characters you play? Have you ever played a character who was really you?
A character is a different person from yourself. I can't say that I ever played anything that was myself.

Who is that?
Who is me? You'll never find out!

Will you at least say what your initials stand for? You've been mysterious about it.
Do you want to hear it from the horse's mouth? The story goes that "E" stands for "Edda" from the Norse legends and "G" stands for "Gunnar." All Norse kings' names begin with G. So my name was Edda Gunnar Marshall. But when I was in the second grade the teacher called me "Edna" and all the kids laughed at me. I explained this problem to my third-grade teacher, who told the kids my name was Edda, not Edna, and they still

laughed. So the only way to solve this matter was to use my initials, E.G.

So is this the real story?
No, I never tell the truth about this. I also say my name's "Egregious Gregarious Marshall." And when people laugh I say, "I didn't laugh at your name. Why do you think mine is funny?"

Isn't it provocative to have two initials?
What about W.C. Fields, e.e. cummings and A.R. Gurney?

At least with Gurney people also call him Pete. Speaking of whom, didn't you just finish doing his play, *Love Letters*?
Yes, with Colleen Dewhurst. Actually, I'd wanted to buy *Love Letters* when I first heard about it, but I was told it was sold. So later on, when they wanted me to do it in New York, I said, "No." But then they asked if I would do it with Colleen in Boston and I said, "You bet." And we did it.

You said she was a very giving actress.
Yes. She did *Love Letters* like a person who's been through a hell of a lot, and that worked very well against my upper-middle-class waspish attitude about things.

How does it affect you when you don't get a response you expect from the audience?
Some actors say, "What the hell's the matter with them? They're sitting on their hands." I say you keep playing.

And reviews?
I don't read reviews because they have nothing to do with you. If reviewers could write plays they would. They review them instead. And they can't help you.

How do you feel if your director or producer doesn't like your work?
When I was in my first Broadway play, *Jason*, which Samson Raphaelson wrote, I was in my 30s and I was playing a 72-year-old man. After our first run-through, George Abbot, who was producing it, said, "I don't know what you're doing. But it's not funny." Well, it turned out that I was a big hit. Every critic men-

tioned my small part. I saw Abbott some time after that and he said, "Worked out all right, didn't it?"

So you are able to deal with criticism now?
Yes. You can say something and I'll say, "You have a point there." But I know some actors who can't survive because they can't take criticism.

What do you think is your chief strength as an actor?
My ability to adapt. When I was a boy, my minister wanted me to join the seminary. But I wanted to be an actor. He said, "You're not fit for it. Your voice is thin and you're no Rudolph Valentino." And then I thought, "Does that make me a good minister?" So then I studied voice and speech. I had to equip myself. You may have a God-given gift but you can't handle it unless you have the tools, the technique. If I see something lacking, I try to acquire it or adapt to it.

Is that what being a great character actor is about—to be able to adapt to different kinds of roles?
Yes. You have to put that sort of person in your mind. Why does that person want to do that? Where does it come from? There has to be some motivation for the way the character behaves.

What are your weaknesses?
I played *Macbeth* and I found that physical movement on stage doesn't come easily for me. I've studied fencing, but I'm not good at sports and I never was. I always wanted to be able to ride, so I studied riding in Vienna. I had a marvelous outfit. But there was something missing in me—the coordination.

So you've never done any Westerns?
Actually, I've been in a couple. One was *Broken Lance* with Spencer Tracy. And the other was a remake of the *Oxbow Incident*. I sat on a horse for three days doing close-ups.
Do you know what it's like to sit for three days on a hard saddle?

What do you like most about acting?
Working with good materials and good people. And I've

made money at it. But I don't like doing movies. It's boring. I don't know how anyone can stand making movies. I worked for 12 weeks on one film. We were always waiting around. How can you enjoy that?

What do you do while you're waiting?
I read letters. I collect the letters of Joyce, Ezra Pound, and Michelangelo. I went back to them the other day. In one letter Michelangelo was telling his brother that he didn't like the six shirts he had sent him. And he'd say things like, "Well, I met the bishop. I'm supposed to do this commission. Maybe I'll get a little money for it. I need that money to pay the rent." Or he'd say, "I'm building my house," and he'd describe the plumbing arrangements and so forth.

Then the letters help you get to know these people?
Yes. They're like diaries. You find out what people were doing at the time. It's not from the imagination. Here's this problem, I have these shirts and I don't like them. Also, you learn what living was like, how things were born—how governments were started. While you're waiting around on a movie set, you can read two or 200. I'll read things like the correspondence between James Joyce and Ezra Pound. Or Pound's letters to T.S. Eliot about what to take out of *The Wasteland*.

Is that why you were attracted to *Love Letters*?
Yes.

Are you a letter writer yourself?
Yes. People tell me I shouldn't write letters. But I disagree. I think you can tell more in a letter than you can tell in a telephone conversation.

You've been acting for a long time. How has your work changed?
It gets easier in one way. George Scott and I talked about this. You have your technique and you've learned some things. And what's harder is now that you know more you have to do more.

How has your life affected your art and vice versa?
Kevin McCarthy and I have both done *Love Letters*, and we

were saying how people who have lived do this play better. You bring your understanding of life to your work. When John Gielgud was doing *King Lear*, he was talking to Cordelia and tears came down. Someone said, "Mr. Gielgud, how can you cry every night?" He said, "I have difficulty not crying."

Do you feel that with *Love Letters*?
Yes. I have no difficulty with the emotion; it just comes up. Because of what I've lived, I guess. I think that comes from living, from understanding, from not being too judgmental of other people.

Have there been roles that changed you in some way?
The wonderful language in *Godot* made me think more. And after doing it for a while, I could talk in Beckett's language.

What did it make you think about?
The existentialists. I got very involved in their writing, which gives you a better understanding of yourself and your place in the universe. That sent me off in a different direction.

What about mentors? Have you had any?
I guess you could say O'Neill was a mentor. We had long talks and he had me reading a lot. He even read a series of short plays I wrote called *Ways, Means and Ends*. He said he wished he could write like that. Because my plays were short.

What was the most special thing about O'Neill?
His philosophy: "To thine own self be true." He thought you should be yourself. You should unify, not fragment yourself. He had a tragic vision. He thought optimism and happiness "were the biggest pipe dream of them all." But when he'd talk about tragic things he'd always laugh. His brother James would fall dead drunk down the stairs and he'd laugh talking about that. He had a tragic sense, but he laughed about it.

Is that what you liked? Because you don't seem to have that dark side.
I do have it. I think I just sublimate it. I subvert it.

A quiet dark side.

Like I said this morning, "The ranks are thinning. All my contemporaries are dying." Only four of the actors from *Twelve Angry Men* are alive. And there's Kevin McCarthy. But he's four months older than I am. He should go first. You've got to accept it. Some people say, "Why me?" Well, who else? Who would you rather?

Do you think about your life and your age a great deal?
No, I just can't believe I'm 76. I don't think of the past so much—which is a blessing.

Was there something in particular that O'Neill said that really had an impact on you?
He said, "Don't sell yourself out." But I modified that to say, "Not in the theater." You can do TV and movies, but the theater, that's your religion. That's your church.

Did your family have a big effect on your acting?
A friend and I used to walk down a road in Maryland on the way to a swimming pool. We'd talk about life and girls. And he said, "Aren't you glad you weren't shy when your mother asked you to recite for the folks?" How does it start? No one urged me. My minister tried to discourage me. It was something I wanted to do.

How does it start?
I don't know. It was always there. They asked Shaw, "When did you first want to be a writer?" He said, "I never wanted to be, I always was." And so was I—I was always doing things, rehearsing things.

Has there been a part that you've always wanted to do?
It hasn't been written yet.

What about a play that you see differently now?
There is one—called *Queen After Death*. I did it about 30 years ago. A friend thought it would be perfect for me. So I agreed to do it before I had even read it. And as we rehearsed it, I realized I didn't know what it was about. They wanted me to continue with it and I said, "I really can't and it would be dishonest because I don't know what I'm doing up there." But I recorded

the entire thing and then years afterward I found the tape and I played it.

What was your reaction?
I said, "My God, this is a wonderful play. Why didn't I understand it? I'd like to do it now." So I told the producer, T. Edward Hambleton, and he said, "Well, it's a pity I'm no longer producing plays."

What did you say?
Well, I didn't sweat about it!

Frank Pierson: "I've spent a lifetime looking for partners. I would have loved to have found my Billy Wilder to be an I.A.L. Diamond to."

> With *Cool Hand Luke*, Stuart Rosenberg still thinks that character is Jesus Christ and I think he's Camus. But Stuart filled the movie with all these Christian images ... The cross figure keeps coming up throughout the picture. And it's absolute bullshit. It had nothing to do with my intentions.

FRANK PIERSON
Screenwriter

Fresh out of a hospital and still in pain after knee surgery, Frank Pierson nonetheless was full of energy and eager to talk about two favorite topics—creativity and screenplay writing. His own scripts include some bona fide classics: *Cat Ballou*, which he was hired to rewrite and which earned an Oscar nomination for best adaptation; *Cool Hand Luke*, also nominated for an Oscar, and *Dog Day Afternoon*, which won the Oscar in 1975. Pierson also co-wrote the script for 1990's highly acclaimed *Presumed Innocent*.

Pierson's noteworthy credits as a director include *King of the Gypsies*; the 1975 version of *A Star Is Born* starring Barbra Streisand and Kris Kristofferson, the third largest grossing musical ever filmed, and an NBC movie, *The Neon Ceiling*, which won Emmies for the performances of Lee Grant and Gig Young.

Sitting on his patio, with a breathtaking view of the Pacific Palisades, Pierson recalled how—although scripting was clearly in his blood—he did not start writing for TV until he was 33. His mother's autobiography, *Roughly Speaking*, was a '40s best-seller. She adapted it as a screenplay for Warner Brothers, then became a contract writer for Warner and RKO.

Pierson, meanwhile, saw combat during three years with the Army in the Pacific. He came home, earned a Harvard degree in cultural anthropology and, in 1951, went to work for *Time* and *Life* as a writer and field correspondent.

In 1958 he turned to TV, just as the Golden Age was waning. One moment he would write for a show such as *Playhouse 90*; the next moment the show would be canceled. For several years he produced, wrote and directed episodes of such shows as *Route 66*, *Naked City* and *Dr. Kildare*. His colleagues included John Cassavetes, Robert Altman, Bob Rafelson, Burt Schneider, Paul Mazursky, Howard Fast, Sidney Sheldon and Carl Reiner. "We were all fired more or less the same day," Pierson said.

So he went across the street to Columbia Pictures, signed on for *Cat Ballou*, and the rest is history.

Do you find that each time you write a screenplay it gets easier—or that you're facing a blank page every time?

Every time you make a movie you have to find the style for it, and then you have to find out how to do it. It's like everyone is starting all over again and you accumulate a certain amount of knowledge about the things that you're good at and the things that you'd probably best not try. But when you sit down it's a blank slate every single time. The act of finishing the movie is the act of finding out how to make it. And then you really wish you could throw it all away and start all over again. But Woody Allen is the only one who has the luxury of doing that.

Can you talk about writing *Presumed Innocent*?

I learned about the artificiality of mystery writing, which I'd never done before. You have all the information, and it is more an issue of which information you choose to share with the audience and with your characters and how much the various characters know about each other as you go along. That is a very artificial way for me to work. I prefer to work on a more unconscious level in terms of writing the scenes and even constructing the story, even though I do work from an outline, unlike a lot of other screenwriters. So I found it a peculiarly unsatisfying experience. I don't think I'll do another one like it.

What was your relationship like with the director?

Alan [Pakula] and I had a lot of differences about the story, which is one reason I insisted he also put his name on the screenplay. He did some things I did not agree with. I wanted to cut 30 pages and leap into the story much later. I just felt that the audience was going to guess it was the wife who did it, and I was much more interested in another aspect of the story.

Which was what?
Scott Turow, the novelist, lied to his readers the first day of the trial. The main character, Rusty, sees evidence that shakes him up. It occurs to him that his lifelong faith in the system may have been misplaced, that he may be ground up and thrown away. It's utterly devastating, because his whole philosophy of life has been denied validity. So that night, he goes home and his wife says, "Come on up. Let me rub your back." And he says, "No, no, I have to stay up." For the first time in years he lights up a cigarette. It's one of the best chapters in the novel.

When does this take place?.
It's about page 200 of a 500-page-novel. He's thinking about his life, about how he always believed in the system and about how he failed his wife. It's revealed in the chapter that he told his wife about his affair, how they battled it out and it was all put behind them. He realizes in the end that there's nothing he can do about the situation, except simply stick with it, and that if he is considered innocent all he can do is try and live his life in a better way. It's a terribly moving piece, because you know he had to think this through for himself. It's a devastating turning point in his life, where he's losing all his life's beliefs.

And that's the story you were interested in telling?
Yes, but a couple hundred pages later in the novel, you discover that that's not the reason he sat up all night. He sat up all night because he saw evidence in the courtroom that day that told him, unequivocally, that his wife was the one who did it. Well, that is such a lie to the reader, the kind of thing that I don't believe you can do to an audience. But the director said that the book worked the way it did for an enormous number of people and we shouldn't fool around with that. So he didn't want to make this change.

How would you have changed the script?
I was going to do that first day in court where he comes home and, just as in the book, his wife tells him to come upstairs but he says he wants to be by himself. Then goes right to the toolbox

in the cellar because suddenly he realizes that they have a tool in the house which makes wounds that are difficult to identify. I actually found [an example of] this tool. Anyway, there's blood and hair on it, and we realize that he realizes that his wife has done it. He walks upstairs, puts the tool down by the kitchen sink and mixes himself a drink. He hears a noise, turns around and his wife says, "What are you going to do?" And it all comes out between them.

That scene was in the movie.
Yes, but at the end. I wanted to move that scene up where she says, "I'll testify for you, I never meant for it to go this far. I don't know how I could have been this insane." She would give essentially the same speech that she gives at the end. And he says, "It wouldn't do any good, nobody'd believe you. They'd think you were trying to save me. It's too late, all we can do is get through this to the end."

The rest of the movie would become a drama that has to do with two people knowing that at the end of it there has to be some resolution. Will he let his child know that his wife is a murderer? Can he leave his child with this woman? How is she going to appease the guilt that she feels, while at the same time having to preserve an absolutely perfect front in the courtroom? But Pakula felt that that was a completely different story. And it is, indeed.

It's a more character-driven story.
You're dead right. In fact, we rehearsed scenes with Harrison Ford that way and everything worked. But Pakula wanted to do the book, so we did.

Do you regret having done it that way?
I was working as a screenwriter for Alan, which means you're a hired hand. I wouldn't second-guess that, no. If I were going to direct it by myself? I don't know whether that would have worked any better than what he did. And the movie was a success.

The audience could have known more about the characters, especially the wife.
Well, part of the problem was, as I said, that he shot an enor-

mously long screenplay—about 150 pages. And a screenplay should only be about 115 pages. I see certain things just flashing by because he had to cut too much, like some of the beginnings and endings of scenes. It's amazing to me that the audience understands it as well as they do. So I guess we did a pretty damn good job, because it still works. Nonetheless, I'm so aware of what's missing that I can't judge it for myself at all. But I do love the way Bonnie (Bedelia) read that speech at the end.

What movies did you write that were satisfying?
Dog Day Afternoon. It was brilliantly directed and acted. And there was the issue of craft. Well, let me back up and speak generally. Knowing how to make the movie is an issue of solving problems. You have one problem after another and the first one is how you begin. What you're saying to an audience is, "This is the way we're going to spend the next two hours of our lives together."

Does the audience need to know right away what kind of film they are watching?
Definitely. They need to know very quickly what it is that's going to be happening with them, and also to feel secure that you're not going to bludgeon them or bore them. But there was another problem with the beginning. We had a situation in which three people are setting out to rob a bank. Guns are out and it ain't funny. There's a machine gun in a case, and when you look at John Cazale you are seeing a homicidal character who is dangerous because of his infantile attitude toward life. And so the problem was, how do you let an audience know that it's all right for them to laugh?

How did you let them know?
By carefully crafting the initial sequence. Three guys go in, the guns are out, there's danger and they're waiting for the proper moment. When the last person is let out of the bank and the tension is building, this other kid sidles up to Sonny and says, "I got bad vibes here." A little ripple goes through the audience. Then he says, "Whaddya talkin' about for Christ's sake, the banks are gonna be closed," which was an odd line in that context.

So you have moments when the audience can laugh.
Right. And then you keep going. You build tension, and then he finally pulls out the automatic gun, points it at the teller and says, "I'm gonna blow your fuckin' guts all over the walls." This was the moment when we knew that the whole thing was going to turn in everyone's face, and from there on anything could happen.

Are there visual or technical things you can do that give the audience permission to laugh?
Yes. When you do comedy, you light everything from edge to edge so everybody can see everything, so there are no surprises. The technical aspect has become so damned important in film. You look at a movie like *Prizzi's Honor*—which was a success and it's a lovely picture; but in the theater I went to, the audience was constantly sitting forward in their seats and saying, "What? Did she say that?" Because the dialogue has a slight little spin to it. Nothing is quite the way you expect it to be.

But it was meant to be a comedy?
Yes. And of course John Huston knew that, but Jack Nicholson claims that he never realized that it was a comedy.

But you're saying the sound track interfered with the comedy?
Yes. The problem for me was that the balance between the various tracks was out of sync. The dialogue was down and there was an odd spin to it, so they were not meaning exactly what they were saying. Consequently the audience was straining to hear the whole time, and you could see from their body language that they experienced the movie as a drama. You watch a comedy from down here and a drama from up here. But Huston was a darkly ironic character, so he sometimes tripped over the comedy. *Beat the Devil*, which has now become a cult classic film, was an absolute disaster when it first came out because nobody got the idea at the beginning that it was supposed to be funny.

How did you come up with the idea for *Dog Day Afternoon*?
I got it out of an FBI report of a real robbery somewhere in Virginia. The robber came in and put the gun in the head teller's face and said, "Give me all your money." And you know those

little triangular signs that say, "Next Window Please"? The teller put one of them up! So I stuck that in the screenplay. That was going to be the joke on which we would build everything, and then everything would unravel. The whole point being that in the middle of the worst things that happen in our lives, life goes on, people need to go to the bathroom! And how do you cope with those things? Intrinsically it's funny, which constantly releases the tension as we get to the end where we know something dreadful is going to happen. But I hope we don't know exactly what it is.

So once you found the beginning did things become easier?
Not really. Because when we started rehearsing, and the teller pushes out the sign, the director, Sidney Lumet, asked who told her to do that. She said that it was in the stage directions. And he said he didn't see that. And then I said, "But that's the beginning of the joke." And he responded, "But that would be funny." And then I knew we were in trouble. I suddenly realized that he was not thinking about this sequence in the same way I was.

Which had to do with giving the audience permission to laugh?
Exactly. I'd been working on it for months. But it was a screenplay that Sidney didn't receive until it was complete. If we had been working on it together as we had in the past, we might have agreed more. So we went ahead with the sign. But when we got to the dress rehearsal and Al [Pacino] had the rifle in a box which was for long-stemmed roses, he couldn't get it out of the box without the damn thing getting tangled up in the ribbon. Of course that was funny, and that went right into the script. Then the problem was to convince everybody to take the sign out, because you couldn't have both. There's a certain order in which things happen.

Did you ever meet the person whose character Pacino was based upon?
No. He was in a contract dispute with Warner Brothers over his share of the net profit, so every time I visited the prison, he refused to see me. I just had to proceed on my own by interviewing his family and everybody who'd ever known him, including the people in the bank. But that became so confusing because it

was like they were talking about a different character. Some said he was kind and loving, some said he was brutal, and some said he was funny.

But he was all of that in the movie.
The thing that was difficult was finding some common element or spine to that character so it would all make sense. I got to the point where I almost quit because I couldn't figure him out. There wasn't anything but the newspaper reports, which described what he did and said. But if an actor asked why he was behaving a certain way, I had no answer. So I went through all the research material one last time and I began to realize that there was one common element to everyone's comments.

Which was?
Everybody felt he had betrayed them. So I looked up the meaning of the word betray—it means you have made a promise or a contract to someone and have failed to deliver on it. Then I realized that the people who felt most betrayed by him were the people to whom he was the closest. And finally the character who began to emerge for me was like a wizard.

In what sense?
He imagines that he has the power to fulfill your dreams and hopes. He can make you whole and then you will be able to give him back the love that he desperately needs and which he expressed to you. Of course this is impossible under the best of circumstances, and especially for this neurotic, working-class guy from Brooklyn.

How did this specifically translate into action?
He would never let his wife, who was grotesquely fat, diet. Because it would be like an admission that she was fat. So he'd say, "Honey, you're not fat. You're just the way I like 'em." After a while it led to a kind of infantilization of her. And this kind of behavior made sense in terms of the bank robbery itself.

How so?
Because Sonny marries this homosexual who imagines that he needs to have his woman's body freed from his male body by a sex change operation. So Sonny robs the bank to get the money

for this operation so his lover will be happy. And the lover's reaction is, "Jesus Christ, I didn't ask you to rob a fucking bank! Are you outa your mind?" So now you have a dramatic character that you know how to write. He's the kind of character who says, "Are you comfortable? Is there anything I can get for you?"

And do the other characters respond to that?
The needy ones do, which leads to a bonding that is built around a tacit understanding that you're going to do this for me. And when he's unable to deliver, they begin to back away or complain; and he says, "I did everything for you and I get back shit." And they respond with, "I never asked you for anything," which would erupt into a fistfight or whatever. And everything in his life went that way, with him feeling bruised. Now you have a character you can move through this situation in the bank, and any situation. You know what he's going to do.

So that's the common thread that you were talking about.
Yeah, exactly. And that makes it possible to write the individual scenes, and it also leads to the next step, which has to do with constructing the story. Because I want the eventual retribution to come about because of the very thing that makes Sonny what he is. In other words, it's not just the mere fact that he stayed in the bank too long and someone tripped the silent alarm that got him into trouble. He stayed in the bank because of the kind of person he was. He could have gotten out with what little money there was.

You mentioned the idea of constructing a story.
There are two major turning points in a film. You trap some people in a situation, and there's a period where everybody could get back to square one if they just didn't go on being who they are. But at some point, somebody does something and they can never get back to where they were before, but they don't know where the future lies. Then you have the period of uncertainty where essentially the characters are exploring alternatives of extricating themselves from the situation, of resolving it in a new way, of bringing about a new synergistic resolution to things, and again their inner problems and mutual antagonisms get in the way. Then you get to the second turning point which can occur anywhere in here, and sometimes very close to the

end. It's where they suddenly realize, "Oh, this is how it's gonna go," and now we're going to go from there to the end.

Is that part of the technique you use as a writer?
Yes. Of course, you take a play like *Waiting for Godot* and you realize that it does not have any of those things, so all generalizations are false. But as a working method, this is more or less how I go about it. I was looking for a way in which that moment when they're trapped in the bank seals their fate. And it's brought about by the very thing that brought Sonny there in the first place—his insistence, his desperate need to be of help—to worry about things like, "Should I let them go to the toilet?"

How much rehearsal did you have for this film?
We had the luxury of three weeks of rehearsal because we were able to hire the cast for the run of the show since everybody was virtually in every scene and we essentially had just one location. But about four days into it I'm sitting with Al Pacino in his living room and everyone has these long faces and the producer is saying, "Look, what Al's talking about is really just a dialogue polish." At which point Al gets down on all fours and runs around the room barking like a dog. And I said, "You know, I don't think Al is talking about a dialogue polish."

What was he talking about?
It turned out that he did not want to play a homosexual and I asked specifically what he objected to. There's a scene where Sonny and his lover have to say goodbye. In the film, the scene plays over the telephone. But I originally had written it to play in the street with Al standing just inside the front door and Chris Sarandon standing just outside the bank with the police officer holding him by the belt so he couldn't be pulled into the bank and added to the hostages. There are 2,000 police officers, and behind them the entire neighborhood screaming, "Faggot!" And so these two people have to play the one scene in their life that most cries out for privacy in this maelstrom of derision. And they succeed in getting through it and ignoring it. At the end they kiss each other on the lips. Then the crowd goes really crazy and snaps us back to reality.

How did Pacino respond to the kiss?

He said, "I'm not gonna do it. I'm not gonna play any scene where I have to be in the presence of the guy." I actually invented a way that we could show their wedding, and he said, "You can't show them together at all. All the stuff about the sexuality of their relationship and the joke is out." So I said to the producer, "Let's do what we did when Al quit the first time—send it to Dustin [Hoffman]."

I didn't realize that Pacino had quit once before.

Yeah. He had just come from *The Godfather* and was exhausted. I guess this thing was bubbling in him at that time, but he hadn't identified if for himself yet. He said he thought it was a terrific screenplay but he couldn't do it because he was too depressed.

But you talked him into it?

Actually, we sent the script to Dustin. And when Al heard that, he asked for it back. He said, "Look, before you do that I'd just like to say something to you. You've had relationships, I know you've been married a couple of times. And when you're playing the really big scenes in those relationships, especially when things are falling apart and all you can do is get out of it the best way you can, how often does sex come into it?" I said, "Never." And he said, "Look, you cannot take away from the audience's mind the fact that a man married a man. But why can't you just write a story about two people who love each other and can't find any way to get what they want?"

How did you respond?

I said, "You sonofabitch; why didn't you say that six months ago when I had time to deal with it?" Al said, "I really wish you would do it—if you agree." And I said, "Absolutely. You're dead right." It turned out rather easy to do. What I was left with were two scenes between the two of them on the telephone—one in which Sarandon kisses him off entirely, and then the Sarandon character calls him back.

In the course of that conversation we discover that ultimately the reason Sarandon calls him back is because the police have threatened him with being an accessory after the fact. He's trying to get Pacino to say that he was not part of it, and of course Pacino is betrayed again. So what you see in the arc of those two long phone calls is a little mini-film which parallels the arc of their real-life relationship. But those phone calls defy all cinematic rules.

How so?
You're not supposed to break scenes up like that. But not being able to show them together was a brilliant inspiration on Al's part. It saved the movie. It would have been funnier, but it's funny enough. And it ran the danger of appearing to be homophobic.

Is *Dog Day Afternoon* your most satisfying film?
Yes, because it's the closest to what I wrote and I did my best work. One of the difficulties in my career as a director is that I've given myself some rather bad scripts.

Such as?
I'd rather not say.

You did write and direct *A Star Is Born*.
I co-wrote it. The screenplay was originated by Joan Didion and John Dunne. They claim they never saw any of the original versions, but I have to politely say that I just don't believe them. What they did was a rather harder-edged and documentary approach to the same story set in the rock music world. Well, the minute Barbra came on board it changed right back into the romantic melodrama that it's always been, and what always made it work. What I did was take off the hard edges and go back to the 1936 version. Dorothy Parker, among other people, worked on that version.

Can you talk about the directing end of things?
Some director once said that writing was either the first half of the directing process or directing was the last half of the writing process. That's perfectly true. I've spent a lifetime looking for partners. I would have loved to have found my Billy Wilder to be an I.A.L. Diamond to. But I was never able to, so consequently you go through life kind of hit or miss, and it's amazing how close you can be and yet how far apart.

I mean, with *Cool Hand Luke*, Stuart Rosenberg still thinks that character is Jesus Christ and I think he's Camus. But Stuart filled the movie with all these Christian images. After Paul Newman's eaten the 50 eggs and he's passed out, we see him sprawled out as a figure on the cross. The cross figure keeps coming up throughout the picture. And it's absolute bullshit. It had nothing to do with my intentions.

Do you feel the film worked?
Yeah, I think it's a good film. And it still holds up. But there are scenes that I look at and say, "Oh, Jesus, if that's what you wanted to do I could have written you a scene that would have worked so much better."

Can you talk more about the unconscious process?
When you approach a tough scene and you don't know what the solutions are going to be and you discard all the ways it's been done before—the easy ways, the melodramatic ways and the tricky ways—you say, "How am I going to solve this? Where is the idea going to come from?" At that point the only place it's going to come from is the unconscious.

You've made a connection, I assume, before you've committed yourself. There's something in the material that lures you and you don't know what it is. It's the writing of it, and the making of it, that helps you find out what it is. What is this connection I feel here? That answer is going to emerge in a dream, or in a nightmare, or when you're driving on the freeway, or when you're just sort of doing exercises.

Where do you write?
At home. And I have an office as well.

Are there particular hours that you like to write?
From 10 to 12. Then I have lunch and spend the afternoon going over what I wrote that morning. And I might be back at the computer at 11 or 12 o'clock at night. So it's never away from your thoughts.

Do you write every day?
Yes, even on people's birthdays and holidays. Laptops are a godsend because the most important thing about writing is to addict yourself to it. So that you cannot not write, in the same way that a heroin addict cannot *not* prowl the streets to find the

goddamned heroin. And that will make you constantly focused on it. Every day, you're going to have to put something down, because otherwise you're going to kick your dog, you're going to be rude to strangers, and you're going to estrange your wife.

And you find that two hours every day works for you?
Yes. I devote myself to putting down the thoughts that have been occurring to me the rest of the time. Or if nothing else occurs, I ask myself the most elementary questions—like what is the conflict between the two characters? Or what would this person do if they were confronted with such and such? It's amazing how often something will emerge that winds up in some form in the screenplay. But as a writer you don't know where this is going to come from. All you can do is simply open yourself up in any way that you find to do it.

Such as?
By getting drunk, by taking dope, by simply staring out the window, or reaching over and gently stroking your Oscar, like a talisman. Because the unconscious from which this idea is going to emerge is the very place that we defend against. But we have to take the plunge, going there amongst our demons. All of a sudden something emerges and you say, "My God, nobody's going to understand that."

Can you think of a specific time when that happened?
Yes. The very much quoted line from *Cool Hand Luke*, "What we have here is a failure to communicate." That came out of my looking out over the Pacific Ocean and trying to think of what I wanted him to say. All of a sudden that line came. And I looked at it and I said, "Oh shit, that's good." But then my next thought was, "This redneck can't say that." So I spent the rest of the day writing a little explanation that I put into the stage directions which said that in the Florida prison system, in order to gain advancement, the bureaucratic process required prison officers to take a certain number of courses in criminology and penology at the state university. So we understood where he would hear words like that.

Did anyone ever question the line?
No, to my astonishment, they didn't. But the point is that

instinct came out of somewhere, and my first impulse was to expunge it. Then I justified it and then I realized it didn't need to be justified. But that's what I mean about the unconscious aspects of the writing process that make it very difficult. We are probing into those areas which we defend against.

The director, at least from my experience, has difficulty in a different way. That comes when you're on the floor and you've got a sequence that's not working. You don't have the time and you can't figure out how to make it work. That's when it's really hard because you can't make the actors play something when you realize that the damned thing isn't right. So you improvise.

Can you think of an example of when that happened to you as a director?

The Looking Glass War was a movie that we prepared over a long period of time. It was based on a John Le Carre novel. To get the picture made, the producer and I had to cut this and change that. We had four days of reading rehearsals before we went off to Spain to start shooting. But it wasn't working, so finally we cabled the studio and said, "Look, it's not gonna work and the best advice is to cut our losses and stop production."

Were you able to stop it?

No, because by that time the people who ran the studio had gone off to the West Indies to a retreat. So we got back a cable saying, "Best first week ever seen. Continue the good work. Congratulations from Columbia Studios." We had to somehow hold ourselves together for four months while we finished the picture. Making a film under those conditions is really shattering.

Nicholas Kazan talks of writers as "receptacles" and how you have to get yourself to that pure state. How do you do that?

That's what I mean about you get drunk, you take drugs, you massage your Oscar if you have one, or you meditate. These are reasons writers are terrible people to live with. If you have small children in the house you should not write in the house with them.

Did your writing affect your family life?

No question about it. But I'd prefer not to talk about it. All I can say is I've spent a lot of years in deep analysis to deal with this. And, you know, if I were in the state of mind that I think I'm in now when I was 20 or 25, I certainly would have dealt with it in a more constructive way and protected my family from the demons that were aroused in me and drove me crazy. During the first part of your career, as Nick puts it in a sort of nice way, the writer is a receptacle—but that's almost a reverence that he's paying to the pain and terror he endures in that state.

Can you talk more about your analysis?
I went into analysis because there was somebody in me that was trying to kill me, and I had to find out. Otherwise, I knew that I was not going to live. So I went in a state of emotional crisis. But once I got past that, because of the particular person that I went into analysis with, I began to realize that there was something far more to it, that it could be a kind of voyage to the spirit, an exploratory voyage that at first I was very scared of. I was afraid that by investigating the process I would destroy my ability to write. A friend of mine once said, "What are you going to do when you're not angry anymore?"

But you were able to work that out.
Yes, but it took me a while. And I was already 45 when I started therapy. I asked the analyst why he started working with me at such an advanced age. And he said something that was very pleasing to me. He said, "Because I sense in you still a flexibility and an ability to change."

Did that help with your work as a writer?
It helped me with my whole life. But I diverged from something I started to say. And that is, in the early phases of one's career, when you're confronting these things, you don't know whether you can write a scene that actors can play. You confront that moment when nothing is coming and you're thinking, "Jesus, I've taken their money, maybe I'm going to have to send it back. Or I'll just call my agent and get myself out of this."

And that's what you went through when Pacino wanted you to rework your script?
Yes. I was ready to call my agents before I went back and took

one last look at that mass of material so I could understand who that character was. Early in your career you reach for the easy things—the sitcoms, the Westerns, the genre stories—which provide you with ready-made elements. If you're going to probe in these areas, it can drive you nuts. Sometimes you have the feeling that no one understands you and you wind up driving your Porsche in the mountains all night long.

What does delving into "these areas" mean to you?
I still don't like to think about it consciously; but I've discovered there's a certain kind of character to whom I'm attracted. That's the lonely outsider. I look at the people I've written best, and they're all outsiders. Rusty, in *Presumed Innocent*, is a guy who—despite the fact that he has built all the accoutrements of family and social amenities and life philosophy, which is intertwined with the way in which he lives—is absolutely alone.

Do you feel that essentially most writers write the same story over and over?
Yes. The question is, when do you become tired of it? If the story is good enough, it has enough variations.

What did you learn from therapy that helped you with your writing?
Oh, a complete revision of the psychodynamics of my family life as a kid.

Which was?
My father was a very glamorous character, a very handsome guy who was called "Pop," which is a demeaning name for a father. He couldn't keep a job and he was always doing crazy things. In 1930, when he couldn't find a job, he played a Santa Claus who jumped out of a plane with a parachute, bringing symbolic presents to the children of Stratford, Connecticut. He was the one who always wrecked the family and my mother was the strong woman who suffered but hid it all underneath this terrifying, brilliant exterior. She wound up writing her autobiography, which was made into a movie with Rosalind Russell playing her and Jack Carson playing my father. So she became a screenwriter and had a career for about eight years at Warner Brothers.

But you said your understanding of the family changed.
I realized that the dynamics were not really that way at all—my father completely hid himself in order to allow her to play that role. And to the extent that the family had any stability at all, he was the strong one and she was the one who was absolutely out of control. That's simplified, but there was a major re-evaluation of my perception.

Was there a turning point in your work as a result of your therapy?
I don't think so. I just worked faster and better. And fortunately I can do those things that interest me—to the extent that the business allows anybody to do that.

Do you think the business has changed a great deal?
I think it highly unlikely that we could get *Dog Day Afternoon* done now. In fact, (screenwriter) Bob Towne was saying the other day that he could get *Shampoo* made but he didn't think he could make *Chinatown* now.

Another difference is each studio used to have an identifiable style. There was an MGM musical as opposed to a Columbia musical, or a Warner Brothers film noir as opposed to a Columbia film noir. But now the studios are all broken up and each movie is a unique thing. Some are the inspiration of the writer, some are a producer's idea, and the director tries to bring it into fruition.

We're just emerging right now from a period in which Disney has been trying to reinstate the old corporate authorship style. But it doesn't work very well for them, because if you want to make a movie which you control you are less likely to hire someone with an enormous run of successes behind him, who will tell you how to do your movie. You'll hire someone right out of film school whom you can tell what to do. And then when he fucks up, you'll hire another one.

Also, isn't there quite a difference in salaries between the established and new writer?
You can hire 10 writers for $150,000 apiece instead of one writer for a million-five. And by the end of that period there are so many drafts that no one knows who did what to whom or why. Anyway, that's sort of the general background situation

against which we all work. But when you come right down to making a film, you eventually get led into the same psychological area from which all creativity derives.

Which is?
Seeing things that you've looked at before in new combinations and in new ways that elicit a very strong emotional reaction. A lot of psychologists and philosophers around the turn of the century were examining the issue of creativity, particularly in the area of comedy.

Why comedy?
Because it's easiest to deconstruct the process. Comedy is a very intellectual exercise. Laughs are very carefully crafted and planned. They just don't happen spontaneously. That goes back to the famous old joke—dying is easy, comedy is hard.

It's sort of like the difference between surgery and internal medicine. In surgery you lay back the skin and you see the muscles and it's a procedure which is out in the open. Whereas in internal medicine you're looking at vague signs and the temperature is going up a little bit, but you don't really know why. Because the construction of comedy is a more craftsman-like procedure, it makes it more accessible in terms of trying to analyze it and deconstruct it to see how it works, so that we know what it is that makes us laugh.

What do you think your strengths and weaknesses are as a writer?
I like to work with character. Like most men, I don't write women as well as I would like to, but I think I write them better than a lot of men do. One of the difficulties in answering this question is that some of the best screenplays I've written have not been made.

Such as?
In 1980 I got a commission from Warner Brothers to do a story about three out-of-work steelworkers in Pittsburgh and what happens to them. They are the middle generation—too old to be retrained and too young to have sufficient stake in the pension fund. So they've got to find a strength inside themselves. Each one of them crumbles and then finds an anger which is going to lead him to revenge himself. The main couple have their love for

each other, and they'll find a way. I loved that screenplay and was crying with love and affection at the end. But these were the Reagan years, and the studio found the story terribly depressing and wouldn't make it. If I had gotten it done three months earlier I think we might have gone into production.

When you look back over your career do you have any major regrets?
Woody Allen once said, when somebody asked him a similar question, "If I had to live my life over again, on the whole I'd do everything the same except maybe I wouldn't go see *The Magus*." Regrets? Yeah, enormous regrets. Existential regrets in the sense that going through life is a matter of doors either remaining closed or slamming closed on you. You have so many choices when you're born, depending on what class you're in. I was very fortunate for a lot of reasons, and there were a million doors opened. But suddenly you realize that door's closed, and I'm never going to be able to do that again. And so there are a few along the way that I wish that I had opened at that time.

Do you know which ones?
No. I'm saying it's an existential feeling of loss which may only mean that my appetite is too big.

Do you think that different people have varying degrees of creativity or need to express that creativity?
I think some people have one creative moment in their life and then there are people like Robin Williams, where everything is exploding at every moment. But in either case, creativity has to do with seeing associations between two feelings or a feeling and an idea, which have never been seen or thought of before in this new context—which then gives rise to an evolutionary new idea.

That is only a crude way of expressing Henri Bergson's theory of creative evolution. The creative process is very destructive because those new levels of understanding destroy everything in the arena. Our level of understanding before that is gone. After Newton made the connection between apples falling off trees and the rotation of the planets around the sun and realized they were all related in one grand scheme, nobody could ever think about the universe in the same way again.

❝ In some jobs you make one design and stamp it out 100,000 times. But each piece of fish, meat and vegetable is slightly different. It's impossible to have duplicates. ❞

JIMMY SCHMIDT
Master Chef

Jimmy Schmidt was working on race cars and pursuing an engineering degree at the University of Illinois when he stumbled on a new recipe for life. Gourmets can thank the university's foreign language requirement for their good fortune.

The Illinois farmboy decided to learn his French first-hand. While in France he discovered French cuisine, which led him to remarkable entrepreneurial and aesthetic achievement.

Schmidt, only in his mid-30s, sat in the dining room of his Rattlesnake Club in Detroit and talked of his remarkable career path and of how creative juices flow in the kitchen.

He followed his mentor Madeleine Kamman from France to Boston. The late Les Gruber, legendary proprietor of Detroit's then world-renowned London Chop House, discovered the young Schmidt toiling in Kamman's kitchen. In a masterstroke of judgment, Gruber soon made the 22-year-old his head chef at the Chop—and the awards soon started pouring in for both.

The young chef we sat down to interview had become the father of two children, writer of two newspaper columns, author of a cookbook called *Cooking for All Seasons* and operator of three restaurants, with a staff of more than 200 and a gross of $5.5 million in 1990.

Though Schmidt looks like the boy next door, he clearly doesn't think like one. His mind seems never to be at rest—which became evident the moment he started to talk about his work. Just as the interview got under way, Schmidt noticed several customers who had just finished lunch and were about to leave. He stopped them to talk, but business—not lunch—was the topic.

You once said that food affects people on the unconscious level.

Food activates all the senses. It's just like advertising—if you can get all the senses involved, you can get the people involved.

How does it activate the senses?

Through visual effects, smell, and the feeling of hot or cold temperatures on the palate. By activating the senses you stimulate mind and memory, which sends a very strong signal to the subconscious. If you say chocolate to some people, they immediately visualize it and ask, "Where is it?" The same thing happens in wine tastings. Food can be very sensuous. That's why people who enjoy food can get really excited. You can actually have a relationship with it.

You've said that a lot of you is in each of your dishes. How are your moods and memories reflected in your cooking?

When I create food, I usually start off with kind of a warm feeling by thinking of something very pleasant.

"I need to be excited, challenged. It's a forward move. When I'm melancholy I wind up designing old food."

Like what?
Like love, family relations, or friends, or a pleasant memory like sitting in the South of France watching the sunset. Or sitting high in the Rocky Mountains and drinking wine. I try to re-create the aura or the mood generated by those circumstances.

And then what?
Then I'll find certain ingredients that will help me create that image in a salmon or scallop, for instance. And as I add other ingredients I try to visualize that image.

Are there particular ingredients or foods that affect you? For

instance, you said some people respond to chocolate.
Pretty much everything.

Is there anything that you don't respond to?
I don't eat sea urchins or a lot of the funny things like that.

Why not?
They're just a little scarier. They don't evoke such a positive response right off the bat. But everything else is great.

Was cooking an important part of your childhood?
No. I got involved in cooking as a lark. I went to engineering school. And to catch up on my languages I went to France. I thought a good way to understand the culture and the people would be to understand the French through their food, since they love it—they worship it.

Why do you think that is?
I think they're very passionate and very emotional people. And I think the geography of France affected their relationship to food.

In what sense?
France has three primary food regions, which created three styles of cooking. The first was the southwest, which contained the fat and the lard; the second was the northeast and the central part of France, which developed the butter cooking; and the third group was the South of France, which was known for its olive oil. France was rich enough to have all three regions, and each region exchanged ingredients with the other.

What about other countries?
Most countries are isolated. They only know one thing and that's what they get used to. If you go to Italy, it's almost entirely olive oil. The milk spoiled very quickly because of the higher temperatures, so it was much safer to handle it by turning it into cheese. If you go to Spain you'll find the land's very poor, so it's mostly olive oil—and some lard in the poor areas. But France had those three regions. And each created its own distinct style, yet those ideas were able to be blended.

Would you say that going to France was a turning point in your life?
Yes. That's where I started cooking and studying under Madeleine Kamman.

How old were you?
I was 18. I graduated from high school early, when I was 16. Then I studied engineering for two years before I went to France. I met Madeleine there. She got me involved in cooking. I followed her back to Boston for 2 1/2 years and then moved to Detroit because I still intended to become an engineer. I decided there wasn't time to work as a cook and an engineer. And it was more fun to get into cooking.

What did you like about cooking?
The creativity angle, because you could come up with ideas and turn them into the product very quickly. And I like having the authority to express ideas, to be able to test my knowledge. It's not like straight math where you add things up and it's the sum of the products. You're able to achieve an exponential result by the combination of texture, colors and flavors that would accentuate the dish. And it can be really exciting.

What's most exciting about it?
The ability to translate ideas into food. And it requires constant attention. In some jobs you make one design and you stamp it out 100,000 times. But each piece of fish, meat and vegetable is slightly different. It's impossible to have duplicates. And even if you do have duplicates, they could not be picked at the exact same time. They have different air exposures, different amounts of humidity. It requires a very sharp attention span to watch each piece, to make sure they all come out ideally. And that's very challenging.

The other interesting thing about food is that it's not very forgiving. If you just kind of throw it around, it comes out like it's been thrown around.

So you have to be sensitive to its needs, like a person.
Exactly. You have to be very attentive to its chemical and physical properties.

What do you like least about cooking?

That it's gone in a flash. Also, I find the customers' varying range of interests difficult to deal with. You end up serving people who have no concerns and people who have every concern—usually at the same table and over the same dish. Food is very subjective. A lot of people's tastes are developed around the foods they had as a child and the positive and negative experiences they had.

And you find that difficult?

Right. When I first started cooking at the London Chop House in Detroit I was very involved with the creativity part of it, wanting people to get what I got out of the food. I would put my soul into the food for each person who would come in. I could be in love with an imaginary woman in one dish, for instance. But each person would take out their own feelings and their own memories. They might say, "This reminds me of something my grandmother made." And I'd stand there thinking, "Your grandmother? How'd you get that out of it?" That's when I realized it's very much a personal thing.

It's like abstract art.

Right, which has its benefits. I can put in whatever I want and the other person can take out what they want, which is kind of safe.

You said before that people's tastes are developed around the food they had as a child. Can you give an example?

Sure, liver. Liver creates violent reactions.

What image does that conjure up in people?

Punishment. They didn't get any dessert—they had to sit there all night. Or lima beans and brussels sprouts. I had a writer in Denver [where Schmidt operated a restaurant for four years] come in, a pseudo restaurant critic. He actually wrote an article about the restaurant, but not totally from a critic's point of view. He wrote six or seven paragraphs about how we should be shut down for serving brussels sprouts as vegetables. He said that brussels sprouts should be outlawed and that the seed should be thrown away.

Was he serious?
Yes. So foods do trigger violent reactions. There's also a guy who's still mad at us today because he was served polenta and he hates polenta. For some reason he expected us to know that. I don't think he'll ever come back. Food is very personal. It's obviously your lifeline. And some people take what we serve them as a personal insult, like it's an attack on their body. Some people can get very strange.

Did this guy who hates polenta tell you he was mad at you?
He didn't tell me, but he let my maitre d' have it. He said, "How dare you serve polenta to me! I've come here a number of times and have specifically said that I don't like it and this is an insult to me and obviously you don't care about me as a customer or any of your customers." He's very educated, collects art and runs a very large company. I think he referred to polenta as corn mush, so somewhere in his childhood his mother fed him corn mush for breakfast and he didn't get his Fruit Loops or something.

So in a way you're dealing with a person's psyche on a daily basis.
Yes. And there are a lot of those things in a person's psyche that are hard to erase. On the other hand, if you look at food more positively, you think of desserts. You can do anything with desserts—you can even break every rule in the book. But if I take someone's steak and I flip it upside down and put the sauce on top instead of on the bottom I've got a riot on my hands. You can take chocolate and make little raviolis out of it and no one cares.

Why do you think that is?
Desserts relate back to childhood as a reward for being good. If you eat your dinner you'll get dessert. Each person has his own favorite dessert, but chocolate seems to be one of the most popular because it's also a luxury item. Most kids weren't running out and getting chocolate. Chocolate produced blemishes. A lot of teenagers wouldn't eat it for fear of acne. And there are many adults who are still careful when it comes to chocolate. They'll have a salad with no dressing and they'll have their fish broiled dry and then they'll have 10 orders of ravioli chocolate. They scrimp in certain areas so they can have something that

will give them a pleasant thought. Some people just like cakes. Maybe the only time they got a cake was on their birthday.

What's your favorite dessert?
Strawberry shortcake—it always sparks my memory.

Why is that?
Because as a kid the more strawberries you ate, the less you had to freeze later. It worked out great. They were right out of the garden. That was the only time my mother actually baked.

Was your mother a good cook?
No. She'd put everything in the water and put the steak in the pan and then turn it on, so everything was gray! There were some vitamins left when she got done.

What are your best memories?
Looking for black walnuts and in the spring looking for wild asparagus and mushrooms and all these other things that are just around.

Do you have any bad memories?
Liver and lima beans. My mother used to go over to the University of Illinois—which had big agricultural farms—and get liver and cook it up for like six weeks. It wasn't really a punishment. It's just that you always had it and it was inedible.

So you never serve liver?
Actually, sometimes we do. I like liver now—but medium rare.

What about lima beans?
No way. I was forced to eat a lot of those, which resulted in my sitting at the table trying to wish them away. I felt justified because lima beans are high in cyanide. Certain varieties are very poisonous.

You said your mother gave all the food a gray quality. How have you used color in your cooking?
Well, if you look at the actual setting of this restaurant you'll see everything's in natural form. The tables are all white and

very simplistic. The only place you really see color is in the flowers on the table. The color in the chair matches the brick tones and the water tones. The entire design comes from Frank Lloyd Wright's philosophy that you're in harmony with your space. So we use outdoor colors like greens and browns. All the woods except the chairs are cherry. The floors are Brazilian cherry, which is harder. And there's green marble, which has good earth tones. All of this gives people a real sense of calmness.

Do you think that creating a certain environment plays an important role in a person's response to food?
Yes. My teacher, Madeleine Kamman, showed me that. She gave me a respect and love for the ingredients you use and an understanding of the balance between the foods that you create and the world around you so that you don't scare people and shock them. They should be at peace with their environment.

What things would scare people?
Wild combinations. Or placing a sauce on top of fish or beef that has no flavorings or character. You can't just take ingredients A, B, and C and put them together and think you have a dish. It's not that simple. You have to look at the textures, the colors, the flavors they introduce and make sure there's a happy marriage.

Again these are the things I learned from Madeleine. Her philosophy is to maintain a balance with nature, to look at what flavors occur in nature and how life really exists. For example, you have to think about what a salmon would be eating and what kind of environment it would be in rather than taking a piece of salmon and throwing it in with some veal, where you get odd results. Madeleine is also well educated in geography, architecture and history, so she could pull out all the historical points.

Can you give an example?
Take a veal shank. It's helpful to know that, historically, people who raised the veal gave up the animals in payment for use of the land. They were the serfs. They ended up with small parts of the cows, the shanks, which were considered the lesser cuts. You combine that knowledge with the fact that most of the veal was slaughtered in the fall because the animals were birthed in the spring—unlike today's modern manufacturing through arti-

ficial insemination, so that veal is produced all year around. But when they were born in the spring, natural evolution came through. The tomatoes became ripe and the lemons reached maturity. And the serfs had a feast with the shanks.

So that's the philosophy of the dish. And it's important to catch the emotional spirit of the dish so you can elevate it to the glory it should have.

Can you talk about the use of contrast in cooking?
To bring forward your primary focus—the salmon, for instance—the ingredients you select need to have contrasting textures. Your palate is unable to determine the differences between an oyster and a scallop when they're poached. It's like painting with off-white and white; there's very little difference, especially in comparison to painting with white and black. So that the whole plate doesn't look brown or green or red, you need the contrasting of textures.

So texture plays an important role.
Right. Texture is the eye of your palate. To delineate between different foods, you either reinforce textures or make them seem changed in a certain perspective. If you want the scallop to seem firmer you put something softer with it. If you want it to seem silky, you put something coarser with it. Then you get that crunch and that's reference point one. And then you taste the scallop and that's the other extreme, and you get a contrast. If both judgments are occurring closely on the palate, it's hard to delineate between the two.

And you're saying that it's important to delineate.
Yes. It keeps the dish from becoming boring. After the first sensation the attention span of the average person is greatly reduced. You can think four times faster than you can hear, so people aren't very good listeners. It's the same thing with their palates. You can think a hell of lot faster than you can eat. You can't consume it as fast you can even think about it.

In the eating process people become very bored. When I mix up dishes, the garnishes and sauces, you'll never get the same ingredients on each bite. So those slight nuances allow the dishes to remain on the palate for a longer sense of time. In your mind the first and last bites are the same thing.

Do certain foods stimulate certain things?
Usually crunchy foods are very calming. Potato chips create a vibration in the inner ear, which allows for a utopia type of feeling. In Weight Watchers they try to steer you away from crunchy foods. You can't eat just one. It's the crunch that's important; the food is secondary.

Is the reverse of that also true—that soft foods create chaos?
I don't know. Very soft foods, like mashed potatoes, even though they're considered comfort foods, relate back to your mother feeding you rather than how they feel on your palate. Usually they're the most boring foods on the palate. More potato chips are sold than mashed potatoes.

So people like the calm but not the maternal comfort.
It's more psychological than physical. You have to get a balance.

You talked about the use of color in terms of the restaurant itself. But how is color used in terms of the presentation of food?
As far as plate design goes, I believe in Ansel Adams's theory of black and white photography, the theory of gradation—your darkest color becomes black and the lightest becomes white. Similarly, when your eye perceives food, the darkest color becomes burnt. So I have to get darker plates. The green on this plate reads black. The darkest color represents certain things, such as the cooking process—grill marks on a piece of fish are such that it was given a searing at a high temperature which is then equated with being cooked. If the fish comes out pale you think it isn't cooked.

So the food has to look like it has been cooked?
Right. For example, you have the dieter who wants fish without breading or butter. But then they say it doesn't look cooked so they send it back. You know what we do? Take a little thing of paprika and salt and sprinkle it. Then they're happy. The food has to look like heat was applied to it.

It's important that you have a darkening of food. Poached food is not big—it doesn't color. Grilled is more popular than poached salmon. When you close your eyes, you can't really tell what you're eating. That's why contrast is important—again because it activates the senses.

How much does the design of plates affect someone's relationship to the food they eat?
A great deal. Even something as simple as using large shapes on a plate is important, because then it's easy to identify what those shapes are. Otherwise they might interfere with your visual perception of the food. You might go out to dinner with friends and because of the design of the plate the food looks different—and you think the waiter didn't bring you what you ordered. Also, through the design we try to enhance good color balance. If I put a grilled piece of salmon on a pale green plate, it will look burnt or severe.

Are there colors that you usually stay away from?
Blue doesn't work for foods—it tends to wipe out all the greens and yellow hues. Browns and blacks are pretty safe. Oranges are OK. Good natural colors are good. Green is OK. Black is great because it sets up the Ansel Adams type of thing of black and white. Other colors that don't naturally occur in nature and food are good—such as red.

Why is that?
Because there are very few things that are really red. And you really don't want to put red things on that plate. If you put a strawberry on it the strawberry looks pale. If the strawberry looks better than the plate, the plate looks faded. If you use a red plate, there aren't many foods that have that color naturally in them; so you don't run into that conflict. There are too many foods with green, yellow and some orange qualities that a blue plate would wipe out.

Back to the setting of the restaurant itself . . . I think ideally we try to have a good sense of order. All the lines are clean and defined—the table layouts are in straight lines. This allows people to relax, even if they're used to chaos. It's very important that you put everything at ease and create a positive environment that will allow people to reach a comfort zone so they'll let all their senses be activated. Then they can have a memorable meal. A lot of other things are out of my control. So you do the best you can.

What other things are out of your control?

A guy comes here and says to his wife, "I don't love you anymore and I'm outa here." You know no matter what you serve, forget it! It's over. One person I used to work for used to hang out with Jimmy Beard. I'd take [my boss] dishes and he'd say, "This is no good." Finally I took him some strawberries that I knew were great. And he said, "These are shit." So I said, "Just tell me when you had the best strawberry so I know what I'm looking for." And he tells me 1939. I asked where he was and he told me the South of France. I said, "What were you doing there?" He says, "I had this great date with this French woman and we were drinking wine and eating these strawberries and they were the best strawberries I ever had." So his reaction to the strawberries had to do with a memory and not the strawberries themselves.

Do any of your moods affect your cooking?

Absolutely. When I'm in a bad mood, forget it. I have to be in a fairly good frame of mind and then I can create that warm feeling of fond memories. I'll think of sitting in Monte Carlo a couple of months ago when I was in a better situation.

If you're in a bad mood what do you do?

You try to cheer yourself up. You just take your mind out of here. Just leave the restaurant.

What about melancholy?

No, that's not where the strongest energy comes from. I need to be excited, challenged. It's a forward move. When I'm feeling melancholy I end up designing old food. Actually it does work OK, as a contrary point. Because I was working on this old 1938 concept, updated. I put myself in that period of time and the shapes, sizes and smells that came forward were coarser and more masculine, like an old steak house. Then the feeling of melancholy worked out, but it's not great for creating forward food.

By forward food you mean modern food?

Right. Melancholy helps me create old stuff, like a big plate of greasy onion rings. What I'll do is reverse directions, strip the food down and put it back together with modern ingredients and modern technology which triggers the same response.

How would you apply that to greasy onion rings?
If I updated them they would be super clean and you could eat as much as you want because there would be no cholesterol. So you have to capture the memory of the past, rework it so that it fits the evolved mind of today and palate of today, and then take it in that direction. Most of that is mechanical. It's semi-creative.

What place evokes the most positive memories for you?
Paris, because of the old buildings. They have an enduring quality. And I think they challenge me to create things that will endure, rather than "this is the trend." Paris has a lot of memories. It's so vital. I guess it's a sensory overload because there are so many buildings and so much around you and you don't slip back into the mediocrity of the suburbs. I hate the suburbs.

Where do you live?
The suburbs!

Can you talk about the use of smell in cooking?
I remember returning to the States after being in Paris and everything was so clean over here, without smell. Also, the American nose is not trained to smell everything that's going on.

Do you work with smells a great deal in your own cooking?
Yes. First of all, we focus on the food smells. We choose flowers that do not have a scent, or have a very low scent, and we allow smoking only in certain parts of the dining room. We don't allow cigars. I think smells are extremely important. A lot of people remember people by their perfumes, their scents. You can trap bees by the mating smells.

How do you specifically use scents?
Technically all the volatile oils, which are the scent carriers in the food, can't escape low temperatures. So we use high temperatures to sear and low temperatures to penetrate the scent and flavors, especially in larger pieces. And we try to cook things very little, to keep those nuances going.

Are there particular scents that people respond to?
It depends. Floral scents usually don't work because most people associate lavender with soap or perfumes. But there are sorbets with lavender. It can be great, but you walk a fine line. If you use too much it tastes soapy. Many other products use those scents to produce a better association. For instance, when you smell cinnamon, you think of gingerbread cookies. But mothballs don't recall a food. We've logged all these scents and colors.

What do people respond most strongly to?
The milder and sweeter scents. Tarragon is popular. Clean, green flavors like chives, parsley, thyme, rosemary, savory, oregano—you get into more of the turpentine or evergreen plants. They can scare people away, too—because they can be quite strong. You take fresh rosemary and rub it on your hands and it's everywhere.

So you don't want it to be too strong?
Right. You have to use herbs and spices mildly. Or you can apply little amounts of heat to them and dry off part of it. You take a rosemary sprig and throw it in hot olive oil for a couple of seconds and it's great. It's crunchier, so it's easier to eat.

What is the most important sense?
It depends. Each has its own category. Smell is one of the most important. But for Americans that may be secondary. Visual is very important because people do eat with their eyes. And texture and taste are important.

Taste is further down the list because it's duller. I can give you 10 dishes and 10 wines and say, "Tell me what each one of these are." It's hard to discern. But if I gave you the essential oils in a cup and we had a smelling test you'd probably pick out most of them. You'd tell me what a banana smelled like. The sense of smell is quite astute.

Temperature is also important. Some people have to have boiling hot coffee.

Why?
They're just used to having the sensation of heat in their mouth. I don't like hot food that much. It depends. You throw that curveball of temperature and it may not come to the person

at that exact point to stimulate their taste the way they want to. Some people like to take fries right out of the fryer and eat them right away. And if you give them this great bread with low temperature they won't like it.

How do you respond to the different needs of people?
You find out the most central pattern that works well. We heat all the plates and we try to keep the temperature up and to keep the oven as hot as possible. You can always cool something off, but it's harder to reheat it.

What was the smell of the farm you grew up on? You have an incredibly strange look on your face. What were you thinking of?
The farm, the barnyard, and the animals. Those are the smells I associate with the farm. Also I think of the fall. Many of the scents come out in the fall, like apples being pressed for cider. A lot of those activities, like ripening the fruits, have a very strong smell.

Are those memories with you a lot when you're cooking?
Yes. It's very important to capture that fresh flavor. Let's say you're cooking a dish with oranges. In order to really get the flavor you'd use orange juice and you'd turn it into an orange butter sauce. But it won't taste like oranges unless you add a lot of lemon juice to reinforce it, because the oranges are lower in acidic quality. When you eat one they're quite acid. But by cooking it you break down acids. So by adding lemon juice you create what your mind would estimate an orange would taste like. You have to play around with your mind's eye—what you think it should be.

Tell me about your book.
A lot of people wanted me to write a book that was a collection of recipes from the restaurant, which I didn't want to do. I thought it might be interesting to write something that revolved around the seasons—capturing foods at their peak. Because foods that are in season taste the best. They're available, economical and your parents probably introduced you to them in a certain season. Summer is sorbets. December is plum puddings or chocolate desserts. I can serve you veal shank in January but I

sure can't do it in spring. There are certain things that have evolved over the course of time in your life, and in your ancestors' lives, that have shaped what you eat and how you react to foods today.

You mentioned that your mother is not a good cook. How does she feel about the work you're doing?
You have to understand I left engineering school to do this. My picture was in *Women's Wear Daily* in 1976. I was working in one of the hottest restaurants in the country and my mother was sending me these little matchbooks that say, "Get a job, learn a profession—radio repair." I used to get those all the time. It wasn't until the last few years that my mother related to the fact that cooking is a viable profession, one to be gainfully employed in.

What about your dad?
He's very calm, very methodical. He loves to eat.

I read that you always wanted to write a mystery novel. Is that true?
Yes. I like the precision of intrigue, being able to set up a lot of things happening simultaneously. And then I like to collide them at a certain point. That's what mysteries are all about. You do the same thing with food. You take very fresh ingredients as well as ingredients that you've cooked for awhile—for stocks or sauce bases—and you take meat that is aged and fish that is fresh and you collide them all at the same time.

So you like that collision?
Yes. Timing is the key, so that everything collides at the right time.

How have you changed over the years?
When I started out I was very aggressive. I was trying to make a mark and I was trying to force the food. I'd take certain ingredients and I'd grind them out. The dishes would come out OK but they lacked soul, they lacked a sense of belonging. Then I realized that if you set up the right environment, the right mood, it flows. Now I can sit down and come up with five to 10 pages of ideas for recipes in half an hour. I'm more at peace with

myself and I can recognize what I can and what I can't change. And the whole dining environment allows me to focus very tightly on the creativity point of view and come up with some great dishes.

Where do your ideas come from now?
I don't know. They just come out.

At any time?
Yes and anywhere. But now my brushstrokes are longer, more peaceful and definitely more mellow.

> People wanted to know what poem I'm working on and what pieces I'm doing for the next two years. For what? It's not their business. If it's not in the bookstore, it's mine.

NTOZAKE SHANGE
Poet/Playwright

The doorman summoned Ntozake Shange to the lobby of her Philadelphia apartment building. Shange appeared in jogging attire, explaining that she had been up all night. An interview sought for several months finally was about to occur.

Shange led the way through a corridor to her two-floor apartment, then down a flight of stairs to her living room/kitchen. There was a picture of her 10-year-old daughter, Savannah, a beautiful angelic face on the kitchen wall. In the living room were two posters—one of Malcolm X and one from Shange's play *For Colored Girls Who Have Considered Suicide/When The Rainbow Is Enuf*—which brought fame to Shange at the age of 27. Between these posters was a TV set, flickering the faces of two beautiful blond actors in *The Young and the Restless*.

The juxtaposition of Malcolm X and a popular white soap opera provided a metaphor for Shange's contrasting sides. She was born Paulette Williams in 1948 in Trenton, New Jersey. Her father was a surgeon and her mother was a psychiatric social worker. From an affluent, privileged and protected childhood she went on to Barnard and earned a master's degree at the University of California. The other side, Ntozake Shange, has transformed rage into unforgettable drama. When asked where all this rage comes from, Shange said, "It's been there all the time, but I was just trying to be nice."

There were problems, despite her parent's affluence. At the age of eight, when her family lived in St. Louis, she was bused to

© Al Hirschfeld. Drawing reproduced by special arrangement with Hirschfeld's exclusive representative, The Margo Feiden Galleries Ltd. New York.

FACING PAGE: Ntozake Shange (far right) in 1976 Hirschfeld drawing of *For Colored Girls* cast. It was a smash success, but Shange has "had to keep it away from me" to be "able to write beyond it."

●

an all-white neighborhood. "I was not prepared for it. I was rich and somewhat protected. Now I was being harassed and chased around by these white kids. My parents were busy being proud." After one very difficult day at school she came home and drew a hopscotch on the sidewalk. In each box she wrote, "For Colored Only."

In 1971 Paulette Williams got rid of her middle-class "slave name" and took her new Zulu name, which means "She who comes with her own things" and "She who walks like a lion." Five years later, *For Colored Girls Who Have Considered Suicide/ When The Rainbow Is Enuf* opened at the Public Theatre. When it moved to Broadway the following September, Shange was an "overnight" success. This choreopoem, as she called it—a combination of dance, theater and poetry—was performed by seven black women, including Shange, simply dressed in leotards. Performing without a set, each woman told a chilling story of rape, abortion, abuse and poverty.

This unforgettable play so profoundly affected Shange's interviewer that she wrote her own first play. Apprised of this, Shange's face took on a troubled look. Her audiences have not let her grow beyond *For Colored Girls*, Shange said. She did not want to discuss her time as a young writer, when she wrote such words as: "Ever since I realized there waz someone callt/a colored girl an evil woman a bitch or a nag/i been trying not to be that and leave bitterness/in somebody else's cup." She wanted instead to discuss what has happened since that time.

For Colored Girls has had such a profound effect on so many people. Can we talk about its origins?
I have no relationship to that play at all at this point in time.

Because it was so long ago?
It was long ago and it was a brutal experience for me. I've had

to keep it away from me with whatever little sanity I've managed to maintain. It's a very consuming kind of experience that is no longer mine. I keep thinking about Gloria Swanson and the movie she was in.

Which one?
Sunset Boulevard. She's caught up in the image of herself that's gone. And when people ask about *For Colored Girls*, I think: "If I keep talking about it, I won't be able to write beyond it and I won't be able to function outside of it." I've tried really hard not to do that.

So this was not the play to bring up!
No. But I think it has a lot to do with creativity.

How so?
Because it has to do with moving forward creatively and moving my audience along with me. I'm not saying *For Colored Girls* was a curse, but it's hard because the audience always wants to go back to that time and that play. But I can't allow that, so I don't. I never even read from *Colored Girls* anymore.

You used the word "brutal." Can you talk more about that?
Ever since that play, whenever I go into rooms anywhere around the country a myriad of people have all kinds of ideas about me. I don't know any of them. I find it very disorienting and I don't like it.

Because they think they know you.
Because they think they're sharing intimate moments with me. I don't know who they are. I've never seen them before. How they think they got me and what they think they have of me may in fact not exist.

Can you talk about the process of writing—whether you're writing *Colored Girls* or your newer works.
I told my writing students when they do interviews not to give away process. But I think I know how to do it where people can't take it from me.

**Does that happen when you teach? Do you feel like you're

giving your process away?

Oh no. I don't teach myself. I'm teaching other writers. It has nothing to do with me. My passion about it might be apparent in a classroom. So it's reaffirming for me because I know I'm in the company of other people who do things that I like.

What is the process of writing like for you? How does it start?

Well, I'm a poet who does a significant number of readings a year around the country. Sometimes I take other people with me, like the band. And what's important is how I experience my poems and the order I've placed them in while I'm performing in front of an audience over maybe a six- or eight-month period.

Do you ever change the order of your poems?

Absolutely. I change it depending upon how long I'm supposed to read, where I'm reading, if I have all white people, if I have all old people or old black church people, whatever. And during this six- or eight-month period I find out as I'm reading what lines are getting stuck in my throat. And this usually means there are too many words. Or I find out what lines leave me feeling like I'm hanging in the air and I'm not supposed to be in the air at that point.

And then do you start revising?

Yes. Just the process of reading the same kind of poem or the same set of poems over one season allows me to figure out what can go in and what has to go out. And eventually I know the order. And no, we do not change it anymore because it will work for everybody most of the time. Musical segues or choreographic links from one poem to another, are also set.

Once everything is set what do you do?

I go to someplace like the Kitchen and do a performance piece.

And the entire process usually takes about six to eight months?

And then another three months to get lights and real choreography and a real score. So it's a long process. And since I'm not like Brecht, I don't want to carry an entire theater company around with me all year long. So that means the people I'm working with are interrupted by other projects.

Is that one of the most difficult parts of the way you work—the time involved, especially because of everyone's schedules?
That and trying to find a world or creating an arena where I can do what I do and have people stop telling me it's a huge poetry reading or it's a small theater piece. For a poetry reading my work looks really spectacular, but when we go into a theater it looks very strange and sparse. It's none of that. It's the same thing I've been doing for 20 years. So that's the process.

What about before you take your work and your troupe on the road? What happens when you first sit down to write? Where do your ideas come from—your life?
Oh no; it's not my life. My life is not that interesting. It's really not. I'm a mother of a 10-year-old. Nothing to get excited about there. Let me see—well I don't think ideas come to me. I'm not that abstract. I get some kind of visceral sensation and then I have to figure out how I can make other people have that. So it goes backwards.

Not that I'm not theoretically involved in my work. I am. But I don't have to think about that. To work on the galleys I can decide what I really want it to look like on a page. And I can decide what kind of diction and syntax I want to deal with.

Even though a lot of that's done already. You don't want to change the shape too much. I think two or three times I have done a series of poems where I had a formal shape in mind for them.

Can you give an example?
I knew one of my poems came in three sections, like a triptych in a cathedral. The poem, in fact, was about mourning the black neighborhoods and the kind of community I was raised in. And it was about a lack of respect for our geniuses and our artists and just our hard-working people. And so I named the sections after pieces by Duke Ellington, and I had an improvisation section. I put key signatures and time measurements in and that way, if somebody was interested in the history of black music or jazz, they could, in fact, have guidelines from me and would be able

to hear what I thought I was hearing when I was writing the poem.

So you have different kinds of ideas.
Yes, but I don't get an idea like I'm going to write a poem about a mother and a daughter. I might get a really powerful kind of sadness so I can relate then to loss and then to mothers, and losing daughters who became women or whatever—that's how it would go. I would then say, "How would that happen? What situation would make you feel a sense of loss?" And then I could figure out what to write.

You talked about a visceral situation . . . and there is a kind of rhythm and energy in your readings.
That's what my poems should be creating. I don't have a mind/body separation. If I'm upset, my body's upset; if I'm happy, my body's happy. So if I'm intellectually stimulated, I sweat. I'm still moving, thank goodness, as that one whole being.

Do you think most artists work that way?
It's always alarming to me that people separate their work from themselves—or they separate their thoughts from their own breath. I find that just incredible. That would make me feel crazy. I know when my own writing isn't working or when it lacks a certain integrity when you can't coo in a particular image I've created or you can't do solace to yourself in it. What I can really share with people is a sense of a language we live in.

Meaning?
Meaning creating some area where I really believe you learn what I mean, not what I say but what I really mean. Most often that's an experience that takes place on an unconscious level. So I try to write myself into other people's unconscious. So they lose control, then they let me have it, so that I can give it back to them. That's what I mean by the language we live in. Not the language we speak, which is a dishonest language.

What's dishonest about our language?
It doesn't have gender identification. So it's assumed there's a

man speaking. And in our verb "to be" we do not separate time and space, or temporal time from intimate time, or human beings from objects. So when I say "I am" and I say, "This is a glass," I say both with the same kind of intensity. And therefore half the time we're lying. So it's not the word itself that allows me to know what you're saying.

It's the unconscious level created by the word.
Right. And you see the world that I feel best in is with visual artists or dancers or musicians. I stay out of relationships with verbal people. I feel very happy with people who don't talk much!

Do you show your work to others while it's in progress?
I show it to the musicians I work with, or dancers. I do not show it to people who are not working on it with me. I don't see any reason to do that. Why would I do that? Are you going to do something with it? No? Then give it back! That's the problem with writing workshops. I went to a couple of them and I never understood what those people were doing.

Because people were criticizing your work who were not involved in the process of creating it?
Right. Either your poem is working for you or it's not. You can hear for yourself if it's working and then go out in the world and do it. If they don't like it, they'll say so. If they don't understand it, they'll tell you. If they think it's boring, they'll start talking on top of you. I stopped teaching creative writing for awhile because if I'm not going to allow just anybody to criticize me why would I encourage other people to do that to each other?

But aren't you teaching now?
Yes, because I pick the people whose work I would have wanted to read anyway. But I don't want to know the ideas of people whose work I'm not interested in. Why would I clutter my life with their thoughts?

One of my students—I don't even want to call them students—told me she had been studying with somebody somewhere who told her she should be less emotional. I said, "My God, why would you have people being less emotional? Where are these people going to put their emotions if they can't put it into poetry? They can't put it into newspapers; they can't put it in the kitchen. Where are they going to have it?" She said her feelings were hurt. And I told her she had written a fine poem and told her not to go back to that other teacher!

What kind of writing interests you?
I've gotten into science fiction. I used to not know what they were talking about. Now I'm dealing with quasars and black holes and cosmic strings. I'm interested in the interactions of the membranes and the surfaces of the protons because that's where most of the real creative movement takes place.

How has this affected your work?
It's allowed me to understand more of where I am without having to take it through someone else's cultural nexus.

Is there a particular author you're interested in?
Yes, Sam Delaney. In one of his books you're on a planet where if you have a question you get the answer by having the thought. And you get it from electronic foreign air called "general information." Isn't that wonderful? You don't have to spend years trying to figure out the answer. You think the thought and you get the answer. This is a wonderful way to live.

You once said that you were interested in Simone de Beauvoir.
Yes, she was a writer in her own right and I liked her and Sartre—that was in my naive days. I thought they had a good atypical relationship.

And you don't think so now?
Well, I just got her biography, and as smart as he was he didn't do right by her.

Didn't they have separate apartments?
Yeah, and I thought that was a great idea. I never would live in a house with anybody again—except my child.

How has your work changed in the last 20 years?
I stopped fooling around with things that I don't really want to do. At a certain point I thought it was important to figure out

if I could write for the theater all the time, or if I could write novels. I didn't have privacy to try these different things when I was 25 because I was publicly known. I don't know if that was good or bad. I think in a way that was awful. So now I just do what I want to do. And it doesn't matter if you like it or not.

What are you working on now?
I'm doing a piece on a bridge which is nearby and I'm calling it *The Bridge Play*. I decided I'd run the ads in the personal section and say, "You're invited to a public display. I am running for all women who have had to run anywhere. I'm running for my life." The sound track will be my mother's bridge party. So when I put it all together I'll be running to the sound of her bridge party.

Why are you using that as your sound track?
Because I want to unite female urban rituals.

What are the rituals in your life?
Well, when my friends come over to see me we don't play bridge, so it looks like we don't have adult rituals. But we do. We either go to the gym or we go running or we dance. So I want to show that we do have something.

So you'll be uniting your running with your mother's bridge party?
Right. The other idea I'm dealing with is women's lack of access to public space, like the Central Park jogger and/or women who have to work at night and come home by themselves. We get afraid to be on our own streets. I just want to take back some space, to take back the bridge.

Where will you start "running" from?
I'm running from where they wrote the Constitution and they decided we were three-eighths or five-eighths, what was that—two-thirds of one white man? So that's how many votes we counted for in the Electoral College. I'm running from there to Camden, where 60 percent of the black and white children live below poverty level. And it's important that I'm running, because I will probably start to look bizarre by the time I get to the middle of the bridge. I'll be sweating as I pass all those pret-

ty women, those women who look the way we're supposed to look all the time.

Will you do this regardless of who comes?
Yes, I'm not even putting the ad in the arts section. I'll just put it in the personals column and see who comes.

Did you once care who came to hear your work?
Yes, I wanted to have an audience. But I don't feel I need one now.

What about the critics? Do you care about their opinions?
No, I don't need them. Never did. Because I have verification from the community I work in.

Which consists of?
Musicians and dancers. Musicians work with me because I can handle them on the stage. They don't overpower me. That lets me know, "Hey, I don't care if you've gotten it or not. My peers have gotten it." Dancers can dance in the middle of my poem; they think they know who they are. If they can do that, what other kind of verification do I need?

So you don't have friends whose criticism would affect you?
What do I care? I say, "That's OK, your name's not on that so you don't have to like it. I wrote it." My mother used to criticize my work, but she's stopped. Probably because she knows I won't change what I wrote. I might write something else you'll understand. That's why you have more than one poem in your book. You didn't get it, OK, let's keep moving.

Do you feel your mother gets your stuff now?
Absolutely.

Has she been supportive?
Immensely. I had to go to a press interview in Washington last week, and I was so nervous my hair fell out. So I called my mother and said, "You have to go with me to Washington because they want me to do all these interviews, and that makes me very, very crazy." I get very, very paranoid 'cause people are asking me all kinds of questions.

Are interviews often very difficult for you to do?

They can be. When I was doing one of the interviews last week I felt like I was repeating myself. And I thought, "When did I say that?" The agent sends me out on five interviews, so whatever story I have in the morning, five interviews later you'll get the same answer. When I was talking about having brutal experiences before, that was part of it, too.

In what sense?

I wound up being emptied out after a bunch of interviews, so I decided that wasn't going to happen anymore. So I would make up some answers after the first interview of the day and then I would keep them for the other interviews, unless someone asked me something that I could actually talk about without having to dig deeper. Because the next level of thought is more intense and more private. And so if I kept answering the questions, I became very weak and enervated by the end of the day. And I just decided I wouldn't do that anymore.

Unless someone asks you the right questions?

I don't know if there are any right questions. That's what's hard about interviews; you're just around strangers and questions all day. That's why I wanted my mother to come to Washington with me—there was someone there I knew and someone who knew me.

You're raising your daughter alone?

Yes.

Has she affected your work?

Yes. When she was first born it meant I couldn't travel much. I couldn't do a lot of elaborate stage pieces because I couldn't go anywhere and be in rehearsal. I could not go away from my house because my child had to go to school. So I had to figure out things to do. It made me realize what I really value is the experience of writing and performing and not so much what people want from me or what they think they want or what they think they saw. I don't care. If I don't like doing this, then I don't need to do it. So having a child has clarified what I want living to be.

Do you think people have a lot of expectations of you?
Yes, especially when I first moved to Philadelphia and was raising my daughter. People wanted to know what poem I'm working on and what pieces I'm doing for the next two years. Why? For what? It's not their business. If it's not in the bookstore, it's mine. And I don't have to share that.

But you're saying you feel a pressure from people to share what you're doing with them?
Yes. I went to an art show up the street and someone asked me what I'm working on. I said, "I'm not working on anything. I'm looking at a painting." And I said to my shrink, "I'm not working when I go to a museum to look at art. I don't have to talk to these people. Why don't they leave me alone?" And the ones that really kill me are the people who actually get angry when I say I'm raising my daughter.

Why do they get angry?
I think, first of all, it's because they have so little respect for motherhood. And . . . people's fantasy of being an artist is you have to give up things. I ain't giving up nothin'. Or they think that children have to suffer or not be as important as poetry. That's ridiculous. I have a reasonable family life here. I cook dinner. We get up, we have breakfast. Whatever their distortion on what an artist's life is supposed to be like or what my obligation is—that's their fantasy, not mine.

Do you think that motherhood and being an artist feed each other?
Yes, but when you have toddlers, there's an intense isolation for five years. I experienced more isolation at that time than I had ever known. People who don't want children around don't come see you. Women who haven't had children yet don't come see you. So you're really left there with whatever you can make up for yourself. During those five years I learned a lot. I learned how to enjoy myself without necessarily having to write about it.

Did you write less?
Yes. And I realized I don't have to write about everything.

Some of it I can just experience and enjoy. And that was a new thought for me. I had never just experienced something. I had always written it down. So my journal changed shape in that sense. I only write in it when I feel like writing. I don't have to document every day any more. That happened because I couldn't write all the time because my baby was nursing. I couldn't even hold the pencil, so I had to do something else. So I thought, "OK, we have to just get through the hour. We can't write now."

Was that difficult?
Well, when you're a young writer you have to write right now. But as a mother I realized I couldn't always write because my child had to have dinner right now! I remember when I first understood that. I mean I thought it was OK if I couldn't go out at night, but I thought it was the most ridiculous thing in the world if I couldn't get up and write a poem because my child had to nurse now. After a few years I didn't have the need to write all the time. I could set aside time and then go write. But at first, when I was nursing my child, I had to figure out ways to get my own nourishment for myself.

How did you get some of that nurturing?
I learned about things I didn't know at all. When I went to Texas I learned how to ride horses. I gave myself something I had never had and had always been intrigued by.

And that helped nurture you?
Yes. And I got some of my power back. 'Cause I was controlling a 2,000-pound wild animal. So I must be OK. I'm not just a housewife—I can ride a horse.

Did having a child affect the kinds of things you wrote about?
Yes, I think I felt freer because if I could relate to the kid I could talk about anything I wanted. Who was going to stop me? Also, I wanted to write about ethical issues. Things that happened to black children that didn't happen to other children. There were issues about mothering and parenting at large in the world. And I thought, "My God, there are no guidelines for my child. There's no poetry about this."

So how did that affect your work?

It made me really try to focus on very large aesthetic and ethical problems that I was dealing with so that my daughter would have a record of how her mother did this and what her mother thought about that. She'd have a record that wouldn't be crammed in with my grocery list, and it wouldn't just be random thoughts in my journal. The thoughts would be refined and she could share them with other girls so that they'd have a thread that they could agree with or not agree with. But they would have a core of some kind to move from. In that sense I had a focus that I hadn't necessarily had before.

Do you have any doubts about your work?

Oh yeah. I don't know why people read what I write. I have no idea. I'll go through days when I'll say "Everyone talks. How in the world could they think what I write is so amazing?"

Does that get in your way?

I don't know. Because I don't write every minute of the day. I still have to make dinner. It becomes less of an issue when it's less of my life, when it's not the priority. It's not all I have to do. Maybe I'll make a pie. OK we'll cook this way. We make very good pies. That's how I move it away. OK, so we can't write today. We really are blocked. We don't have a thought. Let's make some soup. So we cook. Whenever I go on big cooking binges it's usually because I'm in between gestation of projects. I'll either cook or I'll weave or I'll stay in the gym for hours. But I don't chastise myself about that. I don't say, "Well, I shouldn't do that right now."

What do you think you need to help you be most creative?

A clean and organized apartment. I can't work when it's a mess. If I'm going to go out of control when I write, then my home has to be together and in control.

What do you think you do best as a writer?

I have a great sense of humor. And all my characters are grounded in cultures of people of color. So when you learn about my characters you are learning about whole people. And I guess what people see as my weakness is that I don't like plot.

Do you see it as a weakness?

No. I don't know the end of my story, so I don't have a plot. It's OK with me. But it bothers other people. I hear it often. It's not really a novel—it's a poet's novel. Call it whatever you want.

What is one of the most important lines you've written?

It's in *The Love Space Demands*: "I thought Berneatha was like me. That she could take anything. Can't nothing kill the will of the colored people. But Lord I was wrong." That was real disturbing to me because I think it's important that I let a lot of people know that I know how fragile we are. I know what hurts. We're not monolithic, we can't take anything. It does hurt to see what's happening to our neighborhoods and our children. There's still some dignity about our surviving that. I know we can't just take anything.

Where did the title, *For Colored Girls Who Have Considered Suicide/When The Rainbow Is Enuf*," come from?

The phrase, "colored girls" was a term my grandmother used. I thought I should give back place and historically correct meaning to that phrase. When we were little my grandmother used to say, "Good little colored girls, pretty little colored girls." So we understand what we mean, not what white people mean. I can't give up language to them so they can take words and make them mean what they want it to mean. So I took it back and made it mean what I thought it should mean.

And the rainbow?

When I was living in California it was the first time I saw a rainbow. It all sounded right to me.

And the suicide?

I used to work at a rape crisis center. I had to deal with a lot of women who were feeling abused or feeling violated and thought what they should do is die. They thought they couldn't heal their violations or adignities. And my position was and still is that the universe is filled with what we need to function. It's not not there. But we're the ones who have to find it.

❝ I could be quite happy, locked in a room forever with a pair of pliers and a thousand coat hangers and someone passing food to me under the door. ❞

KENNETH SNELSON
Sculptor

From a distance, the burnished steel rods appear to float in defiance of gravity; one art writer said that they look as if they'd been tossed in the air and then frozen suddenly in mid-flight. But look closer and you find that the rods are strung together by taut cables. The effect is striking.

Anyone who has been to Pittsburgh, or Iowa City or Osaka, Japan, or a score of other locales, has probably chanced upon one of these free-ranging constellations of rods-and-cables, the best-known work of sculptor Kenneth Snelson. Though many have been exhibited in the world's premiere museums, they are typically too big, too sprawling to be housed indoors. More often they wind up outside, in some public place like Pittsburgh's Mellon Square, or the Baltimore waterfront, dominating the landscape and exciting more than a little curiosity—and skepticism. Some critics say Snelson's work is more engineering than art. But the elegance of his constructions argues otherwise.

Born in Pendleton, Oregon, in 1927, Snelson has nurtured a passion for "making things" since childhood. But after his discharge from the Navy in 1945, his career plans were still unformed. "My brother advised going into business, because then you can do anything," he recalled. "So I enrolled in the University of Oregon and studied accounting. Then there was a teacher giving a terrific Shakespeare course, so I changed my major to English. After that I became interested in architecture and from there I got into design. There were quite a few painting students in the design class, so through them I was gradually drawn into painting."

Snelson spent the summer of 1948 at North Carolina's Black Mountain College, an important mecca of the arts. He studied with German-American artist Josef Albers, and with architect Buckminster Fuller. Returning to Oregon that fall, he took up sculpture, fashioning the first of a series of small wire-and-wood pieces that foretokened the massive steel structures he would later create. In 1965 he had his first gallery show—at New York's Dwan Gallery.

The structures are one of Snelson's three art-related "obsessions," as he calls them. Another is a controversial theory of atomic structure that he has promulgated in words and image since the early 1960s. During our interview, he brought out a part of his atom model made entirely from magnets. It was examined with fascination before the interviewer realized he was playing with fire—or, worse, with magnetism in the presence of his cassette recorder and tapes.

Snelson's third passion is 360-degree or panoramic photography. At first glance, the photographs, made with a turn-of-the-century rotating camera and rendered in long horizontal prints, appear to be more-or-less conventional cityscapes and country scenes. Then the viewer notices that streets that *should* be straight are bent in a "V," vertical lines that should be parallel splay out, and the details at either end of the picture are identical.

Snelson and his wife, Katherine, a psychoanalyst, live in Manhattan; he commutes by bicycle to his studio several blocks away in the SoHo district. His entry in *The Encyclopaedia of World Artists* states that the artist and his wife "have two daughters, Andrea and Nicole." Shown a photocopy of the article, which he'd never seen before, Snelson was greatly amused: the artist and his wife, in fact, have one daughter, Andrea Nicole, who was attending college.

Our interview took place one evening over take-out Chinese food at a small work table in his studio. Snelson is an easy person to talk to—articulate, easygoing, a good explainer. And though he has lived in New York since the early 1950s, he has never lost the relaxed inflections of the Pacific Northwest.

Kenneth Snelson: "I had this picture in my mind of an atom that was jointless, glueless, stringless and weightless—something that was infinitely graceful."

You're best known for those towering steel cable-and-rod structures, such as the one that dominates the Inner Harbor in Baltimore. What do they mean?

I've always been very interested in the fundamental nature of structure and space. I suppose every sculptor and painter is. These pieces isolate the essence of structure. They're a dialogue between push and pull, compression and tension, which are really the only two forces in the universe.

So these pieces represent your view of how things hold together?

Well, they don't *represent* anything; they're exactly what they appear to be. All of the forces locked up in a piece like this are visible. It's exactly the pattern in which the forces reside. It should be thought of as a force diagram in space.

You also seem to play with structure in your panoramic photography. Is there a connection?

My father owned a photography shop in Pendleton, Oregon, where I grew up, and that had a lot to do with my interest in photography. But like my interest in sculpture, the panoramas come out of a voyeuristic impulse.

A voyeuristic impulse?

Yes—a desire to see in all directions at once. I would like to be able to look at my large panorama, *Jersey Shore with the World Trade Center*, for example, and see what was going on in every window in the buildings over there across the river.

Is that why you shoot most of these pictures in cities rather than, say, less densely inhabited settings, like forests?

Not really. It's because it works out better. I mean, sure, there's always the fantasy that there'll be a window you might peer through like a Peeping Tom, but that's incidental to my main reason for shooting mostly in cities, which is that the camera reveals the contradictions of geometry so much more dramatically than in a nature setting.

This business about voyeurism is interesting. I always thought of most artists as closet exhibitionists.

Art *is* exhibitionistic. You're a kid, you go down to the basement to make a model airplane, bring it upstairs, and show the parents, and they say, "Hey, look at this."

But in talking with most artists, even actors and actresses, I've noticed an ambivalence about this exhibitionism, same as in most people. You want attention, but you also know you're not supposed to want to be able to show off like that. Also, you're afraid that what you show them will be rejected.

So how is your art voyeuristic?
I think art is about discovery—and discovery can be as simple as finding out what a spoon looks like upside down, rather than right side up. It can be a child spilling water on the ground to see what will happen. Will it make a mess? Will Mommy get mad?

But on another level, discovery has to do with voyeurism. In all my art, whether it's my structures, or my photography, or my desire to visualize the atom, I am looking to discover the *essence*—to find out how something works, how it hangs together. I suspect it all has to do with some early wish to understand sexuality.

Your work is about sex?
I really think that's what art is all about—getting at the source of that ultimate secret—how things connect. To perfect that kind of connection in my structures gives me the kind of rich delight I imagine a writer takes in making beautiful sentences and in seeing the way words connect.

Yet there aren't too many artists and writers around these days who are interested in structure—or sentence structure—for its own sake.
I suppose you're right. It's probably a question of generations. I'm 65 and I grew up in a time when non-representational work was dominant—painting and sculpture that was just what it was. There was no literature or symbolism intended; there was no story content.

You're talking about the '40s?
Right. But in the last 20 years we have seen a diminishing of the importance of that kind of pursuit—only I'm still interested in it.

Does that set you apart?
Well, I'm not alone as an artist, but it is a bit out of fashion. The style nowadays runs more to art that has a literary theme or makes a political statement. The idea of doing pure abstraction, as it used to be called, doesn't seem to be high on most people's agenda these days.

I know some critics feel there is more engineering and mathematics than art to your sculptures. Is that true?
No. My work has nothing to do with math as far as I'm concerned. Actually, I have a math block that probably has been one of the formative things in my development. I think that's true of a lot of artists—they have deficiencies of one sort and they succeed by doing end runs around those deficiencies.

How did you wind up as a sculptor?
I was studying painting at the University of Oregon following the war, when I discovered that the GI Bill would pay for me to study anywhere. I was an admirer of Josef Albers's work, and he was teaching at Black Mountain College in North Carolina, so I applied there for the summer session of 1948.

There were about 10 of us in a basic design class, where Albers's practice was to give a sort of loose assignment which involved experimenting with wire, paper, or some other material. Then we'd bring in our work and place it on the floor. The pieces were unmarked, so he didn't know whose were whose. One day, early in the term, we had done some wire things, and he picked mine out and said, "Sometimes we find ourselves in the wrong place. Whoever did these is a sculptor." Suddenly, I was given a name. I'd never thought of myself as a sculptor before. I'd never planned to be a sculptor.

Why not?
For one thing, sculpture was not counted among the liberal arts. You got dirty and full of dust chopping stone; it was very blue-collar.

That's an attitude I've always associated with the Renaissance.
Correctly so. But there was a kind of carryover to my day. Painting was considered an intellectual pursuit; sculpture much

less so. In any event, my wire works in the Albers class grew out of gifts I wasn't aware of—the ability to think and work in three dimensions, and the desire to *make* things rather than simply paint *images* of things.

Actually, I think all art begins with an unquenchable need to *make* something. I've always joked I could be quite happy locked in a room forever with a pair of pliers and a thousand coat hangers and someone passing food to me under the door.

You feel that unquenchable urge is universal among artists?

Among productive artists, yes, whether it's an urge to paint something, build something, tell a story. Because otherwise, you're simply not going to spend all the time in isolation that's necessary to create.

What about when you were a child? Would you rather make things than, say, play ball with the other kids?

I don't even know that it was question of "rather." There was just a strong urge and a need . . . it was more important to make that model airplane than to go out and play baseball. Besides, baseball bored me.

Were you a loner?

Not at all. I was president of my high school class. I was bent on being popular, as every kid is. But all during that time I was consumed with this need to make things—pictures, structures, simple machines. I integrated it nicely in high school because my father owned a photography shop, so I became popular as a picture taker. There's nothing to make you popular like taking pictures of people and giving them a copy.

So the need to "make something" is at the heart of creativity? That sounds a bit circular.

Well, there's also a need to avoid boredom—or, in my case as a kid growing up in a small town in Oregon, a need not to be upstairs with the family where the bickering was going on. It came too from wanting to get approval for the time I spent alone producing something that I could carry upstairs and maybe interfere with the quarreling for a while. One way or another, the creative process, in most people, starts with some childhood need. Usually some compensatory need.

Let's come back to these giant sculptures. What actually goes into making one—from idea to finished work?

I was invited to Baltimore back in '77, to propose a sculpture for their new waterfront restoration. It was going to be the biggest piece I had ever done, and I began to consider a number of questions.

Such as?

Well, it had to be designed to fit the site, which took paths in three directions. Also, since it was going to be accessible to the public, I had to think about public safety and what the law refers to as the "attractive nuisance" factor. I mean, if you've ever seen the thing, you know you can walk right up to it—it's in the middle of things, with no protecting rail or fence. A sculpture like this could be an invitation for kids to climb and hurt themselves—so I had to consider how to raise it overhead.

What comes next? Do you draw up a plan, or sketch it out?

Not usually. I did in this case, though, because of the circumstances—the size, the setting, the human traffic. Usually I start by building a small model of aluminum and steel—what's known as a maquette. The tubular pieces are anywhere from four inches to two feet long, and I develop the piece by adjusting and adding cables and aluminum tubes to the model, just as a conventional sculptor adds clay, or a writer adds words.

When you've completed this stage, you have a replica of the structure in miniature?

Yes. From there, I make a bigger model—1/8 scale and very accurate. And on that basis, I order the materials for the final sculpture.

How much of the fabrication do you do yourself?

I use aluminum tubing for the models. I turn it on a lathe here in my studio and cut it with a slitting saw, and assemble it. As for the big structure itself—well, you're talking about one-inch-thick stainless steel parts, so that has to be fabricated in a heavy machine shop. Then I cross my fingers and hope that when we actually assemble the big piece, everything will go together as it is supposed to.

How long does this whole design process last?
Anywhere from two days to three or four months. It depends on size and complexity of the structure. I keep going back, changing and revising the model. And every one of the changes involves a lot of careful and tedious record keeping, because if you mess up on one thing—well, it's like a crossword puzzle. Every part has to relate to every other part perfectly.

How do you get the structure up?
With a lot of help, plus ladders, cranes and cherry pickers. It took 12 days to put up the piece in Baltimore—12 long, freezing days in December. I had 10 art students helping me. I try to use art students because they're so enthusiastic.

Does it go up smoothly?
Almost never. Lots of things can go wrong on site because the steps of assembly need just the right sequence. Often you don't notice a snafu until after you've gone a step too far. Then you have to back up and take things apart to get it where it should be. It's usually just a simple error—getting a number wrong, reading a part incorrectly. There have been times when I was so frustrated I never wanted to go near one of these structures again.

You make it sound quite laborious.
It *is*. But the reason I say I have the determination to do it is because I'm used to pursuing difficult tasks with a sense of delight.

You must be very patient.
I'm terribly *impatient*. I'm so impatient to get it done that I've got to keep at it. So many of the tasks involved in making art—any art—resemble piecework. They are boring and repetitive, but they're a fundamental part of the process.

Critics have recognized all sorts of shapes and images in your structures. One likened a piece to a two-headed giraffe; another saw an insect skimming on the water. Do you work with such images in mind?
No. There's no literary intent in my sculptures. A tube doesn't *represent* anything; a cable is just a cable. Of course, my saying so

358 CREATIVITY

doesn't stop people from reading things into my work, same as the ancients looked into the night sky at a bunch of stars and said, look, that's Orion, or that's Cassiopeia. Give something a name—say, "Young Girl with Wheelbarrow and Jug"—and, chances are, you can find a young girl with a wheelbarrow and jug in it.

But what about the names you give your sculptures—*Forest Devil* or *Easy Landing* or *Free Ride Home*? Don't they suggest specific, vivid images?
It's rather arid to name sculptures with numbers—or leave them untitled. But the names aren't so important. I mean, if I know what the name is, does it tell me anything about the sculpture?

So the critics are wrong?
They're often wrong. I had a show once in New York City—on the East River, at Waterside Plaza—and the *New York Times* critic was quite sour about it. But I had taken a splendid photograph of the thing and it ran with the review. Everybody said to me, "Hey, that was a nice review you got in the *Times*." Which only goes to show that people don't really read art reviews. I find the language of art criticism heavy and obscure and rarely able to convey what a work really is like. Most of the artists I know say they almost never read reviews except their own and those of their friends.

Does criticism bother you?
Sure it does—and not just the kind you see in magazines and newspapers. Some years back, I was in Mellon Square, in downtown Pittsburgh, very early one morning, to take a picture of a new sculpture that had just been installed. A woman passed by and said, "Don't you just hate it? It's visual pollution." I answered: "I made it." And she said, "Oh, God." It's kind of a funny story now, but at the time it was rather troubling.

What's a typical day like for you?
I typically get up around 6 or 6:30, and, if Katherine isn't home in the evening, I'll go on till 10 or 11 o'clock at night. Someone could say, how can that poor man put in 14-15 hours a day like that? It's not a burden. It's what I want to be doing.

Lately you've been spending most of your working time creating computer images of the atom. In fact, there was an exhibition of them at the Academy of Sciences in New York. What's the story there?

For the past 30 years, I've been trying to convince people that the atom ought to be designed better than it is. What the computer does is allow me to make almost magically clear renderings of a picture of the atom I've been carrying in my mind for years.

I saw your show at the Academy of Sciences, and what struck me was that these pictures are a far cry from the dry textbook diagrams I remember from high school and college physics. One was called Atoms at an Exhibition, and showed atoms mounted on pedestals. Another showed atoms floating through a living-room window. Were you trying to be funny?

Well, yes. The computer graphics are not simply didactic illustrations. I try to do them with some whimsy and wit.

But I assume you're serious when you say that this is what an atom would look like if it could be made visible?

Absolutely. Although, if I'd been a physicist, there isn't a chance in hell I would have come up with such an unorthodox atomic architecture.

Why not?

When atomic scientists talk about atomic models they don't mean physical replicas in the sense of a model airplane. They're talking about *mathematical* models that are non-visual stand-ins for real things. But I approach the problem as an artist, not a scientist; I'm coming into the forest from a totally different road.

Since an atom's details are truly invisible, it's considered unscientific for a physicist to picture an atom. The more I studied the scientific literature of the atom, the more I was troubled not simply by the lack of pictures but by the general insistence that pictures are out of the question. They were almost naughty!

Why do you think scientists are so doggedly non-visual with regard to the atom?

Because they're not free to picture what they can't verify through experiment and direct observation. And the very act of observing an atom changes it. Light waves short enough to make an atom visible would blast the electrons away. An electron can't be tracked in orbit the way a planet can.

How does your vision of the atom depart from the accepted one?
Early on, electrons were believed to travel around the nucleus of an atom like planets around the sun. Of course, they're not really planets, but electrical particles that shove one another away. But the unanswered question of how they circulate to build the atom's geometry presented an enormous frustration to atomic physicists.

Finally, in the late 1920s, science declared victory and simply abandoned the search. Rather than continue trying to picture the atom, they settled for a *non-visual* description built on mathematics alone. It seemed to moot forever the original question, which remains unanswered, but is no longer spoken of or very much thought about. And that is, "What does an atom look like?"

Apart from their invisibility, what is it about atoms that makes visualizing them so difficult?
Within each atom, there's a swarm of electrons racing around a nucleus. So you need to devise a proper architecture for the atom wherein the electrons can obey all the quantum rules, complicated as they are, and keep order of some kind while avoiding bombarding one another right out of the system.

The answer offered in my model is that atomic electrons completely avoid colliding with one another in their normal professional life. Instead, each electron travels in its own donut-shaped wave—a tiny ring of matter that fills up space.

Then what are those magnets you showed me?
Well, the magnets are one part of the picture. I was in a Woolworth's one day in 1960 when my eye struck a bin or refrigerator magnets—round ones, shaped like discs—and they provided the initial discovery that started me on this odd voyage. I found that these magnets could fit around a sphere to form north-south mosaics of magnetic linkages. It was this small insight—by what can only be called an artistic leap—that made me curious about their possible connection with atoms.

I maintain that the magnetic force the electron generates by its circular orbit becomes important in how an atom is built. That's where I come up against the scientific establishment—they dismiss orbital magnetism as unimportant and non-structural.

And that was it—your model of the atom was brought to life?
Oh, no. But from that moment I began my 30-year romance with the physics of the atom. That original model, built from refrigerator magnets, was a far, far cry from the atoms of my imagination. These were immaculate, gossamer structures composed only of wave-like traces. Over the next three decades, I can't tell you how many endless hours I spent trying to give my atom shape. I did pictures. I did models in welded steel, wood and plastic, models held together with glue and strings. They never were right.

What was wrong?
I had this picture in my mind of an atom that was jointless, glueless, stringless and weightless—something that was infinitely graceful. These models were *klutzy*.

What do the scientists have to say about your atomic theories?
It's a good thing they don't burn people at the stake anymore. I can talk with laymen about my ideas, but scientists simply won't listen. They are very close-minded. One guy, a crystallographer, said to me, "Well, just because it's beautiful doesn't make it right." People often ask me what I'm doing worrying about atoms—that I'm an artist, after all, and shouldn't be bothering about scientific subjects. One time a museum director explained to me, "You know, we like to keep these things separate."

How does the computer figure in all this?
In the late 1970s, a new generation of graphics computers was introduced that could create the most amazing three-dimensional forms. I wanted one desperately, but you'd have to be NASA or the Defense Department to afford one. So I waited, and over the next few years, the prices came down—at least to the level of a good-sized yacht. And the computers got better—more memory, more powerful, faster. I saw that with one of these computers

I might finally be able to give form to an object that had only existed in my imagination—give it texture, depth, illumination, movement and life.

So you bought one?

By the time it got down to less than $100,000 in 1987, I decided, at the age of 60, if I was ever going to create my fantasy worlds with this revolutionary technology, the moment was now. So I searched for the best state-of-the-art system around, and came up with a Silicon Graphics 3130 with Wavefront Technologies software, a computer created to do 3-D graphics and animation.

Did it solve the problem? Are you now able to create pictures of your atom consistent with how you imagine it to look?

I wish it were that easy. A computer like this can be frustrating. It's terribly difficult to master, you get booby-trapped at every turn and the damn thing is mercilessly, unconscionably time-devouring. But yes, I have gotten the kinds of images I had in mind.

Taking on the scientific establishment as you have—and spending so much time and energy on it—sounds risky.

I think risk is a buzzword too often heard in the art world these days. Every serious artist takes a risk all the time. I design a structure and then have to raise it up on three pedestals nine feet high, 45 and 3/8 inches apart and get it to stay there and not fall down, and yet critics say, Snelson's playing it safe again, doing the same thing he's been doing for years.

On the other hand, I once did a show I was very enthusiastic about—small, kitelike pieces made of bamboo and nylon, mounted on the wall—and gosh, but I got the bitterest reviews. The critics said the pieces were *disappointing*, coming after all these daring, soaring, difficult structures. But after having worked in such a large-scale context, doing this kind of show constituted an *enormous* risk. The same critics who had been saying how important risk is were now attacking me for it.

But what about the risk of failure? Isn't that a factor is some projects?

I don't think in terms of failure. Look at my early models of the atom—the ones that were so unsatisfactory. They did what they were supposed to do at the time. I went as far as I could with them. If I see that it's going to be impossible for me to work something out, I have no problem throwing it in the garbage and saying, "Screw it. I can't do this." Period.

But if I can find any way to do it, any damn way at all, I will do it.

❝ I think anybody who approaches their work with passion and dedication has the potential to affect people spiritually. When I see a great short-order cook with great economy of gesture and grace, I think that's taking a human endeavor to its peak. ❞

GLORIA STEINEM
Feminist and Author

Gloria Steinem once posed as a Playboy Club bunny—but only to expose the low wages and exploitation of women. She is known as a feminist but has supported the underdog in many arenas, and she has rung up many successes in the publishing world.

Steinem supported Cesar Chavez's lettuce boycotts and interviewed him for *Life*; was the founding editor of *New York* magazine in 1968; lost her editorial job at *Seventeen* when she supported Angela Davis's right to teach at UCLA; covered hearings on New York abortion legislation in '69. In '72 she was founding editor of *Ms.*, which had a sell-out preview issue. She appeared on the cover of

© Al Hirschfeld. Drawing reproduced by special arrangement with Hirschfeld's exclusive representative, The Margo Feiden Galleries Ltd. New York.

leading magazines, including *Newsweek*, and became one of the most popular spokespersons for the women's movement. In '74 she hosted a TV documentary series called *Woman Alive*, for and about women. In 1975, Steinem was the only Western journalist invited to address a meeting of Third World journalists in Mexico City; in '77 she was appointed commissioner of the National Women's Conference by Jimmy Carter; in '78 she became a Woodrow Wilson fellow at the Smithsonian Institution; and in '80 she launched the new advertising-free *Ms*.

Despite a very hectic life as journalist and lecturer, Steinem managed to write two best-selling books, *Outrageous Acts and Everyday Rebellions* in 1983, and *Marilyn: Norma Jean* in 1986. Both books dealt with a common theme—the child without a functioning mother, something Steinem shared with Monroe. Both had bright, attractive mothers who were unable to cope, withdrew from the world, and ultimately were institutionalized.

Steinem was 10 when she moved with her mother, then 46 and divorced, to Toledo. They lived alone together for seven years, spending most of their time in the house in which her mother grew up. Her mother, who had been "an energetic, fun-loving, book-loving woman" and had written for newspapers, went through a mysterious transformation. Suffering several mental breakdowns, she became an invalid and was finally institutionalized. Steinem, meanwhile, played mother to her own mother.

"I remember a long Thanksgiving weekend," Steinem wrote, "spent hanging onto her with one hand and holding my eighth-grade assignment *Tale of Two Cities* in the other." It was a nurturing role she would later play with *Ms.* and the women's movement.

Steinem was busy with final revisions of her latest and most introspective book, *Revolutions Within*, when she took time out for this interview in her upper East Side apartment.

Before her parents' divorce, Steinem spent summers at a resort owned by her father and winters traveling the country in a house trailer while her father sold antiques. One of the most important changes in her life, says Steinem, has been having a nice place to live. After a lifetime of taking care of others, she is taking care of herself.

When asked to do this interview you said, "Thank you for thinking of me as being creative." Do you not think of yourself as being creative?

Yes, but not in quite the same way as I think of painters and musicians and poets and novelists.

What's the difference?

Well, a lot of what I do is—how should I say it—it's certainly not purely a product of my imagination. Everybody takes things out of the world and puts them together in a new way. But as a journalist what you take out of the world is much more literal than what a painter takes. Being creative as a journalist is a little more like being an entrepreneur.

How so?

Because you're taking large chunks of existing reality and putting it together so it reveals the underlying concept, or certain common threads. As a feminist or anyone in a social movement, you're really trying to reveal the power relationships beneath what you're presenting. So it's a little different. But I think I'm moving more toward the introspective and internalized work—especially in my new book, which is about self-esteem.

But wouldn't you say the essays in *Outrageous Acts and Everyday Rebellions* are very personal?

The one about my mother is very personal but that's really the only one. I use my experience in the others, but they're not entirely about me. And in the essay about my mother I thought I was writing about her, which is what enabled me to write the essay. I didn't realize I was writing about myself.

The composer Philip Glass says anyone can be creative but an artist affects people on a spiritual level. Do you think what you do affects people that way?

Well, I hope so. His comment is interesting because I would have thought the difference between being an artist and being creative was discipline and time. To me an artist is someone who does what they do full-time, whereas someone who is creative can be creative in a portion of their work or home life. But I think anybody who approaches their work with passion and dedication has the potential to affect people spiritually. When I see a great short-order cook with great economy of gesture and grace, I think that's taking a human endeavor to its peak. Or when I see a great parking lot attendant, who zips in and out, I feel the same way.

He may be creative, but is he an artist?
I think so. Because otherwise artists are only of a certain economic class. And I just don't think that's true. I realize there are so-called primitive artists, untutored artists. But by confining a spiritual affect to music or to art you run the danger of confining it to people who have bought into a certain ethic. I obviously feel Philip Glass innovated, but he innovated in an intellectual way.

What do you think is the most creative part of your work? Is it your work as a journalist, a feminist or running *Ms.*?
It's all the same. I mean the only alternative to being a feminist, if you're a woman, is being a masochist. I don't divide my work up. It's all the same river or the same subject matter, but sometimes it comes in different forms.

Such as?
Thinking of solutions to problems is creative and so is thinking of how to phrase an idea so it does not just plug into old brain cells in people's minds but can be perceived as something new. I consider myself an organizer and I think organizers are artists because you're trying to make social changes by looking at the available raw materials and resources that you can put together in a new way. That's how you inspire people's imaginations and help them to change. People have to imagine change before it is possible.

Can you give an example of when you feel you've been the most effective and creative?
I have traveled a lot for the last 20 years lecturing and so on, and out of trial and error and just my own temperament, I've developed a certain style. I'm sure I need to keep working at it, but I believe that a successful lecture is when the audience doesn't need me anymore. My purpose is just an excuse to bring people together and get them talking to each other. And after about a half an hour into a discussion which follows a lecture,

when somebody on one side of this hall with 5,000 people stands up and asks a question, and somebody on the other side answers it, then I feel like I've done my job. I don't think that that is the attitude of many lecturers. They feel that they're there to give what they have to say and that's it.

But you take a step beyond that.
I hope so. The whole idea of a movement is to empower other people, not to continue an old relationship in which a predictable person has the power, including the power to speak. I always tell people when they come together, "You have all the ideas and humor and outrageousness and whatever you need right here." I invite them to turn the question-and-answer period into an organizing session.

You have a very particular way of thinking. What do you think contributed to that in your background?
I don't know, I just got born a female human being. I didn't become myself in some sense, not that I have yet, but begin to become myself until I was in my middle 30s, because there was no women's movement until then.

What does "beginning to become myself" mean?
I think understanding why I got involved with certain movements, like the civil rights movement and the farm workers. All my life I identified with whoever was having a bad time. I think for women that's very often true. We identify with every other group that's discriminated against. But we don't understand why, because we're not encouraged to take women seriously. So even though a white woman might very strongly identify with the civil rights movement it doesn't occur to her that women are a serious group and there's a reason for that emotional identification. I think that was true for me, too.

Were there people who influenced you in your life?
Not so much when I was young, except maybe Louisa May Alcott, who I think should not be underestimated, because she was a feminist and even in her children's books some of that comes through. Where else but in *Little Women* are you going to find an all-female group who like each other and discuss art, life, literature, war, and peace. But perhaps the fact that I didn't go to

school when I was little has had the greatest influence on my life. I think that I was lucky when I see what school does to children and their self-esteem and creativity.

At what age did you start going to school?
I think I started when I was 12. Until then I'd gone for some months, I'd go for September and October and then around Halloween we'd leave. I never went for a whole year.

And you say this has had the greatest influence on you?
I used to feel a little freakish that I hadn't gone to school, but the older I get the more I think it was lucky. And working on this book on self-esteem I've been reading all these surveys that show that kids' self-esteem goes down the minute they enter school, especially girls. And then in higher education their self-esteem plummets.

Why do you think that is?
Well, we're not learning about ourselves. We're getting very good grades for studying our own subservience. We're memorizing what troubles we're in, spouting it back, elaborating upon it—whether it's Aristotle or Freud or whoever. It's actually in their cases about hating women, despising them, wanting to kill women.

Then how did your education come about?
I just read haphazardly. But I had a huge vocabulary because I read all the time. You don't need much information. My math is still horrifying.

We were talking about influences in your life. I know you took care of your mother. What impact did her life have on yours?
I think I'm still figuring that out. I mean the most obvious forms of it are that I'm always very moved by old people. And any story about a mother and daughter together, *A Taste of Honey*, *Gypsy*, you name it, just gets to me immediately. But I think I identified with everybody in the world before I identified with my mother, because that was too close, and I was afraid it would happen to me too.

"It" meaning her emotional breakdown?
Yes.

But you seem to be so different and to have such a different type of life.
I have had a different kind of life, but to have the most different kind of life would have been to marry and have children and still give birth to oneself. I made a choice—not in the sense where I sat down and decided not to have children. I just did day-to-day what I wanted to do. But the 12-Step groups have a saying, "180 degrees from crazy is still crazy."

How does that relate to you?
I responded to my mother's being entrapped with a child and so on by not having a child at all. And I looked after her, so I felt I'd already been a parent in a way.

Do you have any regrets about that?
Not one. I mean I recognize the injustice of it, I recognize that women, including me, end up making choices that men don't have to make. But I don't personally regret not having a child. We ought to be able to have patterns of work and not have children if we want. And men ought to be parents, too. People forget that and I think it's absolutely key. We've spent the last 20 years demonstrating that women can do what men can do, but we haven't yet demonstrated that men can do what women can do.

One of the things that really struck me, in reading your book on Marilyn Monroe, was the similarities in your lives, especially with your mothers.
It's true, there are similarities. When I wrote the book I hadn't been struck by the similarities, I just empathized with her because she was such a victim. But when I read some of the research that I was doing, to understand her better, I recognized myself.

In what sense?
Well one of the books I read was *Your Inner Child of the Past*, which talks about the adult manifestations of childhood patterns of neglect. I was not at all introspective when I was doing the Marilyn book, but the patterns were so clear that I recognized

them in my own life as well as in Marilyn's—though my childhood was not nearly as bad as hers.

But you both did have mothers who had breakdowns and were institutionalized.
I think a lot of women and men have had crazy mothers, because we live in a culture that drives women crazy. And especially if they have been encouraged to give birth to someone instead of themselves—which is what frequently happens to mothers.

You've written about many women. And no matter how different they seem to be, whether it's Marilyn, Jackie Onassis or Linda Lovelace, you seem to be able to empathize with each one of them.
Yes, but you see even though they have led very different lives they each share an invisibility of suffering. Nobody believed Linda Lovelace—Linda Marciano—even though if they went to the movie they could see the bruises on her body. All they saw was her smiling. But it didn't occur to them that she had to smile, that she was like a political prisoner. So her suffering was invisible and I think Jackie's was, too. Because she had money and money is presumed to solve everything.

In a sense each of these women—Monroe, Lovelace and Onassis—had a story that nobody wanted to hear and you were the one who tried to set the record straight.
I think that's what draws me to those subjects.

Are there any other women whom you'd like to write about?
If I ever finish this book I'd like my next book to be about what happens to women in America's families of wealth and power. Because I think we need to look at class again. We think that women are the same class as their husbands and their fathers, which isn't really true. And as a result many women wind up getting all of the resentment directed at the men in the family and none of the power. On the contrary, they're in a situation where the power differential between the males and females at those upper levels is huge. There's more incest in rich families. I feel that their problems are invisible. And I want to write about them.

Can you talk about your new book—*Revolutions Within*?

I have to evolve a way of talking about it. I haven't yet. I started to write it because I felt that there were no books that dealt with both the internal and the external part of change. Either they were New Age books that were telling you that you could solve your problems by internal change, or they were self-help books that were telling you how to dress better or work better. Both of those are blaming the individual or at least putting the burden of change on the individual. Or they were social change books that started with the external power structure, but it seemed to me those things are all connected.

And you said you're more introspective in this book?

Yes. When I first wrote, it was over 200 pages and I realized they were the wrong pages because they were impersonal. I had lost my voice, my personal voice. So I went back and put myself in it.

Was the idea for the book yours?

Yeah, but it's changed a lot. In the beginning it was really an externalized idea. I had seen so many women who were wonderful, smart, creative, courageous women, who didn't think that they were any of those things, so I was writing the book for them. It took me awhile to realize I was writing it for myself.

What do you think you learned about yourself?

I learned that though I had thought I had built a wall between me and my childhood, I actually was repeating patterns.

What were the patterns?

A lot of them were very obvious. I don't know why I never realized it. I was a neglected child so I continued to neglect myself—it felt familiar. I didn't save any money and my apartment was full of boxes. I didn't think I was real, which is a real affect of being a neglected child. That was certainly Marilyn Monroe's case, though she had it much more. So I had to make myself real by being useful to other people. I turned the magazine and the movement—but especially the magazine—into my mother.

How?

Because it was constant caretaking. It was so hard to keep going economically and I was always begging for money, begging for ads, begging for contributions. It was like an invalid. I had plenty of readers so it wasn't an invalid in that sense. But in an economic sense it was an invalid.

Once you realized that, what did you do or not do?
I slowly started to change. It takes a long time. You don't change in a minute. I think on the one hand I always really liked being alone. I need to be alone some of the time. Nonetheless I still felt that when I was alone, I wasn't as real as the world outside. I finally realized that we create the world from inside. So staying home and writing becomes that. It's like practically everything in life, if you haven't experienced it it doesn't make sense; and once you've experienced it you don't need to hear about it.

If you were to start *Ms.* now, how would you not make it your mother?
I don't know, because the only way to not have made it my mother would have been to let it fold and I don't think I could have done that. I'm glad I didn't do that actually. The practical answer to some extent is that we perhaps should have started it without advertising in the first place. But I'm not sure that's true, actually, because we changed a lot of advertising practice by having to be in the world of advertising. And I am not sure that we would ever have been taken seriously as a magazine if we had started out in that way. I think some of it just has to do with taking control instead of reacting. Because I was always reacting.

And you don't feel like you are now?
Not as much.

How do you feel you've changed with time—as a person, writer, journalist?
I think I've become more myself. I always used to try to ask myself the question, "Can somebody else do this?" If somebody else can do this I shouldn't do it. But actually I think I did end up doing things that other people could have done or perhaps done better, because I was so vulnerable to supplying solutions,

to helping people, that I would get caught up in some particular situation. So I very rarely asked myself the revolutionary question, "What do I want to do?" I ask it somewhat more often now.

What do you want to do?
Write. For a long time I was running around doing movement stuff, which was important, but it wasn't writing, it wasn't personal. I think if you follow what you're excited about and interested in, it's a good test of what your internal self wants to do.

The times are very different now. They're much more conservative. How has this affected your writing and your other work?
Actually I don't think it's conservative. I mean we've had two asshole presidents—really almost fascist presidents—but only 30 percent of the country elected them. When I travel around, whether it's lecturing or the magazine, the response is huge and it's much more than it ever was. You can't go to a town where there aren't battered women's shelters and a rape crisis center. It's all there, it's just that we get conned by the media into thinking that the guy in the White House represents us. And of course leadership matters, so Bush has made it okay to be racist again, to be anti-Semitic. People come out of the woodwork who believe that. But there is still a critical mass of people, perhaps the majority of people, who don't believe in his politics.

When you started lecturing what was the response from people?
Ridicule, mostly.

From women and men?
No, no. Well, from some women, but there was always a huge difference in response. In the beginning, when I wrote what was in retrospect my first feminist or overtly feminist article, even the nice people I worked with—Tom Wolfe and Jimmy Breslin and Clay Felker—all took me aside and said, "You've worked so hard to be taken seriously, you mustn't get involved with these crazy women." That made me realize that they didn't know who I was. I was like a mascot.

How did you deal with that kind of ridicule?

Well, there's one thing that's worse than ridicule and that's invisibility. So you just keep going. It may make you angry, it may make you feel humiliated, but there's no point in not continuing, because the alternative is worse.

Invisible was the word you used before to describe the women you wrote about.
I identify with that. Women are invisible or visible in ways that we are allowed to be visible.

Helen Gurley Brown says her idols are Beverly Sills and you. Does that surprise you at all?
It surprises me a little bit, because a lot of things that Helen wants, I don't have—I don't have a rich husband, I don't have mink coats. But I think that that's the insecure part of Helen who wants those things. You know there's a different part of Helen, too.

What do you think are your strengths and your weaknesses?
One thing that's clear is I'm an idea person. I love to think about ideas and concepts. I am not an administrator. I can inspire people, but I can't run a meeting as a chair kind of person. I'm not a long-term planner, I'm spontaneous and so on. I always underestimate how long it takes me to do something. Witness this book.

Also, I suppose that your strength and your weakness are often the same. I mean my strength is my ability to empathize and my weakness is that I so empathize that I don't know what I'm feeling, which is a very female trait. We're empathy sick. We know what other people are feeling better than we know what we are feeling. And as a journalist it's very important to know what I'm feeling. Because if something happens in the present that I find very depressing—because it reminds me of something in the past—I might respond inappropriately, to put it mildly.

Have you been in therapy? You talk as if you have been and yet you're clearly against Freud.
Sending a woman to a Freudian is like sending a Jew to a Nazi. I wouldn't dream of it. Fortunately there are a lot of therapists who are not Freudian anymore. As of about three years ago or so, I did start to see a nice older woman who's just a nice wise

person. I can talk to her and I think that's been helpful.

How has that affected your life?
I just came to the end of my ability to continue my life as it was because I was destroying everything—my life, my time, my health. And I just couldn't continue that way. And since I'm such a functionary, you know if there was an Olympic team for functioning, I would be on it. I had to get to the point where it was almost impossible in order to change.

What do you feel you need to be creative?
Most of all I need a lack of conflict. I hate conflict. And I hate it when there's fighting or disapproval. Some people thrive on it. I think more men than women thrive on it, but I'm sure some women do, too.

But wasn't the women's movement nothing but conflict?
Yes, but I didn't choose it on purpose, and I took a long time getting there, too.

Has any of your writing had a major affect on your life?
This book has affected me a lot. It's been working on me and I've been working on it. And I have no idea whether it works or not. But it's helped me a lot in terms of my inner journey.

Is there a piece of your writing that you favor?
I think that the piece about my mother is interesting to me, because even the things that when I wrote it I didn't believe turned out to be true.

Like what?
For instance, I say that I'll spend the rest of my life figuring out what her life and mine meant. When I wrote that I felt completely duplicitous. I thought I should say that but I actually knew completely that it was not a real statement. But it turned out to be true. So much so that by a couple of years after I'd written that essay I couldn't read it. It was too sad. But I wrote it. I think that happens a lot. You write something sometimes because it's your unconscious speaking. And sometimes it's the reverse, it's something you know intellectually, but it hasn't made the journey from your head to your heart yet. But fre-

quently you say or write or do things you don't understand until later.

What effect did this piece about your mother have on you?
It helped me to understand myself. There's a chapter called "Bodies of Knowledge" in this book. When I wrote it the first time I wrote it externally, as a reporting job. And everybody who read it said I had to write it more personally. So in the course of writing it more personally, I discovered things about myself. I discovered, for instance, that our body image is completely different from our real bodies. And the body image has a life of its own, so that most women who are underweight medically think they are overweight. Men are the reverse. But the separate life of this body image helped to explain a lot of things to myself because I grew up in a family that was vastly overweight. My father and my sister both spent most of their lives weighing over 300 pounds, so I have a very different body image than people have of me.

What is your image?
I see myself as a sort of fat kid from Toledo. Others see me as a skinny blonde from New York.

That was one of the things that came up when you were working on the book?
And aging, too. I began to realize as I wrote this body chapter that women have so few models of aging that are active. And I realized that it wasn't so much death that I was worried about, it was aging. I didn't know how to get from 50 to 80.

Do you know now?
I think at least now I'm interested. Before it seemed like dropping off a cliff because everything that I knew was the plateau of life, the middle of life, where I'd been since I was 13 and pretending to be 18. So from 13 to 50-something I was the same person, I was just an adult. Especially if you don't have children, you miss the measure of time. And now I've gotten really interested in the fact that there is a country called aging that comes after this mid-life plateau, that is potentially much more interesting, and much more free. You know you get rid of a lot of bag-

gage and a lot of hangups and so on. So I'm really interested in this new country.

The last question is, any regrets or any feelings of self-doubt?

Oh yes, all the time. As far as regrets go, I think I've wasted an enormous amount of time doing over again what I already knew how to do. I profoundly resent that I spent 17 years selling advertising. I don't know if I could have done it differently, but I resent every one of those lunches and every presentation at an ad agency, and every one of those trips to Detroit and Los Angeles and Chicago. You got yourself up for it, but it was a waste in many ways. I've often done over stuff that I already knew how to do. And as far as self-doubt goes, I'm certainly in the middle of that right now. I have no idea whether this book makes any sense, whether anyone will like it. It seems so obvious to me I can't believe anyone will be interested in it.

Do you have people who are close to you whom you show your work to?

Yes, and it helps. But it's nobody's responsibility but mine in the sense of, here are all these disparate pieces lying around the landscape that are now put into one. I don't know if they work together or not.

That's interesting because many people in this book do not have those kinds of doubts.

Does Philip Glass have any? I would guess that he didn't because he has this incredible ability to say, "You hate my music? Let me play it for you again."

You're right. But there are also women who do not doubt themselves.

Anything else you wanted to say about changes?

Yes. I think one of the most important changes in my life was having a nice place to live, which I never had until about three years ago. I never had a place that made me happy to come home to.

That's part of taking care of yourself?

Right. Also I just wanted to come back to where we started. I think that creativity is perceived as being a luxury, and that troubles me. The couple who decorate their diner in a wonderful way are being creative. I mean creativity is part of everybody's lives, and in fact if we were living the way humans lived for 99 percent of the life of humankind, we would be singing songs while we worked to keep the rhythm of the work, weaving textiles to have something to wear, making images on our huts. Creativity is a part of everything we do. It should be. But it's become separate, it's become a luxury and that's a mistake. We all need to sing, we all need to make images, we all need to dance, we all need to use all of our senses.

❝ I'm always in an advisory role. I did it at NBC, too, even when I was in charge. One vote in the room—that's the way it should be. I'm always amazed at people who get famous for being overbearing and oversupervisorial. ❞

GRANT TINKER
Independent TV Producer

He believes that the writers, actors and directors have been the sole creative force behind the enduring string of hit television shows bearing his executive stamp. Grant Tinker's honesty is commendable, and his credentials lend weight to any opinion offered. But the list of quality shows emerging from his shop simply is too long to be a coincidence of creativity.

Mary Tyler Moore, Phyllis, Rhoda, Lou Grant, Remington Steele and *White Shadow* all were produced by MTM Productions, a company Tinker co-founded with Mary Tyler Moore, then his wife, in 1970. In just five years, MTM became the leading independent producer, with six weekly series.

After 11 years with MTM, Tinker became chairman of the board at NBC. During his five-year stay, the profits increased tenfold while producing such classics as *The Cosby Show, Golden Girls, Family Ties, Cheers, Hill Street Blues* and *St. Elsewhere*.

No one else has been directly associated with so much solid gold TV.

Now in his 60s, Tinker remains in independent production with his GTG Entertainment. It was in an interview at his palatial GTG office at Culver Studios that he resolutely refused to take credit for the quality of his portfolio.

Others have a different view. In September 1982, the National Conference of Christians and Jews awarded Tinker its annual Humanitarian Award for inspiring "the best creative work from the best creative people, for setting and maintaining the highest standards of quality and professionalism in broadcasting."

In 1986 Tinker won the International Radio and Television Society's Gold Medal, as well as the Distinguished Service Award from the National Association of Broadcasters.

And in September 1987 he received the Governors Award for outstanding achievement, the highest honor granted by the Academy of Television Arts and Sciences.

When asked to do this interview, the first thing you said was: "I'm not creative."
Well, that was the truth.

But anyone who has watched your shows...
But those aren't my shows. That's my point. Maybe I'm creative in the way I recruit some people, or the way I get involved or become associated with those people.

In most of the articles written about you the words that come up over and over again are "quality and creativity." An NBC affiliate said you're "a creative genius who belongs in the creative area."
Whoever said that was very nice, but I think he means I should be doing this as opposed to working in Pittsburgh in a steel company or whatever. I hope that's right. I mean, I enjoy it. I think if I have any claims to fame, and I don't want to sound glib, it's that I have a good eye or ear for people who are creative. I don't mean that I can discover them, but I know when I see them and I'm so respectful to the point of idolatry when it comes to dealing with them. People like to be admired and respected and treated properly, and because I so admire what they do—I'm talking about the good, best creative people—maybe they like to work with me as opposed to working with somebody who beats them with a club.

What you're describing takes a lot of skill. It's not a little thing.
It's about as little as you can get in our business.

What is it that you're looking for when you spot talent?

Cast photo from *Hill Street Blues*. "I was involved with—but I'd never take credit for—assembling that very good cast," Grant Tinker said.

I don't know. Quality is such a slippery word. But I would say sometimes you can actually sit with someone and hear something special in their plans, and you take on faith or instinct whether they can execute what they're telling you. Sometimes it gets all the way to film or tape; and the further along something is, the easier it is to make a judgment.

So there is nothing specific that you're looking for?

No. I don't look for something so much as react to material viscerally. I'm not infallible, by the way. I've reacted favorably to some not-so-hot stuff, or some stuff that didn't work. But when I was at NBC the third time back in the '80s, we managed to turn the place around and get it going again because people thought our judgment was good, that we shouldn't just turn to research or Nielsen numbers for our road map. That was the rule we lived by. We felt *Cheers* was a good show, even though it just lay there for the first year. It was literally at the bottom of the Nielsen heap at the end of the first year.

How hard was it to back a show with such low ratings?

Very hard. It's easy looking back, but at the time you get a lot of pressure from everybody—including the sales department, which says: "I can't sell that, that Nielsen number is so low no one wants to buy it," or, "The demographics are no good." I think that's the fun of the business. It's also the danger of the business. It's a perilous way to live, but when it works, when you do stay with *Cheers* and it succeeds, you get not only the good numbers and the advertisement dollars, but you get credit for having stayed with it and having good judgment. And that's when you have it all in our business.

What about the shows you believed in that didn't last?

I guess my batting average has been OK. But at MTM, where I was most directly involved, as opposed to NBC, where you're sort of a step removed, we had our share of busted pilots and scripts. *Doc*, with Bernard Hughes, and *Phyllis*, with Cloris Leachman, lasted only a year or two and just never really made it. So we had our moments that weren't so lustrous. But right or wrong, you do it faithfully in terms of your own instincts and judgment. You hope that those are good enough together to be right more often than you're wrong.

You have to admit that your shows were some of the most special shows on TV.

That goes back to those creative associations you make. When you get into business with people like Alan Burns and Jim Brooks and Hugh Wilson and Gary Goldberg and Bruce Paltrow and Steven Bochco—it was their work that you're talking about. The proof is that as we all got separated they continued to do good work. They didn't need me to help them do it. So it was my good fortune to be associated with a lot of those people. And I don't want to sound inordinately modest about it, but I have a lot to be modest about when you ask me that question.

But what did you give to them?

Confidence, faith and support. Sometimes the most creative people are the least confident, or they worry and they're anxious about whether it could have been better. They're constantly asking themselves questions. I not only gave them a lot of one-on-one support—I don't mean gave it to them cause I'm such a good guy, I mean I responded to the work they did—but also got sort of justly famous for protecting them from those evil ogres at the networks. I was very good at facing down network bullies—those people who really wanted to tell the talent how to produce their shows, or write, direct, or act in them.

How were you able to face them down?

I had been at NBC twice before, before MTM, and in the second case, in the '60s, I was in charge of programs at NBC. So I'd been on that side, and I knew that you really aren't driving the car. You like to think you are. And it's fine later if you tell people, "Yeah, I invented all those shows on NBC." But I knew it was bullshit and therefore when I got to MTM I figured I had both the credentials and the smarts to tell the network people, when they needed it, to stick it!

Which I assume is quite difficult to do.

It is, because they take it quite hard sometimes. But actually it was sort of fun. I figured that was part of my job. I won't say fun, but it was a challenge. And the tougher the network guy was, and the harder he was to knock down and keep him out of the hair of the creative people, the more satisfying the result.

Can you think of an example?

Lou Grant is a case I can recall very well. We took Ed Asner's character and spun him off into his own show. There was a metamorphosis from this drunk who ran the station in Minneapolis to that more responsible guy doing the newspaper in L.A. This was again the work of Jim Brooks and Alan Burns and Gene Reynolds and so on. When we did that, CBS kind of stared at it.

Why?

They were used to the Lou Grant with the Mary show, which had been wildly successful by that time and very well praised and properly so. And so when we showed CBS the pilot for Lou Grant's own show, they were a little bemused by it.

Can you talk more about the Lou Grant character's metamorphosis?

The role that Ed played in his own show was vicarious. It was removed. One of the problems that we had when we gave him his own show was that we couldn't get our protagonist out onto the street because that wasn't his function as the editor. He was supposed to be back at the office, which made that a hard show to execute.

How did the audience respond?

Like most new shows, it went on the air and it didn't immediately get any audience response. So about halfway through that first season they asked me if I'd bring the writers over. Jim, Allen, Gene and I went over and I can recall it as if it was yesterday. We were sitting in a room with these network guys who had a lot of disclaimers. And suddenly they were telling us that what we were doing wasn't good enough. They got a head of steam up and started to launch into the changes they wanted to make. My creative colleagues were sitting there patiently.

What did you do?

I said, "Guys, forget it. If you don't like what we're doing, which is what we're gonna go on doing, cancel it. We'll go home. Or maybe we'll take it someplace else. There's no law that says you have to keep it on the air. But if you want this show, this is the show you're going to get." And it worked. They all backed down. They probably stuck pins in our dolls when we left. But you can do that, particularly if they respect the creative people. The network executives who have failed are the ones who don't respect the creative people, who really do sort of put themselves in the place of the producer.

Do you have a favorite in terms of any of the shows you produced?
Well, we made 168 of Mary's show. They were awfully good and the characters grew and the actors got better. One reason I liked it best is because of its consistency. We started with Jim and Alan and added Weinberger and Daniels and David Lloyd and Bob Ellison. The same creative people who were with it at the beginning stayed right through to the end of the seventh year, when we stopped doing it voluntarily because we thought that was enough. I'd be hard pressed to put any show ahead of that one as a very satisfying experience. And then there was *St. Elsewhere* and *Lou Grant* and the first Newhart show that we did, about the psychiatrist, and that was a much funnier show than people gave it credit for. It lived in the shadow of Mary's show and as a result wasn't as noticed as it should have been, but it was a good show.

What about *Hill Street Blues*?
We started that while I was still at MTM.

What do you think contributed to that?
I can only tell you one thing—it might have been encouraging Steven Bochco, who was then with us. We had a couple of false starts and we recruited him from Universal. He and a guy named Michael Kozell created *Hill Street*. Fred Silverman was at NBC and we did it for them. The pilot was a knockout.
My contribution was that I suggested a guy named Bob Butler to direct it. Bob brought to that very good script a style which has since been imitated. But that style was not well known or seen before that time. This was 1980. And I was involved with—but I'd never take credit for—assembling that very good cast. It just was one of those great experiences. And then to have that pilot turn out as well as it did! It really knocked people over when they saw it.

What attracts you to this business?

There's something about the whole process that is interesting and frequently exciting when it goes well. It's very seldom that I sit in on, or even observe, a creative meeting that I don't get caught up in the process.

Have you been involved a lot in that end—sitting in with the writers?

Yeah, but I do not want to be confused with anyone performing those disciplines that go into making the end result. I'm always in an advisory role. I did it at NBC, too, even when I was in charge. One vote in the room—that's the way it should be. I'm always amazed at people who get famous for being overbearing and over-supervisorial.

Can you talk about the differences between MTM and NBC?

I've always been in television, and you really sit on one side or the other. You're either devising it and selling it, or you're judging it and buying it. The two are 180 degrees apart in one sense, but they're very much the same. You're just performing a different function. I can remember, in 1969, when I left NBC the second time and I went to Universal. I was almost immediately back in my old office selling to my own successor, or trying to, and thinking, "I could literally be on the other side of the desk." It was a funny feeling, but it took me about 20 minutes to get used to it. It's not that different.

Do you prefer one to the other?

No, I shouldn't say that. I love being a fly on the wall, or maybe a little closer to the creative process. I love to mix it up, mingle, schmooze with creative people, particularly the good ones—and that's the programming end. At the same time, since I started way back when with NBC, I think of myself as a broadcaster, too. I like that end of it—the buy and deliver end of it. Buy a program and get it out to the 200 stations and all of the mechanics that go with that. In a way, those are two different businesses and I'd be hard-pressed to choose between them. Today, I wouldn't be hard-pressed to choose, because they're both gone in many ways.

You once said *Lou Grant* wouldn't be done today.
I meant that the economics are now working against this business. It used to be—as the medium grew along with the audience, and there were only three networks dividing it all up—it was a good business for everybody. The networks, the suppliers, the program people and so on. Now it's not as good a business for the networks. Too much of their audience is fragmented away, and the advertiser won't pay any more because the universe isn't growing. So it comes back to this community where we fail as usual to control the costs, which continually go up.

It's a crazy time right now.
It's more than crazy. For me it's sort of sad. I'm old enough so that I don't have to do it anymore, but I fondly remember the old days. I just had lunch a few minutes ago with Bruce Paltrow, who just happens to be up the street at what used to be MGM. We were talking about the good old days, which used to seem hard at the time—fun, but hard—but God knows were simpler. And there was some gold at the end of the rainbow, if all went well.

And you don't feel there is now?
There isn't. The odds now are so bad. From the time you have the idea and carry it all the way through to on-air and possible success, it's so unlikely that you'll ever break even, that you might as well take the money to Las Vegas and put it on a number.

How do you think you've changed?
I've gotten a lot older and fatter. Right now because of this phaseout of the business I used to be in, and actually got sort of good at after a while, this might not be the right time to say this. But if you'd asked me that in the '80s when I was at NBC or in the '70s when I was at MTM doing those two different jobs, I probably would have told you rather immodestly that I had changed and I had gotten damn good at either of those jobs. When I left MTM to go back to NBC, I remember thinking that we really got it up to speed. And there was a lot of satisfaction in that.

Can you talk about what you did?

Actually my MO is pretty much the same in either case, and that is, let somebody else do it. In the case of the creative people and the programming as I've been saying, it's to go get Brooks and Burns or Goldberg, and then support them in whatever way I can. But in effect watch them do it, delegate it. And similarly at NBC, I just had a lot of great people around. I tried to get them going in the same direction.

Can you talk about the genesis of a show like Mary's?
Mary, because of work she'd done on the special with Dick Van Dyke, was asked by CBS to do a series. And I took that opportunity to leave Fox to start a little company to make that series. I went to Burns and Brooks and I said, "Would you guys work together?" That was a pretty good little stroke of genius. Well, it was smart because they were both very good, so I figured together they'd be twice as good. And they were. And from that point on all I did was say to Mary, "Go to work." Jim and Alan did the rest. I did suggest Ed Asner to them. I said, "Read Ed Asner for the part of Lou Grant," because Ed had never done that kind of work. So that was a small contribution.

The way you describe your job makes it sound pretty easy, and you know it's not an easy job.
It is easy. I don't mean easy. I stay as long at the office as anybody else. But again, I'm not doing the things they do. I move papers and people around, make phone calls to the network, or ask somebody at the network to come see me. It's like being a foreman or some kind of boss. But I think a good boss is a good delegator, which is another way of saying he's too lazy to do it himself. Other people can do it better, and that's true with me. Anybody could do what I do.

Do you really think that?
Well, not anybody maybe; but many people. Some have done it better.

Can you talk about your work with the different actors— such as Mary? Was it hard working with her?
At the time, no. She was great because she set such a good tone by her professional example, to say nothing of her talent. And that show was such a labor of love for everybody. I think it

would be a little harder working with her now.

Very seldom did we have a group of lemons or even one lemon in a group. Most of the people were fun to work with. One of the conditions for me was talent. The more talented the person, the more you would accommodate any eccentricities or weirdness on the part of the person, because you just figure he or she has the right to be a little difficult because that's the quid pro quo, that's the trade-off.

Were there people who were particularly difficult?
One or two, but somehow either they reformed and got nice, or they went away. Life is too short. Sometimes you have to take a hard position, when a bad apple does emerge somehow, or is identified, or when an agent comes in and gets inordinately greedy. One of the positive things that happened was that the work we did with Jim and Alan and the others that followed was so good it acted as a magnet for other creative people. If you wanted to go to work as a writer and become a producer in the '70s, you probably would have selected MTM because such good work was being done by so many people who you knew would be not only fun to work with, but you'd learn from.

Did you know Brooks before?
I had met him at Fox. He was doing a show he'd created called *Room 222*.

And what about him appealed to you?
His talent. He was considerably younger at the time, but he was just such a talented guy. The same thing was true of Alan, whom I met also when I was at Fox under a different situation. Sometimes you're wrong and you meet people who talk very well but it's what they call in a baseball game a "two o'clock hitter"—a guy who can really hit in batting practice but when the game starts he's not very good. So I've made my share of mistakes that way, but certainly not with those two guys.

Who do you think the most important creative people are in making a show?
In television, I think the writers. They're also often the executive producers and have a great deal to say about the casting of their shows.

Can you talk about how a show is put together?

It's mostly about the writing. Somebody may have a certain actor in mind or under contract and a part might be specifically written for that actor. But usually you have a concept which you try to get down on paper in some way that sounds or looks like a show. And then you think about which character should speak which words. And another thing that's really important is when you can put together a family of people—the actors, writer and director—and they're all humble and rolling in the same direction. It doesn't work, but when it does it's a great process to watch.

You named a favorite show. Did you also have a favorite episode?

To give you an obvious and not very interesting answer, take Mary's first show, which Alan and Jim wrote. It was a kind of presentation which was half prose—you know, literally, "Mary Richards comes from Roseburg, Minnesota, and so on." At the time she was supposed to be divorced, but CBS didn't want that. So we changed it to having her come off a failed affair. Somehow they found that more acceptable.

And then they would put some of it in dramatic form, like a scene in Lou Grant's office where Mary goes in for the job interview, which is played endlessly on TV. He says, "You've got spunk." She says, "Thank you." And he says, "I hate spunk." The words from that show never changed from the way they were originally written. The *Hill Street* pilot was another one which was able to visualize the written script.

Were major changes ever made from a pilot to a series?

In *Hill Street* we had to revive Hill [Mike Warren] and Renko [Charlie Haid]. They were shot and killed in the pilot in such a shocking way that you didn't have to have the research to know that the audience just fell on the floor and hated that. So mysteriously, they recovered, and it turns out they had only been wounded and were back at work when we started the series. That was an awfully good pilot.

Were there any pilots you liked that never made it to series?

We made a wonderful pilot in the second year of *Mary*, before we started *Newhart* even. It was called *Bachelor at Law*, with John

Ritter, who was then not very well known. It was about an idealistic young kid just out of law school who went to work for Harold Gould, this corner-cutting lawyer in a one-man firm. And it was the play of this idealistic kid against this old guy who did his thing another way. It was funny. Ed. Weinberger and Stan Daniels wrote it. Jay Sandrich directed it. But because CBS was so fat then, and had such a wealth of material, it didn't get on, and that was actually one of my favorite pilots.

What about it appealed to you?
Its execution. That it was funny. And John was so winning. He'd done a couple of little walk-on things in Mary's show. That's how we knew him. The show was good and it should have gone on. In fact, the show that they put on in its place failed in 13 weeks. So it was CBS's loss.

It seems that one of the main things that your shows have in common is that they're character-driven.
I like that. But I don't invent those characters. I respond to them. Like I said, not all the shows I respond to work. We had one show last year called *WIOU*, which was about a TV station. I have my own reasons about what went wrong—like the way CBS scheduled it and how they too frequently pre-empted it.

Wasn't Mariette Hartley in that?
Yes. And a bunch of other brilliant actors. I loved that show. It had good material with characters I got interested in and actors who brought them to life. If you had to think why about it creatively didn't work, it could have been the franchise was a little harder to sell. It wasn't life or death, it wasn't a cop house or a hospital, where an audience immediately understands the situation.

***Hunter* was another character-driven piece.**
Yeah. I remember when I first saw *Hunter* with Fred Dryer at NBC. It wasn't great literature. It was just a cop show, almost a violent simplistic cop show. I thought, "I like that, too." I like the simplicity of the guy. I get interested whenever there are characters that are well-drawn.

What specific type of characters interest you?

Very good villains are interesting. Funny people interest me. People who can do comedy well and also look good, like Mary, would be a great example. It's very rare that you can find an attractive woman, or man for that matter, who can do comedy well. I think the right answer is the most general answer, which is if they do it well, that's what I like.

Do you have any regrets?
Probably too many. None that I can think of that aren't so sort of personal that no one else would care about them. There are obvious regrets like that pilot I mentioned that should have gotten on. And failed shows, like *WIOU*. Those are always regrets because the same amount of effort goes into them, maybe more in some ways, than into shows that succeed. It's like your children. You care as much about the ugly ones or the not-so-successful ones as the ones that do succeed.

I regret what's happened to the business. That television has sort of been born and flourished and sort of died in 40 years—it seems awfully quick. Not that it won't go on, and maybe it's great to have 150 channels in your home. But I regret all of that.

Would you do anything differently now?
You mean if I had to go back and do it over again? Geez, I hope I would. I would have learned nothing if I wouldn't. But yeah, I'd do a lot of things differently. This might open a Pandora's box. But if I had it to do over again, I wouldn't go back to NBC in '81. That has to do with so many things—like why did I go back to help restore it so GE could just gobble it up, and things I couldn't foresee. Only with hindsight can I say I would do things differently. In terms of what I was thinking and how I felt when I did them, I guess not really.

Are there creative areas that you wanted to go into that you didn't?
I don't think so. I've never had any feelings about movies. I don't know why. There are some shows—other people's shows—that I admire, that I would love to have been involved in just because they were so well done. But we had a lot of those, too. On a batting average basis, MTM probably had as good an average as anybody ever had, and better than most. And certain-

ly in terms of the creative people with whom I associated there, you couldn't beat them.

Is there anything you want to say that I haven't asked you about?
In an interview, you know everybody likes not to come off like an idiot. And I don't like the first-person pronoun too much either. Singular, that is. Nobody likes to see that. Very frequently in interviews when we're just talking in colloquialisms it really reads kind of dumb and self-absorbed and I shrink from that, so I'm looking to you to protect me.

How so?
Just don't make me sound self-absorbed. Some of the other people you're talking to, like E.G. Marshall and Frank Pierson, have more reason to be self-absorbed. All I want is for you to make me sound like—just another guy, OK?

Jimmy Webb: "Writing is at the center of vulnerability. You want to make your mistakes in private..."

> Every time I sit down to write a song, I'm nauseous with the thought that I'm not going to be able to do it this time. I'm in an absolute state of panic.

JIMMY WEBB
Composer

Born in Oklahoma in 1946, the son of a Baptist minister, Jimmy Webb has composed some of the best-known songs in the pop repertoire—including "MacArthur Park," "Up, Up and Away," "Wichita Lineman" and "By the Time I Get to Phoenix." Art Garfunkel, Barbra Streisand, Liza Minelli, Glen Campbell, Lena Horne, Dionne Warwick, Frank Sinatra, Harry Belfonte, Linda Ronstadt, Judy Collins, Joan Baez and Joe Cocker are among the diverse roster of artists who have recorded Jimmy Webb's work.

We expected to meet in the office studio in Manhattan where Webb has worked for years, first with the late Michael Bennett and now alone. Instead, he asked to meet at a favorite hangout—the Old Towne Inn on East 18th Street.

When we inquired after Webb in the dimly lit tavern, everyone there knew him. We sat at a small table not far from the bar. The constant din of diners, drinkers and jukebox music might have been distracting, except that Webb is at his best in this kind of environment.

After the interview, still curious about Webb's office in an ancient cast-iron building with only a single tiny elevator, we arranged to stop by a few days later while Webb was absent. One wall was filled with pictures of Jimmy's family and friends, including Campbell, John Denver and Garfunkel, and two of Ronstadt's cows. There were also a dozen or so photos of James Dean, and a poster in which the actor's eyes, nose and mouth were revealed, on closer inspection, to be various vintage cars.

Another wall, facing the piano, reflected an entirely different mood, with framed pages of Henry Miller's writing.

One of the songs Webb had talked about was "If These Walls Could Speak." In their own way, these walls did.

Where—and how—do you work?

Well, I used to think I had to be in some exotic location to feel inspired, so I'd take my electric piano to Hawaii. Then I would find out that all of my songs were about the ocean and seagulls. They were getting very metaphysical and cosmic, and I realized I wasn't really doing the work. It wasn't pure because I was bribing myself. So I came back to New York and decided to follow Randy Newman's example.

What was that?

He had rented an office in L.A., and, like any other job, he went there every day and wrote. I did the same and what I found is that you can bring whatever inspiration you need into the place where you're working, and anything else is a cop-out. If you have to be in Hawaii or on the QEII to write songs, you're in trouble.

So now you work in an office with regular hours?

Actually, I work from 11 to 8, and usually two or three of those hours are really good. For the past seven years I've had the office at 890 Broadway, where Michael Bennett had his studios. It's sort of a Tin Pan Alley kind of place—three or four pianos going at once and a constant din of shows rehearsing.

Is that distracting?

No, it's very, very exciting—the energy, the sound of it.

You worked with Michael Bennett for several years, didn't you?

I did, and he had a tremendous influence on me. He was really the most creative person I've ever known, and he opened up the second half of my life by showing me how to work with other people.

The second half of your life?
Yes. Before I met him, I was entirely alone with my work, unwilling to share it or to listen to anyone. I was really very arrogant—a stubborn, unpleasant, suffering artist. You know the type. But when I met Michael, he said, "Your talent is never in question in this room," and by doing that, he created a free zone—a space where we could work together without ego or self-consciousness. Knowing I had his confidence set me free to collaborate. I learned so much from him—about collaboration and how to work on *story*, which is something I'd instinctively done with songs like, "By the Time I Get to Phoenix." I realized that I didn't have to confine myself to thinking only about music and lyrics.

Did he ever ask you to do something you felt you couldn't do?
He once wanted me to write a 15-minute ballet, which I was really nervous about. But then I remember him saying, "Every time I sit down to organize a musical and I look at the blank paper, I go into abject terror and panic. I am absolutely convinced I've lost every smidgen of ability and that I'm not going to be able to do it." And he said, "It's real panic and real terror, and real gut-churning nausea, and I'm not saying this for effect. I just want you to know that's what I go through."

Do you have similar feelings?
Every time I sit down to write a song, I'm nauseous with the thought that I'm not going to be able to do it this time. I'm in an absolute state of panic.

How do you get through it?
With determination. And also with the knowledge that you have a good idea. Otherwise, where would you get the strength to take the first step? It's never easy. The first few hours are like tipping a big rock over a fulcrum. Unfortunately a lot of people have an idea but they stop right there. They don't realize the first part is *supposed* to be incredibly difficult.

Does it get easier?
Sure. As the weight begins to shift over the fulcrum and you suddenly get going downhill, there's a great exhilaration. It real-

ly has taken on some kind of momentum and it's going to finish itself. With just a little help from me it's all going to fall into place.

You once said that a song has a life of its own.
Yes, it's God—by one of his many names.

And in order to be creative you have to give yourself over to that?
It's absolutely essential. You start with the idea and then you go through the process of writing it. That's what human beings can do. But when it starts writing itself, some other power is taking over. I would be surprised if most artists don't feel some version of what I'm talking about.

Can you give me an example?
I wrote a song called, "If These Walls Could Speak." It's about an old house we live in that's 150 years old. It started out with someone casually saying, "If this house could talk it would have some stories to tell." And then I remembered my parents and grandparents used to say, "If these walls could speak..." So I started thinking about what if they could speak. And that made me think a lot about family, about children, about people living in a house.

So the song says, "If these walls could speak, of things that they remember well, of parties and people raising hell, a couple in love, living week to week, rooms full of laughter." And then later in the song, after these people have had children, it goes, "If these walls could speak, what a tale they'd have to tell, of sun going down and dinner bell, of children playing at hide and seek, from floor to rafter." Then I thought, "But what am I trying to say?" So I wrote the chorus, which goes, "If they could speak, they'd tell you about these things. They would tell you that I'm sorry for being cold and blind and weak. They would tell you that it's only that I have a stubborn streak. If these walls could speak..."

So it starts out being about one thing...
And when the last line comes, the song suddenly has another meaning completely. Because, what I'm saying is, "If these walls that I put up around myself, if this wall I've constructed between

With Art Garfunkel: "Sometimes I'm accused of writing too rangy. 'Up, Up and Away,' for example, usually has to be sung by five people."

you and me, if it could speak, it would tell you that I really care about you." See what I mean? That's the way the song sort of evolved.

When you first started talking I was going to ask you who the walls were.
They started out literally as the walls of the house, and suddenly one line fell into place and they meant something else—something more. That's when you know God takes a hand in these things. We can't do it on our own. Nobody can.

You talked about the difficulty of developing an idea. Have you ever had an idea that just didn't work?
One January, a year or two ago, I came back from the holidays early and sort of primed myself to get off to a real good start. You know, like just as soon as we get these turkeys and hams out of the way, I'm going to take off like an Olympic racer. By the second week of January I'm going to have three songs. And then absolutely nothing happened. I started working on a song called "Airport Bar," which I lived with until the end of January.

Did you finish it?
No. I just couldn't get it. So one day, at the end of the month, I walked into my office and the song was on my piano. I looked at it and I thought I can't do this anymore. This is making me so unhappy. So I wadded it into a neat little ball, threw it on my assistant's desk, and said, "File that!" I had the most delicious sense of freedom after that. In the next couple of weeks I wrote three songs.

What made you stay with "Airport Bar" as long as you did?
I was always taught to finish what I start. And I'd say that 95 percent of the time, I do. But it's clear to me now that much of the time, that's a dogmatic exercise—and one that can serve as an excuse for not being creative. You satisfy those puritanical standards and go through the process and say, "There, I've done it. My conscience is clear." But whether any real creativity has taken place is questionable. What I learned from that experience is that sometimes it's good to let these things go if they're too much of a burden.

I assume some songs come more quickly?
Oh yes. I wrote "Up, Up and Away" in 35 minutes. When it was first sung, everyone assumed it was about drugs. It was about a ride in a hot air balloon. One radio station in Oklahoma took it off the air and my father was so irate at that that he showed up at the station with Bible in hand and started preaching at them.

You said that determination is what helps you push the rock uphill. Have you always been so determined?
I learned determination from my family. They were cotton

farmers in Oklahoma. My granddad didn't believe in using migrant workers or machines, so we worked from sunup to sundown. I can remember my sisters carrying 20-pound sacks of cotton over their shoulders when they were seven or eight. So now, when I'm sitting at the piano, and my head and back hurt, I think about the way we used to work. And I realize, this isn't work, this is fun. Work is when you come back from the cotton patch and fall asleep at the dinner table, face down in your spaghetti.

And that helps you?
It really does—especially when I'm staying up till 2 or 3 in the morning doing arrangements. It really does get into a physical contest between me and what has to be done. You're all alone and no one can help you.

Does fatigue make you more creative?
Yeah. When I get really, really tired, I get emotional. I think a lot of people do. Sometimes, in order to wear down the defenses, that armor we carry around with us all the time, we have to be tired. Maybe the only time a person is completely honest is when he's exhausted.

Do you often stay up all night?
No, but the occasional all-night session is therapeutic for me. Sure, when I'm doing it I feel like I should be in bed. But when I finally get into that purely emotional state, I realize this is good for me—to be able to feel things this deeply is the most valuable thing I could be doing for myself. I get to a state early in the morning when ideas come very swiftly and vividly and I'm really able to express things.

And that's when you do your best work?
Well, no. It's a paradox because I'm usually so tired I can't write. But I can make notes about things I want to write about. Or I can get to an old feeling or remember something that happened years ago that really affected me—something I've been blocking out. All of a sudden I'm in tears and I'm there again. And when I come back to work with a full night's sleep, I remember that feeling. It's almost like Method acting.

Are you able to work at home?
Very rarely. We have five kids at home.

Many writers are so obsessive that they have a hard time turning off their creative side. How do you switch gears?
Well, I keep notes all the time so I can get back to it the next day. It would be terrible for me to feel that I couldn't think about songwriting at all when I'm not in the office, just as it would seem perverse not to be able to think about my family when I'm in the office. It's just that the reality of being in a house with so many other people, with so many other noises and energies, makes it virtually impossible to write.

Because you need privacy?
Yes. Writing is very private. I have an assistant, Laura, and she is the only person I'm not self-conscious around. She and I have been working in the same room for about seven years. Other than her, I wouldn't be comfortable writing a song with another person in the same room, even if it were a close friend or my wife. I know that sounds strange—how could it be too private for your wife? But it is. Writing is at the center of vulnerability. You want to make your mistakes in private because you know there are going to be plenty of them—especially the way I work.

How is that?
I sing every line, even if I wind up changing it. And sometimes I find myself reaching for a note that isn't very flattering.

Do you ever have difficulties with friends who don't understand your need for privacy?
I did once. I had a friend who thought it was perfectly natural to sit in a room with me while I composed. There's no way I can describe how excruciating this was for me. Then I realized that the closer the friend is, the more important it is for you to be able to say, "Look, this isn't meant to hurt your feelings, but get the hell out of here."

How did he take it?
He was fine. It was much more traumatic for me. I think the other reason privacy is so important to me is because creating something is like a secret. There is a certain professional jealousy

about not revealing how you're putting that particular Swiss watch together. When the time comes, it's good old-fashioned show biz. You want to be able to say, "OK—let's open the curtain." I still get a tremendous thrill from unveiling something I've done—at least, something that's really good.

Frankly—and this may sound a bit perverse—I really get a kick out of knowing I'm going to get a reaction from people the first time they hear it.

Why is that perverse?
I suppose it's the surprise element—knowing that the song is so good it's like a trap I can spring on someone's head. You know, snap it just like that—like it's a loaded weapon. That it gets them where they didn't think it was going to get them.

Do you know when you're writing a song that it's good?
I do now.

Do you know if it's going to be a hit?
I know when it has *potential*. But there are so many factors involved in terms of whether something's a hit, like who records it, or what the political climate of the country is. And of course, there is your status as an artist when it comes out.

Of all your own songs, you've said that "The Moon Is a Harsh Mistress" is your favorite. Why?
Maybe I will betray a bit of ire here. I get so desperately disgusted with being asked that question that I finally just make up an answer! That's the truth. I'm very proud of the song, but I don't have a favorite.

The title is great. How did you come up with it?
Actually, I didn't. I've been a sci-fi freak since I was six. And one of my favorite authors was Robert A. Heinlein. He wrote a short story once called "The Moon Is a Harsh Mistress," which I probably read when I was eight. I could never get the title out of my mind and I always knew I was going to write a song with that title.

You say you always knew you were going to write that song. But did you always know you were going to be a songwriter?

No. Actually, I wanted to be a jet pilot. I couldn't wait to get my hands on a Phantom, but the doctor told me if my eyes kept deteriorating, I wouldn't get into the Air Force Academy. So, at 13, my jet pilot dreams were over. My brother was the 6 1/2-foot-tall all-state basketball center and I was the wimp with glasses. I found out that the only time I could get attention at a party was when I played the piano. So really, it was all about hormones.

When did you start writing songs?
At 17, although I had been playing piano since I was six. My father was a Baptist minister and my mother's dream was that I'd play the piano for church services. And my mother's dreams always came true!

When did you have your first success?
When I was 19. I was working for Motown and got to produce albums for the Supremes, Cher and Thelma Houston. I also worked with the group that later became known as the Fifth Dimension.

How has your style changed since then?
I'm more conventional now and less pretentious. I'm not up there preaching. Now I write about simpler things like the Ramada Inn or a song about my race car called "Too Young to Die."

You've always written sad songs. Why is that?
I guess it's my nature. I started my career writing laments and ballads, and so I know how to do it. But I guess the truth is, much as I hate to admit it, it probably says something about my emotional makeup. I don't think of myself as a sad person. I've enjoyed my life a great deal and people tell me that I can be hysterically funny, though I never remember afterwards. But I do have fun and I don't like to think of myself as morose. But I'm aware that most of my songs do come out that way.

And that bothers you?
I guess I feel guilty about making people feel sad. I don't want to impose that on them. Someone may feel really good and then they listen to one of my songs and their day is ruined. I'm not

always sure I like the idea that I trade in emotionalism. I feel guilty about playing on people's feelings and selling them my emotions and pretending that emotions are a substantial product that is worth anything.

Why? That's interesting.
It goes back to my upbringing—coming from farmers who worked hard, raised crops, put them in a truck, hauled them to town, sold them, and took the money and bought a tractor so they could plant more. It was a substantial world. Writing sometimes feels flimsy.

Is there anything else about your music that troubles you?
Well, sometimes I'm accused of writing too rangy. "Up, Up and Away," for example, usually has to be sung by five people. But then someone comes along like Linda Ronstadt and she says, "I like them rangy—don't stop writing them that way. I get more emotional intensity and deeper feeling by crossing from lower keys to higher keys." So I've never been tempted to change my style. Also, I'm lazy.

But you work so hard.
Lazy people often work hard to prove they're not lazy.

Who has had the greatest influence on you?
My father was a big influence. And John Steinbeck. He had a great understanding of the common man and he makes me feel less alone. He can make people feel something.

And yet you say you feel bad when you make people feel something.
I guess because I make people feel sad. I don't want to make them feel sad.

So that's the hardest thing about songwriting for you?
That and the fact that it's one of the world's loneliest jobs. There's nobody to talk to because if you have someone there, you're really bribing yourself and you're not doing the work.

Like being in Hawaii or on the QEII?
Right. Actually, it only bothers me about three in the morning

when I'm really tired, when I wish I just had someone there to keep bringing me tea. But there aren't many people who will stay up all night and make me tea.

But if you could find someone?

I'd be afraid that I'd get into some sort of conversation with them. But last summer I found a way around it. I was in Istanbul and I saw a beautiful red and purple bird in a cage. I really wanted that bird and so my wife and friends surprised me with it. I didn't realize until I got home that I wanted it so that I'd have someone to be with—not someone who would talk to me or be particularly concerned, but someone who wouldn't be too critical of what I'm doing.

But can he bring you tea?

He's not going to be able to bring me tea, but I'm not going to feel the way I usually feel when I'm working.

Which is?

Like the only living thing in the universe.

Acknowledgements

The interview subjects themselves, of course, are the most praiseworthy individuals connected with this project. They were generous with their time and candid with their responses. We thank them all. Equal thanks go to those subjects who do not appear here. We hope to include many in future volumes.

DMB&B, the advertising company, was mother and father to *CREATIVITY*. Without the agency's interest in the creative process and its abiding curiosity about creative people, these interviews would not have occurred.

Special appreciation goes to Al Hirschfeld, who provided readers not only with remarkable and delightful insights, but also with some of his unique drawings. The Margo Feiden Galleries, and David Leopold, went out of their way to provide the ones we needed.

Editorial assistant Abigail List made an invaluable contribution in checking facts, recontacting interviewees, deciphering muffled passages on audio tapes and giving the manuscript a critical read.

The number of individuals who were helpful in a book involving 28 interview subjects is too large to allow full and proper acknowledgement. Several, however, must be mentioned.

Donna Lee was responsible for our finally being able to track down the reluctant Morgan Freeman, who so amazingly refuses to believe that his contributions to a drama are of a creative nature.

Carlin Glynn made it possible for us to reach so many of the people who came together to make *The Trip to Bountiful*. The results can be found in the paperback *Creativity in Film*.

Viveca Lindfors, Shelley List and Dorothy Dwire opened doors beyond which we found some of our favorite interviews.

Ray Charles White was generous not only with his photos of Tony Bennett, but with his time.

Virginie Roland and Nina Cornyetz also contributed beyond

the call of duty as we sought to make contact with key players.

Mary Boone was particularly helpful in some of our research efforts.

And a special thanks to Allan Bateman, a uniquely creative individual, for his endless hours of brainstorming, support and feedback.

Photo Credits

JoAnne Akalaitis, facing Page 1, by MARTHA SWOPE
Tony Bennett, Page 16, by RAY CHARLES WHITE
April Gornik painting, Page 53, by DOROTHY ZEIDMAN
Martin Garbus, Page 73, by BRUCE DAVISON
Paul MacCready, Page 261, by DON MONROE
E.G. Marshall, Page 278, by FRED FEHL
E.G. Marshall, Page 281, by MARTHA SWOPE
Kenneth Snelson, Page 351, by ANDREA SNELSON